R ..... .JR
PREV...JS EDITIONS
OF THE GHOST
HUNTER'S GUIDEBOOK
BY TROY TAYLOR

Troy Taylor, president and founder of the American Ghost Society, has brought a new level of professionalism to the field with "The Ghost Hunter's Guidebook," which stands as the best and most authoritative book written to date on ghost investigation. Both beginners and experienced investigators should make this book their bible. Taylor gives his readers thorough coverage of the subject and the book is the product of Taylor's own first-hand experiences in numerous investigations. Troy is a careful researcher dedicated to promoting professional, responsible research in a field vulnerable to the media's appetite for the sensational. "The Ghost Hunter's Guidebook" gives the straight savvy. The material is grounded, practical and informative. It comes as no surprise to me that Taylor's book has gained international praise, including high marks from some of England's most discerning ghost investigators.

ROSEMARY ELLEN GUILEY
AUTHOR, ENCYCLOPEDIA OF GHOSTS & SPIRITS

Mr. Taylor gives an excellent starting blue print for hunting ghosts. Not only does he give a run down on the history of spiritualism and early ghost hunters, he also tells the reader where to find ghosts and how to use equipment. Mr. Taylor is one of the more credible authors in this field. He is not a "ghost buster" and does not profess to be an expert in ghost hunting (there are no experts in this field) and this makes him very credible. He presents the evidence he has collected from his experiences and lets the reader judge for him/herself. I would recommend any of his books whole heartedly.

AMAZON.COM BOOK REVIEW

The text of this manual (THE GHOST HUNTER'S GUIDEBOOK) offers a wealth of modern and really valuable information regarding sophisticated detection equipment and investigation proceudures and methods ... should be essential reading for anyone in the field of paranormal research, whatever their level of interest or knowledge of the subject.

ANREW GREEN
AUTHOR & PARANORMAL RESEARCHER

GHOST BOOKS BY TROY TAYLOR

HAUNTED DECATUR (1995)
MORE HAUNTED DECATUR (1996)
GHOSTS OF MILLIKIN (1996 / 2001)
WHERE THE DEAD WALK (1997 / 2002)
DARK HARVEST (1997)
HAUNTED DECATUR REVISITED (2000)
FLICKERING IMAGES (2001)

GHOSTS OF SPRINGFIELD (1997)
THE GHOST HUNTER'S HANDBOOK (1997)
THE NEW GHOST HUNTER'S HANDBOOK (1998)
GHOSTS OF LITTLE EGYPT (1998)

HAUNTED ILLINOIS (1999 / 2001)
SPIRITS OF THE CIVIL WAR (1999)
THE GHOST HUNTER'S GUIDEBOOK (1999 / 2001/ 2004)
SEASON OF THE WITCH (1999/ 2002)
HAUNTED ALTON (2000 / 2003)
HAUNTED NEW ORLEANS (2000)
BEYOND THE GRAVE (2001)
NO REST FOR THE WICKED (2001)
THE HAUNTING OF AMERICA (2001)
HAUNTED ST. LOUIS (2002)
INTO THE SHADOWS (2002)
CONFESSIONS OF A GHOST HUNTER (2002)
HAUNTED CHICAGO (2003)
DOWN IN THE DARKNESS (2003)
FIELD GUIDE TO HAUNTED GRAVEYARDS (2003)
OUT PAST THE CAMPFIRE LIGHT (2004)

- The American Ghost Society -

THE GHOST HUNTER'S
GUIDEBOOK

THE ESSENTIAL GUIDE TO INVESTIGATING GHOSTS & HAUNTINGS

BY TROY TAYLOR

- A Whitechapel Productions Press Publication -

This book, as with previous editions of the Ghost Hunter's Guidebook, is dedicated to the members of the American Society -- especially those members who have remained with us since the early days and have supported our work, research and efforts throughout the years. A special thanks to all of you!

And, of course, this book is dedicated to Amy -- without whom the American Ghost Society, and the other things I do, would not exist at all. I once opened a fortune cookie that had a small slip of paper inside that simple said "true love is like ghosts .... many believe in both but few ever find them". In my own case, I have been lucky enough to find both!

This Book is Published by:
Whitechapel Productions Press
A Division of the History & Hauntings Book Co.
515 East Third Street - Alton, Illinois - 62002
(618) 465-1086 / 1-888-GHOSTLY
Visit us on the Internet at http://www.historyandhauntings.com

First Printing / Third Edition - June 2004
ISBN: 1-892523-04-3

Printed in the United States of America

This book is designed to be a tool in the methods of paranormal investigation. It is not designed to be the final word on the subject but a piece of useful information that can be adapted and used by the individual ghost hunter for his own investigations.
Read at your own risk!

Matters of fact well proved ought not to be denied because we cannot conceive how they can be performed. Nor is it a reasonable method of inference, first to presume the thing impossible and there to conclude that the fact cannot be proved. On the contrary, we should judge of the action by the evidence and not of the evidence by the measures of our fancies about the action.

Joseph Glanville, F.R..S

We do not know what happens when we die, or where we go to, or how we get there. And if we come back ... we do not know how that occurs either. I reiterate that we know nothing about these things, which have puzzled mankind since the beginning of time. Of course, there are theories, and the most brillian intellects have, for hundreds of years, been trying to solve the problems.
They have not succeeded.

Harry Price

There are no "experts" in the field of paranormal investigation, no matter what anyone says and regardless of who claims to be one. Ghosts are as mysterious today as they were in the days of Ancient Rome and will undoubtedly remain so for many years to come....

TABLE OF CONTENTS

INTRODUCTION - 8
A Return to the Haunted House

I. GHOST HUNTER - 20
Harry Price & The History of Ghost Research - Among the Spirits -
Biography of a Ghost Hunter - Borley Rectory - The Blue Book: The First
Ghost Hunter's Guide

2. INVESTIGATING THE PARANORMAL - 45
Introduction to Ghost Research - The Scientific Framework of Ghost
Investigating - Approaches to Ghost Hunting - Getting Started as an
Investigator

3. GHOSTS & HAUNTINGS - 49
What are Ghosts & Where Do You Find Them? - Hauntings - Traditional
Hauntings - Residual Hauntings - Poltergeists - Portal Hauntings - Other
Types of Ghostly Phenomena - Crisis Apparitions - Ghost Lights - Man-Made
Ghosts - Where to Find Ghosts - The Trouble with Folklore - Where the
Ghosts Are

4. FREQUENTLY ASKED QUESTIONS ABOUT GHOSTS - 74
A Number of Questions related to Ghosts & Hauntings, including queries
about belief in ghosts, evil spirits. harmful ghosts, ghosts that follow you and
why, haunted objects, spirit communications, why some ghosts wear clothes,
ghosts that smell & more

5. THE GHOST HUNTER'S KIT - 81
Essential Tools for Ghost Research & Investigation - Basic Items for an
Investigation - Ghost Detection Devices - Geiger Counters - Electromagentic
Field (EMF) Meters - Detailed Instructions for Working with Various Meters -
IR Motion Detectors - High Tech Equipment - Temperature Sensing Devices

6 . SPIRIT COMMUNICATIONS - 104
Communicating with the Spirits - Talking Boards - Using the Talking
Board - Table Tipping - Guidelines for Table Tipping & Seances -

Electronic Voice Phenomena (EVP) - History of EVP - How Real is EVP? -
Experimenting with EVP - How to Get Authentic EVP Recordings

7. GHOSTS ON FILM - 122

Using the Camera to Gather Evidence of Ghosts - History of Spirit
Photography - Ghosts on Film - The Trouble with "Orbs" & Other Image
Anomalies - Mysterious Mists - Apparitions on Film - Digital Cameras: No
Longer Ghost Hunting At its Worst - Paranormal Photo How-To Guide -
Infrared Photography - Photography Hints & Tips - Using Video to Gather
Authentic Evidence in Investigations

8. THE PARANORMAL INVESTIGATION - 138

Putting Your Ghost Research into Practice - What to do Before You Get
There - When is it Okay to Call? - Rules for Investigations - Step by Step
Guide to Paranormal Investigations - The Ghost Watch Guide - Examining the
House - Equipment Failures - Afraid of Ghosts? - Interviewing the Witness -
Questions to Ask the Witness - Researching the History of the House -
Getting Rid of the Ghost

9. THE GHOST VIGIL - 169

Conducting Investigations in Cemeteries & Other Outdoor Locations - Tracking
Down Graveyard History - Gravestones & Markers - Surveying the Cemetery
- Researching the Dead - Preparing for the Investigation - Step by Step
Guide to the Investigation

10. BEYOND GHOST RESEARCH - 186

Working with Other Ghost Hunters, the Media & The General Public - Starting
a Research Group - Dealing with Reporters & The Media - Guide to Starting
a Ghost Tour

APPENDIX 1 - 197
WHAT TO DO IF YOUR HOUSE IS HAUNTED
A Guide for Home Owners Who Believe They Are Experiencing Paranormal
Activity

APPENDIX 2 - 205
Forms for Paranormal Investigations

APPENDIX 3 - 209
Dictionary of Ghostly Terms

INTRODUCTION:

A RETURN TO THE HAUNTED HOUSE

Now my suspicion is that the universe is not only queerer than we suppose but queerer than we can suppose .. I suspect that there are more things in heaven and earth than are dreamed of in any philosophy...

J.B.S. HALDANE

We who believe in the psychic revelation, and who appreciate that a perception of these things is of utmost importance, certainly have hurled ourselves against the obstinacy of our time.

SIR ARTHUR CONAN DOYLE

The suppression of uncomfortable ideas may be common in religion and politics but it is not the path to knowledge. It has no place in the endeavor of science.

CARL SAGAN

Do we really need another edition of this book?

That is a question that some of you may be asking as you pick up yet another copy of the GHOST HUNTER'S GUIDEBOOK. To be honest, it's a question that I asked myself as well when I sat down to begin putting together the pile of new notes, changes and editions that I have been collecting since the last edition of this book was published three years ago. Do I need to compile another edition of a book that I have been putting out, in one form or another, since 1997?

As I considered this, I finally realized that I did. When I wrote the first "handbook" back in 1997, there were simply no other books like it on the market. This was one of the reasons that I did it in the first place. People were looking for information on how to hunt ghosts and nearly every book that had been written on the subject was out of print. The first edition of the book was a fairly crude, stapled booklet but it was met with great enthusiasm and over the next several years, I produced various editions, each a little longer and each with additional information. Of course, since those days, there have been a number of books written on ghost hunting and ghost research, often varying wildly when it came to quality and usefulness. There has also been, since 1997, an explosion of websites on an Internet that was just getting started when the first edition of the book came out. Like most of the books on the subject, the websites that you are likely to run across vary drastically when it comes to theories, ideas and how investigations are best carried out.

As you can see, a lot has changed since that first book was published and there have even been many changes to equipment, techniques and theories since the last edition in 2001. My own personal theories and research have also changed since that time, as you will discover in the pages ahead. But even after all of this, the basic idea behind the book has not changed at all. That remains the same - it has the simple goal of providing the reader with the essential information needed to conduct research into ghosts and the paranormal. This goal is deceptively simple however, for the outcome of such research and investigation is not simple at all. In fact, it can be so complex and confusing that many people walk away from the paranormal field every day, scratching their heads and wondering if all of the work and effort is really worth it.

I can assure you that it is but like any other object of endeavor, it is only as reward-ing as the effort that is put into it. Hopefully, this book will show you how to make that effort worthwhile and show you that ghost research can not only be educational and enlightening, but entertaining and thrilling as well. I hope these factors will encourage you to pick up the book again and again and hope that the ideas and theories contained within will spark your interest and encourage you to devise your own theories about ghosts and ghost research. Obviously, I won't have all of the answers about ghosts until I am one myself, but I can pass along my own knowledge, ideas and theories that have been gained by my own past experiences with hauntings. What I hope is that you, as the reader and ghost enthusiast, will be able to do with this book is take away at least one small piece of it for yourself and your own investigations. See what I have done and learn from the mistakes (and from some of the successes) that I have been part of my investigations, and in this way, improve the quality of your own research.

As I will undoubtedly state many times in this book, there are no "experts" when it comes to ghosts and ghost hunting. Ghost researchers do not uniformly agree on what makes a place become haunted, or even about what ghosts actually are. Everyone has his or her own ideas on the subject and mine are certainly not meant to be the final word on it. My ideas and theories come from my own past experiences and as has been seen in past editions of this very book, I often started out with certain ideas about how to do things, only to find those same ideas are cast aside in light of new events and experi-ences. This new edition of the book will be proof of that ever changing cycle of ideas and hopefully, there will be much here that you can put to work for yourself.

What's new in this third edition of the book?
And what can you expect to find in the pages ahead?

In this new edition of the book, I will recount many of my own experiences with ghost research and give you an idea of a system for investigating that has worked well for me. We will also discuss working with witnesses, dealing with ghost sightings, con-ducting interviews, additional techniques for investigations, more on using paranormal detection devices, added information on doing historical research and much more. I have also added more of my own case studies and investigations as examples of what to do -- and what I should have done -- that will assist during your own excursions. We will also take a new look at the use of digital technology in ghost hunting and find out that (finally!) the equipment has progressed to the point that it can actually be used with good results. This is one event that has been a long time coming and in that long-awaited section, I will reveal how newer cameras can now produce a system that can be as effective as a photographic negative.

As mentioned, much is new in this third edition and we will also take an updated look at the "old reliable" aspects of ghost research. This will include ghosts themselves and of course, real life haunted houses. I should note here that the term "haunted house" can mean a lot of things from old decaying mansions to new tract homes but remember that just about any place can become haunted, including churches, theaters, libraries, office buildings and even graveyards. What we call "haunting" activity in such spots can be any sort of unexplained happenings, like apparitions, footsteps, noises, odors and more. For a spot to be considered genuinely haunted, this phenomena must be directly related to the place itself. For example, let's say that a family lives in a haunted house and decides to move out. If the house is really haunted, the next family who lives there should experience the same things as the previous one - which creates some of the best evidence that you will ever collect in a haunted house investigation.

Take note however that there are many different kinds of hauntings. No two cases are ever exactly alike. When conducting your research, you are bound to discover various kinds of activity and sometimes, believe it or not, it will be at the same location!

In some places, ghosts are seen. Some reports claim that they are white, mist-like forms that only resemble a person. They are sometimes transparent and you are able to see through them. In other cases, the ghosts are reported as appearing very life-like. In fact, witnesses sometimes mistake the ghosts for living persons, at least until they vanish into the wall or disappear through a solid door. In my own experience, I have only ever actually seen two ghosts and the sightings varied completely from nothing more than a white light to a figure that I would have sworn was a living person - except for the fact that it entered a room with no exit and vanished. Looking back, I realized that my two sightings were typical of what others have also seen.

Some people, and usually those outside of the paranormal field, are often surprised that during all of the years that I have been searching for hauntings, that I have only seen two ghosts. Most ghost hunters are not surprised though. We know that in most cases, ghosts are not seen in the houses that they haunt. In the vast majority of cases, ghostly noises are heard instead. Witnesses report everything from footsteps to voices, mumbling, whispers, knocking sounds and more. And in other houses, furniture, knick-knacks and solid objects fly about by themselves. At other times, doors open or close, lights and appliances behave erratically or phantom smells come and go without logical explanation. In other words, you never know what you will find in a haunted location and once again, no two cases are ever exactly alike.

In addition to the wide variety of things that you might encounter at a haunted location, there are also a lot of things that you probably won't. There exist a great many unfounded myths and fabrications about ghosts and hauntings. First of all, ghosts are not "everywhere". In most cases, you have to go looking for them because they are not going to find you. Ghosts are usually not out to kill anyone or avenge their deaths. The instances of harmful ghosts are so rare that the few cases that have been documented have caused a huge sensation. Nor, as you may have guessed, do ghosts appear with sheets draped over their heads, rattling chains.

There are many misconceptions about haunted houses as well. For instance, many believe that only old, ramshackle buildings can become haunted. We have already mentioned that this is not true, as many relatively new homes have been known to attract ghosts. Many also believe that ghosts cannot be photographed. Quite to the contrary, there are a number of authenticated photos of ghosts on record. We'll be looking closer at that later in the book and in this new edition, I have provided even more information on how best to capture these mysterious beings with a camera.

Theories about ghosts, hauntings and more will be discussed throughout the book and you will note again that I spoke of "theories" here. There seem to be few clear-cut answers when it comes to ghosts. For decades, ghost researchers have wondered -- what force or intelligence lies behind a haunting?

One view is that a location becomes haunted when some tragedy, like a death or a murder, takes place there. This is apparently true in some cases, but not in all. But are ghosts really the spirits of the dead, come back to haunt us? Are they somehow attached to the places where they lived and died? Or could ghosts be "memory pictures" of the past or "energy discharges" that replay over and over again? Could some ghosts be only the memory of something that is so real that sometimes we can see it? In other words, do we see some ghosts as something that has only been left behind as an image in our heads? Perhaps a friend has died and one day we are walking down the street and look into a window and just for a second, we see him there. The next day, perhaps we see him getting on a bus or driving a car in the opposite direction on a street. Is he really there -- as a ghost -- or is this just a memory that is so vivid to us that we have made it real in our minds?

Ghosts can be any of these things and perhaps all of them, which we will discuss later in this new edition of the book, but no matter what, they are theories. No one has all of the answers when it comes to ghosts but everyone has his or her own ideas on the subject. This is a wonderful thing, as long as each researcher remembers that their own personal theory is just one of many such ideas. Not a one of us, no matter how experienced or how long they have been doing this, can offer the absolute answer. In a field such as the paranormal one, where there are no absolute answers, there is a rush to find solutions to every possible puzzle. And unfortunately, for some it becomes easier to rush to conclusions rather than build off the foundations put into place by others. As you will read many times in this book, there are no "experts" when it comes to the paranormal and it becomes very important to for you to know that we are all allowed to say "I don't know" every now and then.

So, in a field where no absolute answers exist and in a field where ghosts can only be seen sometimes (and by only certain people), how can we prove that these elusive creatures exist?

Here's my first chance to say it... "I don't know". By definition, a ghost is a disembodied personality and as of this time, we have absolutely no physical evidence that the human personality even exists. Science will not admit that such a thing is present inside of the body while it is still functioning, so we are far from scientifically proving that it exists outside of the body (as a ghost) after death. We can only infer this by observation.

It's unlikely that mainstream scientists will ever accept paranormal research as a legitimate science. This is not so much because it is fraudulent, but because they cannot understand it or simply don't want to. In order to establish scientific proof of something, it must be subject to repeatable experiments that can be backed up by a theory that has a mathematical base. A good example of this was proving that the world is round and not flat. The Greek scientist Pythagoras was the first to introduce the idea that the world was round but it would not be for another 300 years before another Greek, Eratosthenes, would create a mathematical theory to back it up. Even so, there was little fanfare about the idea until much later when Magellan actually sailed around the world in 1522. This "experiment", along with the mathematical theory, destroyed the theories of those who still insisted that the Earth was flat.

I think that most readers are aware of where I am going with this. The supernatural does not really conform to the idea of repeatable experiments. We can measure, document and record, but ghosts do not perform on command, which is what scientific proof demands. Ghosts cannot be trapped in a laboratory. If you drag them out of the shadows and expose them to the harsh glare of scientific reality, they tend to vanish.

But can we prove that ghosts exist? The answer, which may surprise you, is "yes"! While we cannot prove them scientifically, we can prove their existence historically. What do I mean by this? Let me give you an example of the "perfect scenario" in proving that a house is haunted:

A family moves into a house and shortly after, they begin to experience strange phenomena. Doors open and close by themselves and when locked, are found mysteriously standing open again. Objects begin to vanish, only to appear again a few days later in unusual places. They are also soon startled to find that the apparition of a man (let's say with dark hair and wearing a white shirt and gray pants) begins appearing in the corner of an upstairs bedroom.

Bewildered by what is going on, they contact the previous owners of the house and learn that they too also experienced the odd happenings and saw the ghostly man. Checking back even further, they further learn that the owners prior to the last ones also had the same experiences. Before this, none of them were aware that others had seen the same thing and had not discussed the events with anyone outside of the family.

While scientifically speaking, no one has "proven" that a ghost is haunting this house but there is "historical evidence" of the fact. In this particular scenario (which is incidentally based on a real case from my files), the witnesses to the haunting had never compared notes on the case and all lived in the house over period of more than 50 years. During each occupancy, the home owners independently saw and experienced the ghost without ever realizing that someone else already had. To add to the real story behind this brief scenario, the actual home owners even identified a photograph of the home's original owner as the ghost seen in the upstairs bedroom. They did this with no hesitation and did not know that anyone else had picked out the same photo.

For those who do not believe in ghosts, they are convinced that anyone who experiences one is either drunk, insane or lying about what they claim has occurred. In a situation like this, every single one of the witnesses would have had to have been mentally ill or possessing an alcohol abuse problem, which they did not. None of the witnesses were aware that anyone else had shared their experience and yet it had been repeating itself for quite a few years. Merely a coincidence? I don't believe so and in fact, I believe that the history in this case has "proven" that the house is haunted.

In this way, we collect historical evidence by gathering witness testimony and details about a ghost that may be present at a location. We can then research that gathered information and match it to the alleged ghost when it was still a living person. Better yet, as I did in the previously mentioned case, we can collect testimony of events that occurred in the house by residents in the past and then match that evidence to current events that are now taking place. Having independent witnesses, of different time periods, with matching experiences makes for some very convincing evidence. Technically, we have "historically proven" that the house is haunted and that ghosts exist.

But are results like this conclusive enough for you?
Do you wonder if it's worth the trouble to become a ghost hunter at all?

There is no question that there are hundreds of us around the country involved in regular ghost research. Many people wonder what it is that we hope to gain from the effort that we put into it.

Many ghost hunters, like myself, started out by collecting strange tales and ghost stories and then decided to see if there was anything behind the stories other than folklore and urban legend. Others are simply driven by the need to look beyond the horizon and past what is generally accepted as the norm. There are also those who seek that elusive answer as to whether or not our spirits have somewhere else to go when our bodies cease to function.

While ghosts are more widely accepted than they were even a few years ago, ghost researchers still have a long way to go to validate the things that we believe to be genuine. This is why we use equipment, investigative techniques and sometimes even advanced technology to hunt for evidence of ghosts. We are trying to find something solid on which we can base the beliefs that we might already have. This validation is essential to the cause, for what good are beliefs to the general public if there is no evidence to back them up? We can be happy and contented that ghosts are real, and never bother to seek validation for our results, but what does this really prove?

To achieve such validation, many researchers have organized and have joined groups in an attempt to combine our efforts. We may not be able to provide enough proof to convince the scientific community of the reality of ghosts, but what we can do is to gather the most conclusive evidence that we can and then dare them to prove us wrong.

I hope that this book can assist you in whatever your quest might be. The main purpose of it is to study ghost research and detail the best ways to gather evidence of the paranormal. And there is one thing about this book that has remained the same since the first edition of it came out -- it is a guidebook to ghost hunting for the average person. There are other guides that are filled with new age mumbo-jumbo, rants about demons and how-to schematics for technical gadgetry but this book has always been meant to be the guidebook for the "common man". There is nothing in this book that cannot be done by those who want to put the effort into it. There are no electronic devices that are far out of the price range of the ordinary person. Sure, we would all love to have the thousands of dollars to spend on a thermal imaging camera but realistically, most of us do not. You won't find forbidden, arcane knowledge here. There are no spells or incantations involved in collecting credible evidence of ghosts, at least not if it is done in a respectable and realistic manner.

But ghost research is just like anything else. It is only as worthwhile as what you decide to put into it. If you just want to be a weekend hobbyist, there is nothing wrong with that. However, you cannot expect to stun the paranormal community with your incredible insight into the supernatural when you go out to do an investigation once every couple of months or so. If you want to put some time and energy into it though, you just might see some amazing results.

There are many things that a good ghost hunter must be armed with. He needs the equipment, thecameras and the tools of the trade. He must know what to look for, how to operate his equipment, what questions to ask, how to conduct his investigation and more. The common factor with all of these things though, is the ghost hunter himself. He becomes the most important tool for any investigation. This person must use his own mind, judgment and powers of observation to the advantage of each particular case. No gadgets, recorders or even guidebooks are going to help in an investigation when the researcher is lacking in personal qualities and abilities.

The ghost hunter must remember that his goals have many layers. Not only is he seeking evidence of ghosts, but he is also there to help the person who called him in to investigate the case in the first place. It may be a distressed person (or a frightened family) and one of the researcher's main responsibilities is to assure this person that they have nothing to fear from the activity that may be taking place. It should be explained that while the phenomena may seem frightening, this is because it is strange, not evil or demonic. One of the ghost hunter's first obligations is to help the witness deal with the activity they are experiencing. They should not be shut out of the investigation, but talked to as a friend and helped to understand what is going on. You see, at this particular moment, the researcher may seem like the best friend they have.

Here are some things to consider before we begin....

Obviously, one of the most important parts of your investigation will be the collection of evidence. I can't stress enough how important it is to be very careful with this evidence --- evidence that you claim to be genuine. We have to be sure that we can back up our claim that what we have is real and authentic.

I have never understood the logic behind collecting paranormal evidence that is presented to ghost enthusiasts and other researchers only. This really doesn't seem to prove anything. Such a practice is like smiling in the dark -- it feels really good to you, but no one else knows that you're doing it. The idea of the research is supposed to be so that you can collect evidence that might sway the mind of the non-believer. How can we do this if we never take a chance and allow someone to try and debunk the evidence that we have? If we are so sure that the evidence is genuine, then we should have no problem presenting it to someone besides other ghost hunters. Our belief system cannot be so fragile that we are afraid of being shown that we are wrong about something. We should have already attempted every possible natural explanation for the evidence that we believe to be real. If someone else suggests another one, then we have that much more ammunition for the next time that something possibly ghostly comes along.

But how do we go about presenting that evidence and how can we be sure that it's authentic? That's where being cautious with your evidence and your claims of authenticity come into play. In a nutshell, a researcher should never claim that evidence is genuine unless he is sure that it is. Unfortunately though, not everyone feels that way.

In the years since the Internet became so widespread (starting in the middle and late 1990's), there has been a surge of new interest in the occult and the paranormal. There have been many new ghost hunters and research groups that have surfaced. I have seen literally hundreds of ghost hunters and dozens of ghost hunting groups appear in the last few years, only to see these same people fade away and lose interest in a matter of months. That's the drawback to this new wave of interest, but on a more positive note, I have also seen a lot of bright, energetic and hard-working researchers get involved in the field as well. These are the ones who stay around and turn out to be a real asset to any research group that they get involved with.

Unfortunately, there are others who stick around too. Some of them have been here since the beginning of the new wave of movement in the 1990's and as much as we would like to see them fade away, they continue to hang on. This type of ghost hunter is not so hard working and presents evidence that is questionable (at best) to the general public and to gullible would-be ghost hunters who are just getting started in the field. I think that all of us are well aware of the damage this does to legitimate researchers and I think that I find these people to be more disagreeable than even the debunkers. These pseudo-ghost hunters are the ones giving paranormal research a bad name, not the debunkers, from whom the general public realizes will come an argument for any valid point that exists.

What happens is that the public mistakenly comes to believe that these sloppy ghost hunters must be representative of the whole paranormal community. Obviously though, they are not. This group mostly consists of hobbyists who are too lazy to do proper research; have never heard of confidentiality in private cases; are too far "out there" with metaphysical theories to recall what planet they are on; or are simply too misguided or ill-informed to understand that camera straps, dust and bugs in photographs are not ghosts.

But don't get me wrong -- some of these folks are nice people and even mean well, so it's never my intention to point fingers at anyone. I don't have all the answers. As I have already stated (and will again), there are no experts when it comes to the paranormal, no matter what people say or who claims to be one. The goal of this book is to pass on information that I have picked up as a ghost researcher and for you to adapt that information to work for you. Hopefully, it might, in even some small way, help to keep you from making the mistakes that some of the previously mentioned "ghost hunters" are making.

I can tell you many times that I am no expert when it comes to ghosts. However, I have been accused of being many things, including arrogant, rude and flat-out wrong. I have also been often referred to as a "skeptic" and that's one that I can agree with. Now, before you think that I have lost my mind, let me explain to you what the actual definition of a skeptic is. It is a person who keeps an open mind about everything. Unfortunately, the true definition of the word has been corrupted over the years to mean someone who is close-minded to everything. I tend to think of these people as "debunkers".

I believe that I am what I like to call "optimistically skeptical", especially when it comes to ghosts. You see, I am a believer in the possibility of ghosts; however, I do not believe that every ghost story has something to do with ghosts. I believe in the possibility of haunted houses, although I rule out every natural cause for a haunting before believing that a ghost is causing the activity. I also don't necessarily believe that ghosts are the metaphysical creatures of legend, but are in reality, a natural part of our world that we just don't understand as of yet.

For these feelings, I am considered an enemy to some and am criticized by many, but I just can't seem to find fault in believing through evidence. That is what I continue to search for, evidence of ghosts and spirits, not weird theories and mumbo-jumbo. And regardless of how differently we might go about it, I believe that those of you who are bothering to read this book also want the same thing. I believe that you are looking for ways to obtain the most authentic evidence of ghosts possible. I hope that this book will provide a little advice, or at least a few tips, on how to find that evidence.

Collecting evidence is so important because just walking around and telling people that we have seen ghosts everywhere does not constitute any proof that they exist. We have to gather the evidence, like a detective, and show that something strange really is going on out there and that it's something that cannot easily be explained.

And this brings us to our investigations...

Believe me, I am not the only person who chuckles when they get letters or peruse the Internet and see the results of some of the "investigations" that are going on out there. As much as I, and many others, have complained about some of the silliness that occurs in the name of "ghost research", the same things continue to happen year after year.

My biggest complaint is this: there are many ghost hunters who are out running around searching for the "what's" and "how's" of hauntings, but have completely forgotten to look for the "why's". You know, why is the location haunted? Why did the history of the location create a haunting? Why is the phenomenon that is being investigated even taking place? Too often, we see and hear of investigators who are merely running around deserted locations taking pictures. I am not sure what the purpose behind this is. Is it to try and capture ghosts on film? If so, that's all well and good, but in the end, what has this proven?

After all of these years have passed, I continue to maintain that this can be called "ghost hunting" but I would hardly call it ghost research. It is not research, nor is it an investigation because nothing is actually being investigated. To be able to conduct an actual investigation, there has to be criteria to go by. There must be an element of organization behind it. The ghost hunter should have a checklist of items that need to be studied at this particular spot. Simply wandering about in a cemetery taking photographs is a lot of fun, don't get me wrong, but when all is said and done, what has actually been learned?

There are many things that should be questioned during an actual investigation. Try answering just these simple questions when you are in the midst of one:

1. What is the history behind the location?
2. What events may have caused this place to become haunted?
3. What paranormal events have been reported here in the past?
4. What phenomenon has been recorded during the investigation?

If you can't answer any of these questions, then you may not have any business being at the location in the first place. What is being done really doesn't qualify as an investigation, it's merely an outing. It may be entertaining, but can you really call it paranormal research?

In the past, I have raised these same points and have been criticized by those on both sides of the issue. Those who enjoy this sort of outing did not feel that I provided enough information on how it should be done properly and those who felt that investigations that are conducted in outdoor locations (especially cemeteries) cannot be qualified as authentic research lambasted me for bringing it up in the first place. So, in this edition of the book, I have included more information than ever before on how to property conduct these investigations, which have been dubbed "vigils", and I have also pointed out how investigating allegedly haunted graveyards can be seen as genuine research. I think that you will find this to be eye-opening if you are one of those who tend to dismiss cemetery research as the province of the weekend hobbyist and not the work of the serious researcher.

Also, along the lines of problems concerning the collection of evidence, we have to mention the issues that have arisen over ghost detection devices and equipment. Before we go any further though, please don't misunderstand me --- I do think that technology (and our adaptation of it) is essential to continuing paranormal research. The more equipment that you can use to actually record and document authentic evidence of the paranormal, the better. The problem that I speak of is not the equipment itself, but the way that much of it is being used.

Earlier, I stated that the most important tool in a paranormal investigation is the ghost hunter himself. It is imperative that he uses his mind, his judgment and his powers of observation to the utmost of his ability. There are no cameras or fancy gadgets that can take the place of a good investigator.

In the early days of ghost research, technology usually consisted of a camera, some string, a jar of flour and whatever homemade device the investigator could come up with. Do I believe that we should go back to those days? No, of course not, and I believe that if ground-breaking ghost hunters like Harry Price had possessed an infrared video camera in his day, he would have been using one of them in place of his jar of flour. However, we also have to concede that some of the most amazing and compelling evidence of hauntings came from this period. It was a time when researchers were forced to reply on their own abilities and common sense. Unfortunately, many ghost hunters of today feel this is no longer necessary. They are under the impression that going to a "haunted" spot and taking pictures and waving an EMF detector around constitutes an investigation. Honestly, I don't feel that it does. I feel that is leaning on a "technological crutch" and not actually conducting research.

Interviewing witnesses, examining the location, collecting evidence and waiting around for something to happen are what make an investigation. These should not be things of the past. They are in fact essential, despite the fact that they are not done as often as they should be. People are always in a hurry and impatience seems to prevail in every walk of life, including in ghost research. The incorrect use of cheap, digital cameras is a perfect example of this. Some would-be ghost hunters simply walk around snapping images and wait for "orbs" to appear, thinking this is what ghost hunting is all about. EMF meters are also abused. These same people believe that merely waving a meter about constitutes hunting ghosts, but it doesn't. Such actions don't really qualify as investigations, no matter how much some would like them to. Believe me, there is nothing wrong with digital cameras and EMF detectors, but only if they are used correctly. So often today, they are not being used correctly and in fact, are being horribly abused.

The point is this -- if we relax our standards, what do we hope to gain? We simply need to make sure that if we are calling ourselves "researchers" and "investigators", then this is what we actually are. Anyone can be a "ghost hunter", but we have to be sure of the legitimacy of what we are doing. If this is just entertainment for you, that's great. You'll get out of it exactly what you put into it. But if you want to take the next step and actually begin "investigating", then that can be accomplished too. The choice is always yours. It's all about what you are prepared to do.

Hopefully, this book will assist you in taking that next step. This book, no matter what the edition, has always been about discovering the basic skills of investigation. It's not all about "gee-whiz gadgets" and fancy cameras. Most of it is about putting what we can learn together into practice.

Just remember that paranormal research is finally getting to the point where it is almost plausible to the public at large. They are beginning to see the flakes, weirdo's and phony psychics for what they really are. This small (but still visible) minority is actually made up of the dwindling few and they are not the spokespersons for everyone interested in the paranormal.

What we can do is to make a concerted effort to display the best information that we have and the most carefully scrutinized evidence that we can. Who cares if we are criticized for being too cautious? It is better to be too careful than to make foolish mistakes that can destroy the precious credibility so desperately needed in this field.

At the close of this introduction, I should tell you that you should not be too surprised if it takes awhile before you can actually find some of the elusive "genuine evidence" that we have been discussing here. It often takes a long time to find the authentic cases that you are looking for, but perhaps this book will help you to tell the difference between the natural and supernatural events you encounter.

Before you get to the point of having to decide between them though, you are likely to discover some very strange or very scared people who have, for all sorts of reasons, come to erroneously believe that their house is haunted. You will discover creaking floorboards, banging water pipes, mysteriously "haunted" microwaves and folks who are just plain "nuts".

Being a ghost hunter can be a long, strange trip sometimes, but when you find that one great case out of 100, you'll be very happy that you decided to stick with it after all.

Happy Hunting!

Troy Taylor
June 2004

1. GHOST HUNTER

HARRY PRICE & THE HISTORY OF GHOST RESEARCH

"HAUNTED HOUSE: Responsible persons of leisure and intelligence, intrepid, critical, and unbiased, are invited to join rota of observers in a years night and day investigation of alleged haunted house in Home counties. Printed Instructions supplied. Scientific training or ability to operate simple instruments an advantage. House situated in lonely hamlet, so own car is essential. Write Box H.989, The Times, E.C.4"
Advertisement in the LONDON TIMES, 25 May 1937

There is no doubt in my mind that the practice of Spiritualism literally created the need for paranormal investigation. It would be because of the claims of the Spiritualists, concerning their alleged contact with the dead, that the need for investigations of such claims would come about. These investigations were not done so that the Spiritualists could be exposed as frauds (although this sometimes happened) but because the evidence that was being presented had to be questioned.

The investigations that followed, and which later began to focus less on mediums and Spiritualists and more on hauntings, set the standard for the ghost hunters to come. They established the need to question the evidence of ghosts, ruling out all possible natural explanations for the activity before accepting that it might possibly be real.

In the chapter ahead, we are not going to dwell for long on the Spiritualist movement or even on the investigators who attempted to expose the frauds and duplicate the phenomenon the mediums were creating. Instead, we are going to focus on the background of the man who most influenced the field of paranormal investigation as we know it today. This man's name was Harry Price and, although disliked and distrusted by many, there is no denying that he was one of the most influential figures in the formative years of ghost research. He was a highly charismatic personality whose energy and enthusiasm for the paranormal made him the first celebrity ghost hunter. Price was instrumental in bringing ghost research to the general public, realizing that only by making the research entertaining could he attract the attention of the masses. Because of this, after his death in 1948, jealous "colleagues" would attack not only Price's research, but also the man himself, staining his reputation for years to come.

Price was regarded as an embarrassment during his time and effects from this still linger today. Despite more recent work supporting his claims and methods, many British researchers still regard Price as something of an enigma. Because of his flamboyant manner and continuous self-promotion, Price made a number of enemies within the psychic research field. Much of the resentment revolved around the fact that Price had no real scientific training but was still so skillful at what he did. Price was a deft magician and an expert at detecting deception, so he was not taken in by many of the fraudulent mediums that plagued paranormal research of the time. His success was a slap in the face to what many considered the "established" psychical researchers.

Regardless, his work is considered groundbreaking for many today and his investigations at the house known as Borley Rectory became some of the first documented attempts to track down the ghosts of a single haunted location. I have never made it a secret that I have a great admiration for Harry Price and his work and continue to challenge those who disregard him to show another investigator who has so shaped the methods that we continue to use today. If you are not familiar with his work, you should be and the pages ahead will reveal just how influential he remains.

AMONG THE SPIRITS

To understand the era when Harry Price began his work, and the initial investigations that set the stage for his research to come, the reader must first understand the influence of the Spiritualist movement on the times. As mentioned, most paranormal investigators of the late 1800's and early 1900's started out testing the alleged psychic skills of Spiritualist mediums, attempting to decide if the phenomenon they produced was genuine or fraudulent. Price was one of the investigators who came along during the movement's second heyday, which occurred just after World War I.

The Spiritualist movement, like jazz, was purely an American invention.

Although the idea that man was able to communicate with spirits had existed already for centuries, modern belief in such a practice came about in March 1848 in Hydesville, New York. The movement, which would come to be known as Spiritualism, would remain strong for nearly a century, enjoying its greatest revival after World War I. The practice was founded on the belief that life existed after death and that the spirit existed beyond the body. Most importantly, it was believed that these spirits could (and did) communicate with the living.

Spiritualism was born at the home of the Fox family in Hydesville but legend holds that the house was haunted before the Fox family came to live there. In those days, between 1843 and 1844, a couple named Bell occupied the cottage. In the last few months of their occupancy, a young local woman named Lucretia Pulver handled the household chores. She acted as a maid and carried out the cleaning and cooking duties for the Bell's.

One day, a young peddler came to the door of the house. He was a friendly young man and he brought with him a case of merchandise. These goods consisted of pots, pans and other useful items for the home. He stayed with the family for several days and it has been suggested that perhaps he enjoyed a closer than was proper relationship with Mrs. Bell. A short time later, Lucretia found herself fired from her position in the house. No explanation was ever given but apparently, there were no hard feelings about her dismissal. Mrs. Bell took the girl home in her wagon and before she left the house, Lucretia purchased a small kitchen knife from the peddler's selection. She left him instructions to deliver the item to her father's farm, but the knife never arrived.

Barely a week later, Lucretia was surprised to find that Mrs. Bell was again requesting her services. Thankful to have her job back, she reported for duty the next morning. The peddler who had been staying with the family had departed but she found that a number of things he carried in his case were now in the possession of Mrs. Bell. She simply assumed that Mrs. Bell must have bought the items from the peddler before the young man left for parts unknown. Nothing seemed to be out of the ordinary, but that would soon change.

Shortly after returning to the house, Lucretia began to notice some particularly strange things had begun to occur. Unaccountable noises, like knocking and tapping, came from the room that the peddler had once occupied. On several occasions, she also heard footsteps pacing through the house and then descending the stairs to the cellar. Not surprisingly, Lucretia began to feel frightened and nervous when left alone in the house. She would often send for her brother, or a friend, to come and stay with her and usually, the strange sounds would cease. However, on one occasion, they continued for hours and scared Lucretia's brother so badly that he left the place and refused to return. One afternoon, while in the cellar, Lucretia stumbled and fell over a patch of freshly turned dirt. She was slightly hurt and Mr. Bell explained that the mound of dirt had been dumped to cover up "rat holes".

A short time later, the Bell's moved out and the Weekman family moved in, along with a relative, a Mrs. Lafe. The length of their residence in the house would prove to be a short one. One day, Mrs. Lafe entered the kitchen and as she closed the door behind her, she spotted the apparition of a man in a black frock coat standing across the room. She screamed in terror and the figure vanished. Soon, they all began to hear the rappings and footsteps in the house. They would come during the daylight hours, but mostly they were heard at night, bothering everyone as they tried to sleep. Finally, the odd happenings proved to be too much for them and they abandoned the place.

Then in 1848, the Fox family moved into the house. John Fox and his wife had two young daughters, Margaret and Kate, and they settled temporarily into the cottage. Fox was a farmer who had come to New York from Canada and had purchased land nearby. A home was being built on the new property and he moved his family into the cottage until the other house could be completed. Their stay would turn out to be very eventful.

Within days of moving in, the noises began. The banging and rattling sounds pounded loudly each night, disturbing them all from their sleep. At first, John Fox thought nothing of the sounds that his wife and children reported and were so frightened by. He assumed that they were merely the sounds of an unfamiliar dwelling, amplified by active imaginations. Soon however, the reports took another turn. Kate woke up screaming one night, saying that a cold hand had touched her on the face. Margaret swore that rough, invisible fists had pulled the blankets from her bed. Even Mrs. Fox swore that she had heard disembodied footsteps walking through the house and then going down the wooden steps into the dank cellar.

Fox, not a superstitious man, was perplexed. He tried walking about the house, searching for squeaks and knocks in the floorboards and along the walls. He tested the windows and doors to see if vibrations in the frames might account for the sounds. He could find no explanation for the weird noises and his daughters became convinced that the house had a ghost.

On the evening of March 31, Fox began his almost nightly ritual of investigating the house for the source of the sounds. The tapping had begun with the setting of the sun and although he searched the place, he was no closer to a solution. Then, Kate began to realize that whenever her father knocked on a wall or door frame, the same number of inexplicable knocks would come in reply. It was as if someone, or something, was trying to communicate with them.

Finding her nerve, Kate spoke up, addressing the unseen presence by the nickname that she and her sister had given it. "Here, Mr. Splitfoot," she called out, "do as I do!" She clapped her hands together two times and seconds later, two knocks came in reply, seemingly from inside of the wall. She followed this display by rapping on the table and the precise number of knocks came again from the presence. The activity caught the attention of the rest of the family and they entered the room with Kate and her father. Mrs. Fox tried asking aloud questions, such as the ages of her daughters and the age of a Fox child who had earlier passed away. To her surprise, each reply eerily accurate.

Unsure of what to do, John Fox summoned several neighbors to the house to observe the phenomenon. Most of them came over very skeptical of what they were hearing from the Fox's, but were soon astounded to find the ages and various dates and years given in response to the questions they asked were correct.

One neighbor, and a former tenant in the house, William Duesler, decided to try and communicate with the source of the sounds in a more scientific manner. He asked repeated questions and was able to create a form of alphabet using a series of knocks. He also was able to determine the number of knocks that could be interpreted as "yes" and "no". In such a manner, he was able to determine the subject of the disturbances. The answer came, not in private, but before an assembled group of witnesses, that the presence in the house was the spirit of a peddler who had been murdered and robbed years before.

As it happened, one of the neighbors who had assembled in the house was the former maid of the Bell family, Lucretia Pulver. She came forward with her story of finding the dirt that had been unearthed in the cellar. The story now took on a more sinister tone. John Fox and William Duesler went to the area that Lucretia described and began to dig. After more than an hour, they had little to show for their trouble but an empty hole and sore backs. That was until Fox noticed something odd beneath the blade of his shovel. He prodded at the object and then picked it up. It appeared to be a small piece of bone with a few strands of hair still clinging to it. Spurred on by the gruesome discovery, he and Duesler began to dig once more. They found a few scraps and tatters of clothing, but little else. They were far from disappointed though, as a local doctor determined that the bone appeared to be a piece of a human skull. They were convinced that the presence in the house was indeed the ghost of the luckless peddler.

Shortly after, the story of the Fox family took a more dramatic turn. The two daughters were both purported to have mediumistic powers and the news of the unearthly communications with the spirit quickly spread. By November 1849, they were both giving public performances of their skills and the Spiritualist movement was born. The mania to communicate with the dead swept the country and the Fox sisters became famous.

Over the years, the credibility of the Fox family was often called into question. As no real evidence existed to say that any peddler was actually killed in the house, many accused the family of making up the entire story to support their claims of supernatural powers. It may come as no surprise to the reader that the Spiritualist movement was riddled with fraud, but was the story of the murdered peddler merely a ruse to prove the powers of the Fox sisters?

It's possible that Margaret and Kate, had they not died years before, would have been vindicated in 1904. By this time, their former home had been deserted for some years. A group of children were playing in the ruins one day when the east wall of the cellar collapsed, nearly killing one of them. A man who came to their aid quickly realized the reason for the wall's collapse. Apparently, it had been a false partition, hastily and poorly constructed in the past. Between the false brick wall and the genuine wall of the cellar were the crumbling bones of a man and a large box, just like the ones that had been carried by peddlers a few decades before. A portion of the man's skull was missing.

Dead men, as they say, really do tell tales.

Or do they? That's been the mystery behind Spiritualism since it was first conceived. Were those involved with the movement really communicating with the dead? Skeptics, even of those times, were convinced they were not, but the public was not so easily discouraged. In fact, they were fascinated with the reports coming from New York and news of these "spirited communications" quickly spread and the Fox Sisters became famous. In November 1849, the girls were giving public demonstrations of their powers in contacting the spirit world and drawing crowds that numbered into the thousands. Seemingly overnight, Spiritualism became a full-blown religious movement, complete with scores of followers, its own unique brand of phenomena and codes of conduct for everything from spirit communication to séances.

The Spiritualists believed that the dead could communicate through what were called "mediums". They were sensitive persons who were in touch with the next world and while in a trance, they could pass along messages from the other side. Besides these "message mediums", there were also practitioners who could produce physical phenomena that was said to be the work of the spirits. This phenomena included lights, unearthly music, levitation of objects, disembodied voices and even actual apparitions.

All of this was produced during what were called "séances" (or sittings), which were regarded as the most exciting method of spirit communication. Any number of people could attend and the rooms where the séances took place often contained a large table that the attendees could sit around, smaller tables that were suitable for lifting and tilting, and a cabinet where the mediums could be sequestered while the spirits materialized and performed their tricks. The sessions reportedly boasted a variety of phenomena, including musical instruments that played by themselves and sometimes flew about the room, glowing images, ghostly hands and messages from the dead.

While each séance was different, most had one thing in common in that they were always held in dark or dimly lighted rooms. Believers explained that the darkness provided less of a distraction to the audience and to the medium. They also added that since much of the spirit phenomenon was luminous, it was much easier seen in the darkness.

Those who were not so convinced of the validity of the movement offered another explanation. They believed the dark rooms concealed the practice of fraud. These early questioners would go on to become the first paranormal investigators of the era.

But while the Spiritualist movement brought the study of ghosts and spirits into the public eye, it also provided fame (and sometimes infamy) to many of those involved. Not only did the mediums gain notoriety, but so did many of the investigators, and in many cases, the movement led to their ruin. Even the Fox sisters, who had known such early fame and fortune, drank themselves to death and died penniless.

The downfalls of many of the mediums came about because of their exposure as fakes. It was obvious that Spiritualism was riddled with cases of deliberate fraud. It seemed easy to fool the thousands of people who were looking for a miracle and many of the mediums began lining their pockets with money that had swindled from naive clients.

Of course, that's not to say that all of the Spiritualists were dishonest. Many of them, like famous author Sir Arthur Conan Doyle, truly believed in the validity of the movement. At the very worst, many of these believers were good-hearted but gullible and at best, well -- there do remain a few of the mediums for which no logical explanations have been suggested. For as William James said about the medium Lenora Piper... "to upset the conclusion that all crows are black, there is no need to seek demonstration that no crows are black; it is sufficient to produce one white crow; a single one is sufficient." Piper, James believed, was the "one white crow".

Interestingly, Spiritualism was never meant to turn into a faith or religious movement. It was little more than a popular past time at first and the idea of communicating with the spirits was an amusing way to spend a long winter evening. There were a couple of factors that worked independently to cause Spiritualism to be inflated in importance and to be accepted as an actual religious faith. One of these was the rise of the Apostolic Church in America, which also got its start in New York. The idea of speaking in tongues and being taken over by the Holy Spirit appealed to many and the Pentecostal faith (and its many offshoots) is still going strong today. Despite the fact that many ministers condemned Spiritualism as the "work of the Devil", it was not a far stretch for many to accept the possibility of strange events surrounding spirit communication and religious fervor at the same time.

In addition to the Apostolic movement, Spiritualism saw a huge increase in popularity after the Civil War and then, after a slow period, saw another incredible resurgence after World War I. Most credit this to the fact that families were really introduced to the wholesale slaughter of loved ones in a way that they had never seen before. Thanks to Spiritualism, their lost loved ones, taken away so young during the throes of the war, were no longer lost at all. They could be communicated with and contacted as if they were still alive. Spiritualism managed to fill a huge void for the everyday person, who now had something to cling to and a belief that their friends and family members had gone on to a better place.

By around 1900, Spiritualism had largely died out as a popular movement, as it had never really been organized enough to continue, thanks to dissension in the ranks and internal politics among the leaders. The exposure of many frauds also took their toll and with science not being forthcoming about legitimizing the proof of Spiritualistic tenets, the movement began to fall apart. A little more than a decade later though, World War I brought thousands of the bereaved back to séances when the movement went through its second heyday. Public interest soon cooled though and by the 1920's, the era of the physical medium was gone. Most agree that this period was largely killed off by the continued attacks by magicians, investigators and debunkers, who exposed fraud after fraud and gave even the legitimate practitioners a bad name. Soon, the mediums no longer wanted to expose themselves and abandoned the physical medium effects of flying trumpets and spirit materializations and turned to mental mediumship instead.

Mental mediumship can include trance messages relayed from the spirits and while some mediums continue to work with the spirits of the dead, others claim contact with highly evolved discarnate beings that is characteristic of channeling. In recent years, Spiritualism (or rather a skewed, modern version of it) has gained popularity again through television psychics who also claim to be able to communicate with the dead. As was the case years ago, much controversy surrounds these claims and there has been little proof offered that these communications are genuine. However, as with the early days of Spiritualism, many questions remain unanswered.

Psychic investigation began just shortly after the birth of Spiritualism. By the 1850's, science had managed to challenge the hold that religion maintained on society, offering a new version of the truth for people to examine. Mixed into this time period was Spiritualism, with its alleged proof of life after death, and the public became fascinated by it. Not long after though, many of the practitioners of this new faith were exposed as frauds and a division formed between those who believed in Spiritualism and those who did not.

The scientific establishment, resentful over the fact that they had managed to break the hold that religion had on society only to lose their footing to Spiritualism, encouraged the debunking of mediums and had a blatant disregard for anything that even hinted at the supernatural. In spite of this, there were a small number of scientists who had taken the time to attend séances and who believed that there could be something to the strange phenomena that was being reported. They decided to try and apply the laws of science in investigating these reports.

By the late 1800's, there were a number of scientists who investigated the claims of mediums. Perhaps the best known was Sir William Crookes, an eminent chemist. From 1869 to 1875, he investigated a number of mediums, including the famous Daniel Douglas Home. After witnessing a number of Home's séances, he became convinced that the phenomena he saw was genuine and proved the existence of a "psychic" force within the human body. Crookes wrote a paper on Home and tried to have it published in the Proceedings of the Royal Society of London but it was refused. He then used his considerable influence to have it appear in the *Quarterly Journal of Science* instead. Needless to say, it caused an uproar in the scientific community and both Crookes and his work were discredited.

Two scientists who watched Crookes' plight with sympathy were Professor Henry Sidgwick and Frederick Myers. They firmly believed in the possibility of supernatural phenomena. Myers had attended an 1873 séance conducted by Charles Williams, where he had felt the hand of Williams' spirit guide, John King, melt away to nothing while he was still holding it.

It was experiences like this one, combined with the attacks on Crookes, that persuaded Myers, Sidgwick and a friend named Edmund Gurney, to form an association of people who were interested in investigating the paranormal. Among the group's first members were future British Prime Minister Arthur Balfour, his sister Eleanor, Lord Rayleigh and Stanton Moses.

Over the course of the next six years, the group continued their inquiries and soon found themselves mixed in with a small number of Spiritualists and interested individuals who were also attempting to conduct investigations of the paranormal. Finally, in 1882, a committee was formed with Sidgwick as the president. It later became the Society for Psychical Research. The initial membership was mostly made up of Spiritualists and friends of the Sidgwick group like Lewis Carroll, Mark Twain and William Gladstone. They formed six research committees to investigate hypnotism and clairvoyance, telepathy, sensitives, mediums, ghosts and hauntings, and records and archives. The members of the SPR could then devote their spare time to investigating whatever subjects interested them.

The idea behind using scientific research to document the paranormal was to make it as detailed and as painstaking as possible and while such a meticulous approach did not appeal to many of the Spiritualist members, the SPR continued to grow, gaining new members from both the skeptical and supernatural camps, including Sir Oliver Lodge, Sigmund Freud, Carl Jung, Sir William Crookes and Sir Arthur Conan Doyle. In 1885, a sister society was founded in America, which like the SPR, is still in existence today.

Over the course of the next couple of decades, the society managed to weather both scandal and embarrassment, as mediums they endorsed were found to be fraudulent; Frederick Myers got involved in a sex scandal with a female psychic investigator who turned out to be a fraud; Edmund Gurney was found dead under strange circumstances; and in 1888, the founders of the Spiritualist movement, the Fox sisters themselves, publicly confessed to being fakes. Even though the credibility of this confession was in question, it was still used by other scientists to make the SPR members look like fools. By the early 1900's, the reputation of the society was rather tarnished, but nevertheless, still intact.

In the years that followed, the SPR concentrated on the debunking of mediums, until interest in Spiritualism began to die down. At that point, the group turned more toward laboratory work, rather than field investigations, as the American branch of the group had already done.

The SPR is known today as the first large organization dedicated to the study of the paranormal, using scientific techniques to gather evidence. The early society was plagued with problems caused by the controversy of Spiritualism and by smear campaigns launched by scientists who were angry the group was started in the first place.

The mainstream scientists considered the academic members of the SPR to be merely crack-pots, while the other members were simply pseudo-scientists who had no business using scientific techniques in any sort of investigation. To try and get into the good graces of the scientific community, the SPR spent a lot of their time debunking mediums, which in turn got the Spiritualists angry with them too.

In the end, this was all for the best. A group dedicated to the research of the paranormal cannot be aligned with only the debunkers or with the "true believers", but must remain grounded in the middle, gathering evidence which is based on facts and not preconceived notions. In this, the SPR (and many groups who have appeared after them) have succeeded and are able to continue their work today.

It was from the volatile climate of the 1920's that Harry Price first emerged as an investigator of Spiritualist mediums. During this period, Price began to make a name, and also many enemies, for himself.

Harry Price was born in London in 1881, the son of a grocer and traveling salesman. His interest in the paranormal began in 1889 when he saw his first performance by a stage magician. From that point on, he became an amateur conjurer and began collecting what would become an immense library of books on magic.

Price had his first encounter with the supernatural at age 15, when he and a friend locked themselves overnight in a reportedly haunted house. After hearing noises in an upstairs room that they could not explain, and what appeared to be footsteps on the staircase, they set up an old-fashioned powder-flash camera at the bottom of the stairs. About an hour later, they clearly heard the footsteps descending the stairs again and fired the camera. When the plate was developed, it showed nothing but an empty staircase. Price would always consider this his first encounter with a ghost.

After graduating from school, Price worked at a number of jobs, including as a journalist. Then, in 1908, he met and married a wealthy heiress named Constance Mary Knight. He then settled down to become what all of us wishes we could be, an independently wealthy ghost hunter.

By the time that Price joined the Society for Psychical Research in 1920, he had already begun his career as Britain's most famous ghost investigator. He had spent many hours at alleged haunted houses and in the investigation of Spiritualist mediums. He was also an expert magician and soon made a name for himself within the SPR for using his magic skills to debunk fraudulent psychics, which was then in keeping with what was the main thrust of the current SPR investigations.

One of Price's first efforts exposed the work of spirit photographer William Hope, who was making a fortune taking portraits of people that always seemed to include the sitter's dead relatives. Price was sent to investigate and soon published his findings. He claimed that Hope used pre-exposed plates in his camera, which he learned by secretly switching the plates the photographer was using with plates of his own.

It was only chance that led Price into another aspect of his career. One afternoon, while taking the train from London to his country home near Pulborough, Price met a young woman named Stella Cranshaw. The two happened to strike up a conversation about psychic anomalies, during which Stella, who was a hospital nurse, told the investigator that she had been experiencing strange phenomena for years. She said that rapping noises, cold chills and household objects inexplicably taking flight had been bothering her for some time. Price, excited at the prospect of a new test subject, told her that he was a psychic investigator and asked if she would submit to being tested as a medium.

Price, being an amateur inventor, immediately designed new equipment to test the young woman's abilities. One of them was the "telekinetoscope", a clever device that used a telegraph key that when depressed would cause a light to turn on. A glass dome then covered the key so that only psychic powers could operate it.

During 13 séances, conducted between March and October 1923, and always conducted in front of witnesses, Stella managed to produce all sorts of strange, physical phenomena. During one séance, for example, she managed to levitate a table so high that the sitters had to rise out of their chairs to keep their hands upon it. Suddenly, three of the table legs broke away and the table itself folded and collapsed. Needless to say, this ended the sitting.

Price kept a journal of the events and also noted a number of temperature fluctuations during each séance and the fact that Stella was able to manipulate the foolproof telegraph key device. In the end, Stella's career as a medium would be short-lived, but Price's investigations would earn her much respect in psychic circles. In addition, Price's handling of the investigations would earn him prestige and respectability as well.

Price then journeyed to Munich to investigate the famous medium brothers, Willi and Rudi Schneider, at the laboratory of Baron Albert von Schreck-Notzing, a flamboyant investigator. Price was so impressed with what he saw during the séances, that he invited the brothers to his own laboratories in 1929. He was also impressed with the publicity-seeking methods of von Schreck-Notzing and decided to emulate him in his own career.

Soon, Price began testing his own psychics and set about trying to measure some aspects of the séances in a scientific manner. He managed to record strange temperature drops and other occurrences that finally convinced him of the reality of the paranormal. From this point on, he devoted his time to pursuing genuine phenomena rather than debunking mediums, which did not sit well with the SPR.

The relationship between Price and the society had always been strained so Price formed the National Laboratory for Psychical Research in 1923. It would take three additional years for the laboratory to get up and running and would be located in the London Spiritualist Alliance. This was the final straw for the SPR and in 1927, they returned Price's donation of a massive book collection. To make matters worse, after Price's death, it would be three members of the SPR who would attempt to discredit him.

Most of the members of the SPR treated Price with something verging on contempt. In those days, the main officers of the society were made up of the British upper class and most were related to one another by marriage. Price was most definitely not of their class and breeding, as his father was salesman for a paper manufacturer, and this in itself seemed to make his research suspect in many of their eyes. He was simply, in the words of one of the members of the society's governing council, "not a gentleman." He was also looked down upon for the fact that he was not as well educated as other members and had no formal scientific training. He remained a member of the organization until his death in 1948 but he was not always a welcomed one.

In 1926, Price came across the case of a Romanian peasant girl named Eleonora Zugan, who was apparently experiencing violent poltergeist phenomena, including flying objects, slapping, biting and pinching. The girl had been rescued from an insane asylum by a psychic investigator that Price had met in Vienna. Price returned to London, with the girl, and began a series of laboratory tests that were only partially successful.

Testimony and reports from the testing claimed that "stigmata" appeared on the girl's body under conditions that precluded the possibility of the girl producing them by natural means. It was also stated that she was able to move objects with her mind, although no cause could be discovered for her abilities outside of the fact that she had been severely abused as a young child. Eleonora's "powers" ceased abruptly at the age of 14 when she entered puberty.

In 1929, Rudi Schneider, whose abilities were said to surpass those of his brother, traveled to England to be tested by Price. The investigator was still adding new scientific technology to his array of gadgets and one device wired the hands and feet of Rudi, and everyone else seated around the séance table, to a display board. A light would signal if anyone moved enough to break the electrical circuit.

Despite these controls, Rudi was said to have produced an array of effects, including ectoplasmic masses, rappings and table levitations. Lord Charles Hope, a leading SPR investigator, was astounded, as was Price himself. At the end of the sessions, Price declared that the phenomena produced by Rudi was "absolutely genuine" and "not the slightest suspicious action was witnessed by any controller or sitter."

In the spring of 1932, Price began testing Rudi again. In these sessions, he planned to photograph Rudi's manifestations as further evidence of his psychic abilities. Although Price obtained some favorable results, the sittings were not as successful as before for Rudi's talents seemed to have diminished with age. In the fall, Lord Charles Hope conducted more tests of the young man and while he too noticed a decline in his abilities, he still maintained that his powers were genuine.

And then, even as Hope was preparing his report, Price rocked the paranormal community with the announcement that Rudi was a fraud. As evidence, he produced a photograph that was taken during a séance, which showed Rudi reaching for a table. The camera had been set to go off if there was any movement by the medium. The resulting image was grainy and shadowed, but it managed to destroy Rudi's reputation and embarrass the investigators, including Harry Price, who had declared him to be genuine. Those who claimed that Price was simply a publicity-seeking fraud were (and are) hard-pressed to explain why he would have made himself look ridiculous in this matter.

By the time of Rudi Schneider's downfall, the appearance of credible new mediums had all but ceased. Soon, Price had turned his attention from investigating mediums and psychics to investigating haunted houses and bizarre phenomena.

But not all of Price's cases (or publicity-seeking antics, as some would call them) were as successful. One trip took him to Germany where he went to test a spell that would convert a mountain goat into a man. Needless to say, the spell failed and Price was the subject of much ridicule.

Another of Price's strangest (although possibly genuine) cases was that of Gef, the Talking Mongoose of Cashen's Gap, and yes, if you are not familiar with the case, you did read that right -- a talking animal! The case began in 1931 with a disembodied voice claiming to be that of a mongoose, a weasel-like creature. It began at an isolated place on the Isle of Man and according to the Irving family, who lived at Cashen's Gap, this creature ate rabbits, spoke in various languages, imitated other animals and even recited nursery rhymes.

Price personally investigated the case in the company of R.S. Lambert, then editor of a popular radio show called *The Listener*, but the animal refused to manifest until after they had left. The case may have been related to poltergeist phenomena, as Voirey Irving, the 13-year old daughter in the family, was closely associated with the manifestations of the talking mongoose. Price failed to detect any evidence of fraud.

Lambert, who investigated other supernatural cases with Price, almost lost his job over the Cashen's Gap affair. The publicity around the case caught the attention of his employers at the BBC and one of his supervisors concluded that Lambert's interest in the supernatural reflected poorly on the broadcaster's competence. However, Lambert sued him for defamation of character and kept his job.

The Cashen's Gap case was also investigated by Nandor Fodor, a pioneer in the field of poltergeist phenomenon related to human subjects, who interviewed a number of witnesses to the phenomena, many of them hostile to the haunting, but couldn't shake any of the testimony to say that it was not real. Fodor did not accept the explanation of a poltergeist and half-seriously suggested that it might have actually been a mongoose that learned to talk. Many years later, after the affair had died down, a strange and unidentified animal was killed in the area. Some suggested that it might have been Gef.

During this period, Price also made some serious contributions, although they were not as widely publicized. In 1933, he persuaded the University of London to open a library and set up a University Council for Psychical Investigation. The library still exists today at the university and consists mainly of Price's enormous occult collection.

The year 1929 marked a turning point in Price's career, although the case would not be made public for several years yet. It was in that year that he became involved in a case which would take over his life and for which he would become most famous. The case involved a deteriorating Essex house called Borley Rectory, which will be discussed in more detail later in this chapter.

It would be during Price's investigations of Borley Rectory that he would become the best known and most accomplished of the early ghost hunters, setting the standard for those who would follow. He carefully documented both his findings and methods and established a blueprint for paranormal investigations.

Many of Price's accounts from Borley would be first-hand, as he claimed to see and hear much of the reported phenomena like hearing bells ring, rapping noises and seeing objects that had been moved from one place to another. In addition, he also collected accounts from scores of witnesses and previous tenants of the house, also talking to neighbors and local people who had their own experiences with the rectory.

Price even leased the house for an extended one-year investigation that was supposed to run around the clock. He ran an advertisement looking for open-minded researchers to literally "camp out" at the rectory and record any phenomena that took place in their presence. After choosing more than 40 people, he then printed the first-ever handbook on how to conduct a paranormal investigation. A copy was given to each investigator and it explained what to do when investigating the house, along with what equipment they would need.

Price turned the Borley investigations into two books entitled *The Most Haunted House in England* (1940) and *The End of Borley Rectory* (1946). Both books became very popular and entrenched Price solidly as the organizer of well-run paranormal investigations.

Despite what his detractors would claim, the books would set the standard for future investigations and would mark the first time that detailed accounts of paranormal research had been exposed to the general public. While his critics saw this only as further grand-standing, future investigators were able to use the books when researching their own cases.

Regardless of what some may think of his methods and research, Harry Price must be remembered today as a pioneer in paranormal research. He is the one person who so many modern investigators (even unknowingly) emulate today with their own research. Price managed to give "ghost hunting" a place in the public eye and opened it up to those who don't fit into the category of professional scientist or hard-headed skeptic, nor that gullible "true believer" either. If for no other reason than this, we owe him a debt of gratitude.

BORLEY RECTORY

One of the most famous haunted houses cases of all time, and unquestionably the most famous case in the career of Harry Price, was that of Borley Rectory, a deteriorating house in Essex. The last ten years or more of Price's life were dominated by the long, complex and rewarding investigation of this house and its hauntings. None of his earlier cases had ever involved so many people, aroused so much interest or caused him so many problems. His two books that were written on the case became bestsellers and captured the imagination of the public. At the time of his death, he was in the final preparations for a third book on Borley Rectory and interest in the story has never ceased.

There have been critics and attention-seekers who have maintained that the whole thing was a hoax, a publicity stunt that was created by Price. One journalist accused him (after his death, of course) of deliberately lying about the phenomenon and producing some of the activity with a "pocketful of pebbles and bricks". On the other hand, there are those who were actually present when the strange activity occurred who could assure the doubters that the house was truly as haunted as Price claimed.

It would be impossible to retell the entire story of Borley Rectory and give it the space that it deserves in this book. Price needed two entire books to do it and was forced to leave out several hundred pages of his notes. What I will present here is a main outline of events and theories about the rectory and offer it as a groundbreaking case in the history of paranormal research. To some ghost hunters, a haunted house from the 1930's will seem impossibly old-fashioned and out of date but I submit it to you here as one of the first in-depth and documented accounts of haunted house investigation and one that has helped to set the standards that we attempt to imitate today.

The tiny parish of Borley is located in a desolate, sparsely populated area near the east coast of England, near the Suffolk border. It is a lonely place and would be largely forgotten if not for the fact that it is the location of what came to be known as "The Most Haunted House in England".

Harry Price would begin the chronicle of Borley in 1362, when Edward III bestowed the Manor of Borley upon the Benedictine monks, but as much of this history is shrouded in mystery, we will state with more certainty that the manor was in the possession of the powerful Waldegrave family for 300 years. Between 1862 and 1892, the Reverend H.D.E. Bull, a relative of the Waldegraves, was the rector of Borley. A year after his appointment, he built Borley Rectory. Despite local warnings, he built the house on a site believed by locals to be haunted. He was succeeded as the rector by his son, the Rev. H.F. Bull, who remained until his death in 1927. After that, the rectory was vacant for over a year until October 1928, when the Rev. Guy Eric Smith was appointed to the role. However, he quit the rectory just one year after moving in, plagued by both the ghosts and the house's deteriorating state.

There had been strange happenings in and around the rectory for many years before the residency of the Rev. Smith but they had been kept quiet by all concerned. In 1886, a Mrs. E. Byford quit her position as a nanny at the rectory because of "ghostly footsteps". More than 14 years later, two daughters of Henry Bull first spotted what would become the famous "phantom nun" on the rectory's front lawn. The sighting occurred in the middle of the afternoon and would coincide with other strange happenings that were reported by the family, including phantom rappings, unexplained footsteps and more. The young women were repeatedly unnerved by these events but Reverend Bull seemed to regard them as splendid entertainment. He and his son, Harry, even constructed a summer house on the property where they could enjoy after-dinner cigars and watch for the appearance of the phantom nun as she walked nearby.

Rev. Harry Bull often discussed the spirits with his friend J. Harley, who later supplied information to Harry Price. In 1922, Bull told Hartley that in his opinion, "the only way for a spirit, if ignored, to get into touch with a living person, was by means of a manifestation causing some violent physical reaction, such as the breaking of glass or the shattering of other and similar material elements. The Rector also declared that on his death, if he were discontented, "he would adopt this method of communicating with the inhabitants of the Rectory."

The members of the Bull family were not the only ones to see the ghostly nun on the grounds or outside the gates of the rectory. Fred Cartwright, a local carpenter, saw her

A southeast view of Borley Rectory

four times in two weeks, according to his account to Price. Up until 1939, 14 people were reported to have seen the nun, three people had seen a phantom coach and horses with "glittering harness" sweep across the grounds and two others had seen the apparition of a headless man.

In June 1929, two years after the death of Harry Bull and nine months after Rev. Smith came to the rectory, the story of ghostly occurrences in Borley was mentioned in the newspaper. The next day, Harry Price received a telephone call from a London editor and was asked to investigate. He was told about various types of phenomena that had been reported there, like phantom footsteps; strange lights; ghostly whispers; a headless man; a girl in white; the sounds of a phantom coach outside; the apparition of the home's builder, Henry Bull; and of course, the spirit of the nun. This spectral figure was said to drift through the garden with her head bent in sorrow.

Local legend had it that a monastery had once been located on the site and that a 13th century monk and a beautiful young novice were killed while trying to elope from the place. The monk was hanged and his would-be bride was bricked up alive within the walls of her convent. Price scoffed at the idea of such a romantic tale but was intrigued by the phenomena associated with the house.

Price was accompanied on his first visit to Borley by V.C. Wall, a well known journalist, and Miss Lucie Kaye, his experienced secretary. Together, they listened to the experiences of Rev. Smith and even observed some minor examples of poltergeist phenomenon for themselves. Price also conducted a long interview with Miss Mary Pearson, the rectory's maid, who had seen the ghostly coach and horses twice and was firmly convinced the house was genuinely haunted. Later that night, the group held a séance in the "Blue Room" of the house, where much of the manifestations had allegedly occurred, and they were purported to make contact with Harry Bull. Whether they did or not, they were startled when a piece of soap jumped up off the floor with no assistance. The following day, Price held more interviews and spoke with Rev. Bull's daughters and the Coopers, a man and wife who had lived in a cottage on the rectory grounds. They had moved out in 1920, blaming uncomfortable feelings caused by the ghosts.

The events that occurred, and the witness interviews that were documented, were enough to convince Price that something strange was going on at the house. That June day would begin more than 18 years of intensive and overwhelming paranormal investigation. It would be during his investigations of Borley Rectory that he would become the best known and most accomplished of the early ghost hunters, setting the standard for those who would follow. Price coined the idea of the "ghost hunter's kit"; used tape measurers to check the thickness of walls and to search for hidden chambers; perfected the use of still cameras for indoor and outdoor photography; brought in a remote-control motion picture camera; put to use a finger-printing kit; and even used portable telephones for contact between investigators. He was quite impressed by the house and believed that it represented one of the most exciting and fascinating puzzles of his career.

His second visit to Borley came two weeks after the first. This time, he documented the appearance of a religious medal and some other items that seemed to show there was a Catholic element to the haunting. There was also a number of times when bells rang throughout the house, although the bell wires (once used to summon the servants) had been cut many years before. The constant ringing was a source of great worry for Rev. Smith and his wife and this, along with other manifestations, convinced the couple to abandon the house on July 14, 1929.

Over the course of the next 14 months, the rectory remained empty and yet the happenings reportedly continued. According to local accounts, a window on the house was opened from the inside, even though the rectory was deserted and the doors were securely locked. The main staircase was found covered with lumps of stone and small pieces of glass were said to have been scattered about. Locals who lived nearby reported seeing "lights" in the house and hearing what were described as "horrible sounds" around the time of the full moon.

Even though Rev. Smith and his wife moved out of the house because of the ghosts, things had really been rather peaceful up until that point. All of that would change though in October 1930, when Smith was replaced by the Reverend Lionel Foyster and his wife, Marianne. Their time in the house would see a marked increase in the paranormal activity. People were locked out of rooms, household items vanished, windows were broken, furniture was moved, odd sounds were heard and much more. However, the worst of the incidents seemed to involve Mrs. Foyster, as she was thrown from her bed at night, slapped by invisible hands, forced to dodge heavy objects which flew at her day and night, and was once almost suffocated with a mattress.

The activity during this period was more varied and far more violent than ever before. Rev. Foyster kept a diary and later compiled a manuscript that was never published called "Fifteen Months in a Haunted House". Harry Price would later use large excerpts from the manuscript in his books on Borley. There is no question that Rev. Foyster, Marianne, his adopted daughter and later, a young boy who stayed with them as a guest, went through some strange and sometimes terrifying experiences.

Things took another inexplicable turn when there began to appear a series of scrawled messages on the walls of the house, written by an unknown hand. They seemed to be pleading with Mrs. Foyster, using phrases like "Marianne, please help get" and "Marianne light mass prayers".

It had gotten so bad that by May 1931, the Foysters left the rectory so that they could get a few days of peace and quiet. In June, Dom Richard Whitehouse, a friend of the Foysters, began an investigation. He found that things had been scattered all over the unoccupied house and when the family returned, the violent phenomenon began again. At one point, Mrs. Foyster was hurled from her bed three times.

In September of that same year, Harry Price learned of these new and more violent manifestations. A short time later, he and some of his friends paid a visit to the rectory and witnessed some weird happenings of their own, including mysterious locking and unlocking doors and bottles that were tossed about. Because nearly all of the poltergeist-like activity occurred when Mrs. Foyster was present, Price was inclined to attribute it to her unknowing manipulations. He also considered the idea that some of it might be trickery. However, he did believe in the possibility of the ghostly nun and some of the other reported phenomenon. The rectory did not fit into pre-conceived notions of a haunted house, which was one of the reasons that it would go on to gain such a reputation.

Despite the implications of the phenomena centering around Marianne, Price maintained that at least one of the spirits in the house had found the rector's wife to be sympathetic to its plight. This was the only explanation he could find for the mysterious messages. He believed the writings had come from another young woman, one who seemed to be, from her references, a Catholic. These clues would later fit well into Price's theory that the Borley mystery was a terrible tale of murder and betrayal, in which the central character was a young nun, although not the one of legend.

A short time after Price's visit, Mrs. Foyster, Dom Richard Whitehouse and the Foyster's maid, Katie, were seated in the kitchen with all of the doors and windows closed, when bottles began to appear, seemingly from nowhere, only to shatter on the floor. At the same time, the bells in the house suddenly began ringing once again.

The months that followed brought more ringing bells and door locking but after a séance was held, things quieted down considerably. The bells still rang occasionally and items flew about but there was what was described as a "different atmosphere" after the sittings. The remainder of 1934 was quiet but in 1935, the manifestations returned and became more violent. Things frequently vanished and were broken and by October of that year, the Foysters had reached the limits of their endurance. They decided to leave the house and the church decided to sell the place, as they now believed that it was unfit for any parson to live in.

The church offered the house to Harry Price -- for about one sixth of its value -- but after some hesitation, he decided not to buy the place but to rent it for a year. Price planned to conduct an extended, around the clock investigation of the house, using scores of volunteer investigators to track and document anything out of the ordinary that occurred there. As it turned out, the investigation was never that organized. Even so, in spite of often poor record-keeping and periods when the house was unoccupied, the year-long investigation remains a landmark in the annals of the paranormal.

Price's first step was to run an advertisement in the personal column of the Times on May 25, 1937 looking for open-minded researchers to literally "camp out" at the rectory. They were to record any phenomena which took place in their presence. The advertisement read:

"HAUNTED HOUSE: Responsible persons of leisure and intelligence, intrepid, critical, and unbiased, are invited to join rota of observers in a years night and day investigation of alleged haunted house in Home counties. Printed Instructions supplied. Scientific training or ability to operate simple instruments an advantage. House situated in lonely hamlet, so own car is essential. Write Box H.989, The Times, E.C.4"

Price was deluged with potential applicants, most of whom were unsuitable. After choosing more than 40 people, he then printed the first-ever handbook on how to conduct a paranormal investigation. It became known as the "Blue Book". A copy was given to each investigator and it explained what to do when investigating the house, along with what equipment they would need. Because of the historical nature of the booklet, I am reprinting the pages of it here. I believe the reader will find that in many cases, aside from the time period in which it was used, many of the instructions that Price gave to the observers at Borley Rectory are still relevant to investigators today.

From the "Blue Book" by Harry Price:

THE ALLEGED HAUNTING AT B------ RECTORY
INSTRUCTIONS FOR OBSERVERS

INSTRUCTIONS
1. Attend carefully to all written and verbal instructions and carry out to the letter.

2. Each observer should provide himself with the following articles, in addition to night clothes, etc. Note-block, pencils, good watch with second hand, candles and matches, pocket electric torch, brandy flask, sandwiches, etc. If he possesses a camera, this can be used. Rubber or felt-soled shoes should be worn.

3. When going on duty, search the house thoroughly, close and fasten all doors and windows. If thought necessary, these can be sealed.

4. Visit all rooms, etc. at intervals of about one hour, unless circumstances call for your presence in any particular part of the house or grounds. Before going on duty at each period, inspect grounds.

5. Occasionally extinguish all lights, and wait in complete darkness (varying your observation post), remaining perfectly quiet.

6. Make a point of taking meals at the same times each day or night. Depart from this rule if circumstances warrant.

7. Make the fullest notes of the slightest unusual sound or occurrence.

8. Take exact times of all sounds of happenings; also make notes of your own movements with exact times. Record weather conditions.

9. Frequently examine grounds, and, occasionally watch windows of house from exterior of building.

10. If with companion, both he and you should act in unison (in order to have a witness), unless circumstances determine otherwise. If several observers present, party can

be divided between house and grounds.

11. For one half hour before, and half-hour after sunset, take up position in Summer House. Remain perfectly quiet, and watch the "Nun's Walk" on the far side of the lawn. It is this path that a black draped figure is said to frequent.

12. If phenomena appear strong, or if experiencing a succession of unusual events, immediately communicate with one of the persons whose telephone numbers have been handed you. Detail exact happenings. Expert assistance or further instructions, will be sent you.

13. Establish your base in one room, and keep all your equipment, etc. at this post. This will prevent hunting for an article when wanted in an emergency.

14. Keep the electric torch IN YOUR POCKET ALWAYS, whether in or out of the house. Be careful with all lights, matches, cigarette ends, etc.

15. Should strangers call, be courteous to them. Do not permit them to enter the house; do not encourage them to remain; ON NO ACCOUNT GIVE THEM INFORMA-TION OR OPINIONS of any sort. This applies to villagers, hotel staff, etc. equally.

16. Re: Meals. You should come provided each day with sandwiches, etc. and hot drinks in a vacuum flask. Rest can be obtained on the camp bed provided, but excellent meals and beds can be procured at "The Bull" L---------- (2 1/2) miles, or at S----------- (2 1/4 miles). It should be possible to obtain sufficient rest during the 24 hours, but if two are on duty, take turns at resting, and wake your companion if anything unusual occurs. Leave your car in the appointed place, screened from the road.

17. When asked to take charge of instruments, examine them regularly with torch, and record readings and times in note book. Carefully note anything which may appear unusual. Change charts when necessary, marking on each the time it was changed, and date.

18. Spend at least a portion of the day and night (in complete darkness) in the Blue Room.

19. No observer is permitted to take a friend to the house, unless permission has been given and the necessary Declaration Form signed.

20. Your report and notes should be posted to the Honorary Secretary, University of London Council for Psychical Investigation, 19 Berkeley Street, Mayfair, W.1., as soon as possible after you have completed your "watch".

Possible phenomena may be experienced. There is some evidence for all of these alleged manifestations during the past forty years.

BELL RINGING If a bell rings, immediately ascertain which bell, and from what room or place the "pull" was operated. Note if bell pull is in motion, and record duration of ringing, and exact time.

MOVEMENT of OBJECTS When going on duty, see that objects are on chalked outlines, and check frequently. When an object is heard to fall, immediately ascertain in which room object has fallen, and draw rough plan of the room, showing the direction of flight. Estimate approximate force expended, and, if object seen in flight, note speed, course, force and trajectory. Examine object and restore to chalked outline.

FOOTSTEPS If footsteps are heard, try to judge direction, note duration, and record type (heavy, soft, pattering, shuffling, etc.) and at what time they were heard.

FORMS or APPARITIONS If seen, DO NOT MOVE AND ON NO ACCOUNT APPROACH THE FIGURE. Note exact method of appearance. Observe figure carefully, watch all movements, rate, manner of progression, etc. Note duration of appearance, colour, form, size, how dressed, and whether solid or transparent. If carrying camera with film ready for exposing, quietly "snap" the figure, but make no sound and do not move. If figure speaks, DO NOT APPROACH, but ascertain name, age, sex, origin, cause of visit, if in trouble, and possible alleviation. Enquire if it is a spirit. Ask figure to return, suggesting exact time and place. Do not move until figure disappears. Note exact method of vanishing. If through an open door, quietly follow. If through solid object (such as walls) ascertain if still visible on the other side. Make the very fullest notes of the incident. The "nun" is alleged to walk regularly along the "Nun's Walk" in grounds. (See Instruction No. 11)

RAPS or KNOCKS Ascertain exact location and intensity, and whether soft or percussive. Imitate knocks with knuckles or foot, and note whether your signals are duplicated. If so, say aloud that you would like a number of questions answered, and that the "entity" can reply by giving one rap for "yes" and two for "no", and three for "doubtful" or "unknown". Endeavor by these means to ascertain name, age, sex, condition, etc. Ask "entity" to knock at a letter when you call over the alphabet. Information can thus be conveyed, and intelligent sentences formed. Ask "entity" to return, making definite appointment. It is alleged that knocks can frequently be heard in the Blue Room. (See Instruction No. 18)

PERFUMES If air becomes scented, try to identify perfume, and ascertain whether it is general or localized. Look for any dampness.

LIGHTS If lights are seen note mode of appearance, judge exact position in room or grounds, size, shape, height from ground, duration, colour, and whether lambent or percussive. If traveling, direction and trajectory, and method of disappearance. Note whether odour accompanies lights.

APPORTS (Objects abnormally brought or precipitated into house) Note exact time of arrival, if possible, and endeavor to ascertain their origin. Carefully preserve and continue inquiries.

DISAPPEARANCES Note under what conditions the object disappeared, exact time of disappearance, and if accompanied by sounds of any sort. Search for object and note if, how, and when it makes its re-appearance.

THERMAL VARIATIONS Transmitting thermographs are used for recording changes of temperature. These should be read frequently. (See Instruction No. 17)

EXTERIOR OF THE HOUSE

The above suggestions apply equally in the case of phenomena occurring OUTSIDE the house. But Poltergeist phenomena (such as stone-throwing) outside the house may be observed from within the building. The fullest particulars concerning such phenomena should be recorded.

IMPORTANT NOTE

Although some - or all - of the above phenomena may be observed, it is very important that the greatest effort should be made to ascertain when such manifestations are due to normal causes, such as rats, small boys, the villagers, the wind, wood shrinking, the Death Watch beetle, farm animals nosing the doors, etc., trees brushing against the windows, birds in the chimney stack or between the double walls, etc.

End of "Blue Book" -------

During the investigations, the researchers were allowed wide latitude when it came to searching for facts. Some of them employed their own equipment, others kept precise journals and others turned to séances, which would prove interesting over the period of 1935 to 1939. The greatest aid to Price in the investigations was Mr. S. H. Glanville. He and his family took a special interest in Borley and spent many, many hours there. It was Glanville who compiled with great zeal the famous "Locked Box", which contained a detailed record of the Borley story from its beginning to the night of the fire in 1939. Some of the material was eventually published in Price's books and Glanville remained completely in charge of the investigations when Price was not present.

The observers that Price recruited came from all different professions, outlooks and interests but all of them contributed to the pile of data that began to accumulate. Many of them spent nights in the empty rectory, where one room had been set up to serve as a "base" and where various instruments had been installed. Some of them came alone and others came in groups, skeptics, believers and debunkers alike. A good many of them neither saw nor heard anything but quite a few of them had strange experiences. These experiences were wildly varied from sounds to moving objects, weird lights and even full blown apparitions. Very few of them were witnessed by one person alone and the nun was seen by the majority of them.

The corps of observers established beyond doubt that Borley Rectory was the center of some large paranormal disturbances. The number of the disturbances, their variety and the length of their observations also supply an answer to any accusations that Harry Price staged the phenomenon for publicity or other purposes. The vast majority of the observations, accounts and reports were not witnessed by Price at all. Instead, they came from independent observers who often had no idea that others were experiencing the same events at other times.

There were two important developments during Price's tenancy of the house. One was the observation of the "wall writings". These frantic cries for help were often hard to decipher and had first started to appear during the Foyster's occupancy of the rectory. Most of them were addressed to "Marianne" and some non-believers suggested that they had been written by Mrs. Foyster herself, although none could provide a motive for such a pointless hoax. Strangely, the scrawls continued to appear on the walls long after Mrs. Foyster had left the Rectory and Price believed that they provided vital clues to the mystery behind the haunting. The observers who noted the new messages marked and dated all of them so that there would be no mistake as to which were old and which had appeared later on.

The other important development of 1937 - 1938 was the series of séances that was held by Mr. Glanville, his family and several friends. During a sitting with a planchette (a device used for automatic writing), an alleged spirit named "Marie Lairre" related that she had been a nun in France but had left her convent to marry Henry Waldegrave, a member of a wealthy family whose manor home once stood on the site of Borley Rectory. While living at the manor, her husband had strangled her and had buried her remains in the cellar.

Borley Rectory After the Fire -- March 1939

The story went well with the most interesting of the Borley phenomena, namely the reported phantom nun and the written messages. Price theorized that the former nun had been buried in unconsecrated ground and was now doomed to haunt the property seeking rest.

In March of 1938, five months after Marie's first appearance, another spirit, which called itself "Sunex Amures", promised that the rectory would burn down that night and that the proof of the nun's murder would be found in the ruins. Borley Rectory did not burn that night, but exactly 11 months later, on February 27, 1939, a new owner, Captain W.H. Gregson was unpacking books in the library when an oil lamp overturned and started a fire. The blaze quickly spread and the rectory was gutted. It was said that the fire started at the exact same point that the spirit had predicted and that "strange figures were seen walking in the flames."

The building itself was finally demolished in 1944 but the story was far from over.

The publication of Price's first book on Borley, *The Most Haunted House in England*, brought Price a deluge of letters. The wall-writings, the planchette messages and the various reports from the observers led to arguments, new theories and new facts. Price was able to point out the parallels and similarities in a dozen other hauntings. The rectory was now in ruins but this did not keep the interested away. Throughout the years of World War II, visitors often explored the rubble and occasionally spent the night in the eerie remains of the building. In 1941, H.F. Russell, a businessman, paid a visit to the

The burned out Blue Room of the house, which Polish officers rebuilt and used as a location for séances among the ruins. The plank that leads into the entrance was the site of a mysterious "cold spot" that was encountered by numerous visitors.

Borley grounds with two of his Royal Air Force officer sons. While there, he claimed that he was seized by an invisible presence and dashed to the ground. Two years later, some Polish officers spent the night in the ruins and claimed to see and hear a number of chilling sounds and sights. In particular, they saw a shadow on the Nun's Walk and a man's figure in one of the rooms. The Polish officers also rebuilt the floor in the Blue Room and erected chairs and a table where séances could continue to be held.

Other visitors included a commission from Cambridge University, which was formed by A.J.B. Robertson of St. Johns College. He would go on to contribute a long essay to Price's second book on Borley. Robertson and his colleagues were interested in the inexplicable "cold patches" in the house. They investigated the house from 1939 until the demolition of the rectory in 1944. The report that Robertson wrote at the end of the investigation was cautious but stated that: "There appears, in fact, to be something at the rectory which cannot all be explained away. It must be remembered that the investigations described here form only part of a much wider survey which has brought to light very many mysterious phenomena."

Some of the most fascinating, and ultimately relevant, investigations into the rectory were conducted by Rev. W.J. Phythian-Adams, Canon of Carlisle. After reading Price's book, studying plans of the house and photographs of the wall writings and doing a detailed analysis of Borley's history, Canon Phythian-Adams prepared a detailed and convincing account of events leading up to the haunting. He used the data connected to the Waldegrave family, as well as statements from a medium that Price had contacted to try and use psychometric powers on an apport that had been found by an observer in the Borley sewing room, to create his report. He combined all of the various pieces of the

Borley accounts into a tangible story. He connected the wall writings to the séance messages and extracted the symbolic and literal meanings of the information that had been gathered. There had been many other attempts at interpreting the messages, especially the wall writings, and all had concentrated on the desperate attempts the nun had made to try and get the living to do something for her. But no one else tried to do what Canon Phythian-Adams had achieved -- creating a consecutive narrative that sounded convincing.

There would be those who would say that his story (recounted earlier in the story of "Marie Lairre") was nothing more than clever guesswork but Canon Phythian-Adams told Harry Price to dig for the nun's remains and he told him exactly where to dig. In August 1943, in the company of Rev. A.C. Henning; Dr. Eric H. Bailey, Senior Assistant Pathologist of the Ashford County Hospital; Roland F. Bailey, his brother; Flying Officer A. A. Creamer; Captain W.H. Gregson and his two nieces, Georgina Dawson and Mrs. Alex English, Price began his excavations in the cellars of the ruined rectory.

On the exact spot where Canon Phythian-Adams indicated (having never visited the site), they found a large antique brass preserving pan, a silver cream jug and a jawbone with five teeth on it. Dr. Bailey declared it to be a left mandible, probably from a woman. They also found part of a skull. The next day, they also found two religious medals, one of which was made of poor quality gold. Price took the bone fragments from Borley to the studios of A. C. Cooper, Ltd., well known art photographers, who would then document the finds. At the studio, another strange act in the Borley haunting was played out.

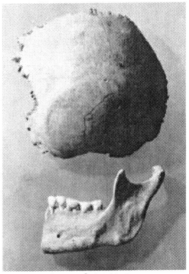

While setting up the skull to have it photographed, it slipped from four hands and broke into four pieces. Moments later, an expensive oil painting fell off its easel with no explanation and crashed to the floor. A clock that had not worked in more than ten years suddenly started back up again, functioning for just 20 minutes before stopping again, this time for good. Five months later, the Cooper studios were destroyed by an air raid. Coincidence? Perhaps, but based on all of the other strange happenings connected to Borley, it was worthy of mention.

In May 1945, a Christian burial for the bones appeared to provide the ghost with the rest she had long sought and a service was later conducted by the Rev. Henning in the small village of Liston, less than two miles from the rectory.

The portions of skull that were found in the ruins of Borley Rectory.

The nun was never seen at the house again but the weird events continued to occur. They were frequent enough that Price made plans for a third book about the site, although it was never completed. As his research progressed, Price lined up 50 new witnesses to more recent phenomena, including Rev. Henning, officials from the BBC, local residents and strangers. It seemed that after the ruins of Borley were demolished, the ghosts moved to Borley Church, where a great many manifestations began to occur in the vestry and throughout the building. Many reliable people heard the organ being played when the church doors were locked and no one could possibly enter. Rev. Henning, then rector of the church, was one of the witnesses and he contributed his accounts to Price for the third book.

Perhaps this was just one of the reasons that the story of Borley Rectory has never really "died". Its legacy remains today and it has gone down in history as one of the world's most haunted houses.

And as for Harry Price himself, his legacy continues as well. His tremendous labors and volumes of research remain controversial but he is not without appreciation. One of those who spoke best of Price, Sir Albion Richardson, Recorder of Nottingham, stated that: "Borley Rectory stands by itself in the literature of psychical manifestation. The large numbers of the public who are interested in these things are under a debt of gratitude to Mr. Harry Price, for without his untiring energy and skilled experience as an investigator, the story of Borley Rectory would have remained unrevealed. The manifestations are proved by the evidence, to the point of moral certainty."

2. INVESTIGATING THE PARANORMAL

INTRODUCTION TO GHOST RESEARCH

Eliminate the impossible and whatever remains, however improbable, must be the truth.
SIR ARTHUR CONAN DOYLE

Man has always been fascinated with the unexplained, the elusive and the unknown. Since the beginning of recorded time, people have reported seeing things that defy natural explanation. In times past, these strange happenings were given a superstitious meaning and taken as signs from the gods, curses or visitations from mysterious creatures.

In more recent times, people have used science as a framework to understand the world and the things that take place in it. Of course, as we have already mentioned, one of the main theories in science is that events can be tested by anyone at any time. In other words, if a scientist makes a claim that he can improve the taste of your food by adding certain chemicals to it, you do not have to take his word for this. You are more than welcome to do your own research on the subject, try the food with and without the chemicals and even get another scientist to do tests that either prove or disprove the claims.

Can hauntings and paranormal phenomena fit into this scientific framework? No, basically, they can't fit in at all. This type of activity is described as anomalous because it completely contradicts all of the standard and existing scientific theories. For this reason, mainstream science tends to ignore any observations, ideas or events that even hint at the supernatural. This way of thinking has always baffled me and I continue to think of it as incredibly blind and narrow-minded. I wonder where the world would be if science had always been this way? Would we still be huddled in the Old World, wondering if we would fall off the edge of the Earth if we sailed too far on the ocean?

BEFORE GETTING STARTED

There are many things to be cautious of when you begin investigating the paranormal. Remember that you have no special privileges as an investigator and that you should always obey laws (such as trespassing) and the rules of society.

1. Always respect a request for confidentiality whether for a person or a location.

2. Never enter any location without permission.

3. If a witness declines to cooperate, always withdraw politely.

4. Always maintain a polite and professional relationship with a witness.

Unfortunately, this narrow viewpoint of mainstream science has become so engrained in our society that most people automatically doubt anything unusual they might hear. For instance, when someone sees a ghost, most people will quickly question their observations and perhaps even their sanity. It doesn't help that this is usually a rare and unexpected event and such things are hardly ever recorded on film. For this reason, it is easy for the public, and for science, to dismiss such reports.

Hauntings are consistently scoffed at by science but how does science explain the fact that there exists a consistent record of ghost sightings and related events that date back for centuries? Ordinary people have reported the presence of ghosts from early times up to the modern day. Could they have all been mistaken, lying or insane? That hardly seems likely and if you have no other reason to maintain an open mind when it comes to ghosts and hauntings, that alone should suffice.

A balance must be struck by the ghost researcher between the hard-edged world of science and the outright acceptance of the true believer. In the vast majority of cases, a natural explanation can be found for the strange happenings that are reported, but once again, can all of those who encounter ghosts be mistaken? Science will say 'yes', but we cannot afford to accept the trappings of mainstream science as total and absolute fact. The theories of the past are constantly changing and being adapted and updated to fit new information. Who knows what might be accepted in the future?

You see, just because scientists choose to treat the paranormal with scorn is no reason why it should not be studied. Their lack of interest in the subject is just the reason why fascinated amateurs need to fill the gap. Don't misunderstand though. There are scientists who do study the paranormal, as evidenced by the excellent parapsychology labs that have existed at universities in the past. There are also other scientists who would like to study it but it is difficult to obtain grants and funding for areas that are not supported by other scientists.

Will breakthroughs ever come? In the introduction to the book, I expressed doubts about paranormal research ever being accepted because science is unable to duplicate the events that occur. However, should even a single anomaly be proven to exist, then the theories that we have now will no longer fit. They will have to be changed completely because they would cause what scientists called a "paradigm shift". While it may be difficult, it is highly possible that such information could come from the research being done by amateur ghost hunters and researchers --- even one who might be reading this book.

In the pages ahead, we will begin to look more closely at actually investigating ghosts and hauntings. Here, you will find theories and clear techniques that will assist you in investigating various types of hauntings and show that ghost research is not just about running around with cameras and meters looking for "orbs" and magnetic fields. It's about understanding the individual cases and looking for a way to resolve them. This book will hopefully serve as a guide to understanding strange phenomena, what is and isn't paranormal and what sort of problems to look for when investigating the unknown. Overall, I hope to pass along information that will help the researcher to strike that balanced and level-headed approach that I mentioned earlier. Only this approach will likely obtain the results that you are looking for.

Here are two approaches that are sometimes used that cause investigations to fail and little evidence to be obtained:

1. THE BELIEVER APPROACH: In this way, ghost hunters go into an investigation with the idea that the house must be haunted. They are sure that the spirit who is present is trying to make contact with the witnesses at the location. These ghost hunters are already accepting that the events reported are genuine and then attempt to prove that their views are correct.

2. THE DEBUNKER APPROACH: In this method, the phenomenon reported is viewed as a misinterpretation of naturally occurring events. These types of investigators are not looking for evidence of ghosts, but are attempting to show that there is no way for the paranormal to exist. They often express themselves by saying that "extraordinary claims demand extraordinary proof"... and while most of us don't disagree with this, such investigators are determined to ignore any evidence that they might find.

It may come as a surprise to you to know that while these two methods are at the opposite ends of the spectrum, they are amazingly similar. Both of them presuppose something about the nature of the phenomenon they are trying to explain. This is not the way that real science works, nor is it the way to conduct a proper investigation into anything, including (as a detective could tell you) a criminal act or in our case, an allegedly haunted house

Throughout the book, you will be urged to keep an open mind. If we can ever hope to actually explain paranormal events, we must research them without prejudice going in. A good investigator must follow the facts where they lead, find out what phenomena is present to study and then study it with the best methods available to him.

Obviously, we can assume as we enter an investigation that the events reported are "probably not" paranormal, but we cannot assume that they "must not" be. We must eliminate the mundane first, before reaching any conclusions about whether the events are paranormal or not. Only after the normal explanations have been eliminated should we proceed along supernatural lines.

The first stage of any investigation is to gather all of the facts. You should interview witnesses and examine the site and exhaust all of the possibilities. This is the first (and perhaps most important) step and unfortunately, this step has led to the conclusion of what seemed to be many promising cases. Incidents that first seemed to be linked to a haunting are often explained away by a presentation of possible solutions. Only if the case survives this first step is it worth pursuing any further. If it does, and the haunting involves what might be recurrent phenomena, then it's time to monitor the area and possibly have a chance to observe the happenings for yourself.

Confused? Perplexed? Overwhelmed? Continue on... the pages ahead will hopefully intrigue you, possibly exasperate you, but most of all, will provide you with what you need to know to begin researching ghosts. Take away with you as much, or as little, of this book as you want. Just be sure to form your own theories, based on your own experiences. This is the foundation for where to begin. Take this information and use it to build on.

3. GHOSTS & HAUNTINGS

WHAT ARE THEY AND WHERE DO YOU FIND THEM?

Nearly every community in the United States can claim at least one haunted house. Some have more than one... In most cases, the citizenry, except for a few knowledgeable individuals, is totally unaware of the fact that macabre dwellings are standing in their midst.

RICHARD WINER

What causes a place to become haunted?

No one really knows. In fact, there are so many types of hauntings from human ghosts to animal ghosts to even ghost ships, that no one has ever been able to come up with a general theory that can explain all of them. Any single theory would have to cover an immense variety of phenomena and it just can't be done. Such a theory would have to explain why apparitions are seen in one location, but not in others. It would have to provide a solution for phantom footsteps, cold spots, strange smells and much more. Developing such a theory is no easy matter, especially as few researchers can really agree about what underlying force causes a haunting in the first place.

However, that's not to say that we should all give up hope. As I have mentioned already (and will again), I certainly don't claim to have all of the answers when it comes to ghosts. I have seen and have experienced some things that I certainly feel were paranormal. On two occasions I believe that I actually saw ghosts and have been in a number of places where I believe that ghosts were present, based on the sounds and sensations that I and others present experienced.

As many readers already know, many things happen in the course of a paranormal investigation that might be caused by a ghost. I know that I can't explain some of the things that I have seen happen by any other way than to say they were caused by some sort of "spirit energy". But was all of this activity caused by ghosts? Perhaps, but then again, perhaps not. You might not believe the strange things that can happen that are caused by natural means. Weird things can, and do, take place that can be easily explained away. In addition, how can we really say with certainty what ghosts can or cannot do?

Many authorities on the subject do not believe that ghosts are literally the "spirits" of people who have died and who have remained behind at a location. While it is a popular belief, many parapsychologists refuse to take it seriously. This is not to say that they reject the possibility that some hauntings are caused by the activities of the dead though. They just don't believe that the ghosts themselves are the actual forms of the dead.

Here's why: they use as an example that many haunted houses show no evidence that a past tragedy or death has taken place in them. And they also add that no evidence exists in many locations to say that any past personality is present there. The house might be haunted, but they don't believe that it is by the spirit of a dead person.

To be honest, I can't say that I agree with this, but I ask the reader to simply judge for himself. I agree that many locations do not boast events that might spawn ghosts, but isn't it possible that the ghosts may have stayed behind for other reasons altogether?

As we will soon discuss, there are likely many reasons for hauntings. The following chapter is meant to be a study of this type of paranormal activity. It will certainly not be the final word on the subject for just like the theory of what causes a place to become haunted, the idea that a ghost (or type of haunting) could be a single, all encompassing thing is a nice idea, but an unrealistic one. Even the word "ghost" is misleading. We use it as a generic term to describe both "spirits" and "apparitions", paranormal manifestations that are actually very different things.

There seem to be several different kinds of paranormal events that have been linked to ghosts. Are they all the work of the spirits? Your own investigations will have to decide that for you. I will present the facts, the theories and the evidence and you can use the information in conjunction with your own ideas and research. Just remember to accept all theories as possible, but question each one of them before accepting them as the truth.

HAUNTINGS

First of all, what is a haunting?

According to the definition, it is the repeated manifestation of strange and inexplicable sensory phenomena at a certain location. But does this mean that a haunting is always associated with an actual ghost? No, it doesn't, as we will explore later on, but for now, let's assume that hauntings are connected to paranormal activity.

There are no general patterns to hauntings, which is what makes them so hard to define. Some phenomena may manifest on occasion or even continually for periods that last from several days to centuries. Other manifestations may only occur on certain anniversaries, in accordance with distinctive weather conditions or for reasons that make no sense whatsoever.

The public assumes that hauntings always involve apparitions, or the ghosts of the dead, but actually, apparitions are connected to a minority of cases. Most hauntings involve noises like phantom footsteps, strange, unexplained sounds, tapping, knocking and even voices and whispers. They can also include strange smells, sensations like the prickling of skin, cold spots and breezes and being touched by unseen hands. Other hauntings can involve poltergeist activity such as furniture and solid objects being moved about, broken glass, doors that open and close by themselves and the paranormal manipulation of lights and electrical devices, circuits and outlets.

Visitors to haunted places often report a variety of emotions, including anger and fear when negative forces are at work. Many cases like this are mistakenly labeled as "evil" or "demonic" (which will be discussed further). Other sites seem to involve friendly, or at least benign, emotions.

While attempts have been made to try and categorize certain types of hauntings, many locations defy this labeling and manifest a variety and a combination of different types. In fact, it has even been my experience that some locations seem to act as a catalyst for activity, sometimes causing visitors to manifest their own unconscious phenomena. This can often give rise to accounts that don't fit into any category at all.

THE TRADITIONAL HAUNTING

The Traditional, or Intelligent, haunting is perhaps the most widely accepted kind of ghost activity, although it's really not as common as you might think. In this kind of case, the spirit or entity involved is an "intelligent" or "interactive" presence in a haunted location. It is there because of a connection to the site or to the people at the location.

This ghost is best, and most simply, described as the personality of an individual who once lived and which has stayed behind in our world instead of passing on at the time of death. This may happen in the case of murder, a traumatic event, a suicide or even because of some unfinished business in the person's life. At the time of death, the spirit refused to pass on because of these events. They may also linger because of emotions that tie them to the earth, from anger to love. It may not have been that the person did not pass on because they couldn't, but because they didn't want to. In other cases, there is the chance that the spirit didn't even realize that he had died. This may occur when a death is sudden or unexpected, like with an accident or a murder.

These spirits are now made up of the energy that once made up the character of a living person. Now that the human body is gone, that energy is all that remains. These interactive spirits are not evil or demonic, as some so-called experts would have you believe. I have never encountered an "evil" spirit during the time that I have been involved in this field and neither have any of my associates, some of whom have been researchers for longer than I have. However, I have run across a few spirits that I would call "negative" though and it's possible that they were the personalities of people who were angry or bitter in life. This often explains the types of activity (or behavior) being exhibited at the haunted location. The spirits are simply human personalities and seem to retain the same traits they had when alive. If a person was kind and caring in life, the spirit will be a benevolent one. On the other hand, if that person was angry or cruel, those qualities are likely to manifest.

The negative spirits can be frightening, especially to people not trained in the paranormal, and in rare cases can actually harm the living. This is generally not the case though and most injuries related to haunted houses occur because of physical objects that are moved or when someone injures himself in an accident because of their fear of the phenomena. Intelligent, yet negative, spirits can be linked to cases involving poltergeist phenomena as well. Soon, we will discuss a type of "poltergeist-like" phenomenon that is linked to a human agent, but standard poltergeists are truly "noisy ghosts" (which is the meaning of the word in German).

Poltergeist phenomena, even though there can be other causes, is usually either linked to a human agent or an interactive spirit. In the case of the intelligent entity, the variety of phenomena can include knocking and tapping sounds, noises with no logical cause, disturbance of stationary objects, doors slamming, lights turning on an off and much more. The ghost usually tends to manifest itself in physical ways, including cold chills and smells. It usually seems to want to bring attention to itself and such cases can literally drag on for years at a time. Human agent poltergeist-like cases usually are of a much shorter duration.

So what do you do if you find yourself involved in a case like this? The fact that some of these spirits have remained behind because of some sort of incomplete business is a hard obstacle to overcome for the investigator. The spirits may have remained in this world because they have left behind relatives or loved ones. Or they may have left unfinished tasks that they feel cannot be completed by anyone else. They may not rest because of some injustice that was done to them or perhaps because of something as simple as wanting to be around to see their children grow up.

SIGNS OF A TRADITIONAL / INTELLIGENT HAUNTING

Most Intelligent spirits will manifest in physical ways in an attempt to interact with those at the location. This will include:

- slamming doors
- windows that open and close
- cold chills and a strong presence

On rare occasions, the spirit will be seen and when it is, it will most likely look as it did when alive. The witness should be sure that the visible spirit interacts however and is not merely an imprinted, or memory, image.

For the most part, the idea of these spirits remaining behind in this world is rather sad, if not tragic in some cases. In all of our excitement over finding a ghost, we also must keep in mind that many spirits are confused over what has happened to them and may not even realize they are dead. Many of them may have died suddenly. Others may try to cling to life, afraid of letting go of the tangible, material world. Because of this, they are drawn back to places where they experienced joy, peace and happiness in life. Many of these spirits may just feel too "alive" to want to pass on to the other side.

These ghosts sometimes need help to be convinced that they don't belong here anymore. They do not need to be "exorcized", as they are not demons, but shown the right way and introduced to the fact that there is more for them in the next world than there remains for them in this one. There are many different ways to accomplish this, although I never suggest that such a thing be carried out by the investigator himself. There are many ways to approach this and surprisingly, a number of people who are skilled in such matters. They accomplish their tasks in different ways, ranging from simple explanations to perhaps a prayer offered by a clergyman of the spirit's faith.

While all of this is very intriguing, critics would charge that it sounds a lot like Spiritualism, but it isn't. In such cases, we can actually historically verify the existence of the ghosts by connecting their current communications, and the rare instances when they are actually seen, to the time when they were among the living. We can take the witness accounts of the ghost and compare them to contemporary photographs or descriptions of the person the ghost is alleged to be.

Another thing worth noting is that the annoyance factor in a case like this will be high. It's likely that the spirit will attempt to get the attention of the living occupants of the location. These spirits can be known for hiding objects, moving things about, turning things on and off, and other nuisances that can be compared to a child seeking attention. It's possible that the spirit may by looking for assistance to cross over or to accomplish a certain task. It has also been documented that the spirit may just be seeking the company of the residents, or even attention from the investigators in the case.

My own experiences with this type of ghost have been infrequent, but all of the cases were memorable. In one case, a young child gave an accurate physical description, including the clothing, of a person that he reportedly saw in his room. At a later time, his parents discovered an old photo of the original owner of the house and were shocked to find that this man's appearance matched the boy's description exactly. What made the case even more interesting was the fact that the spirit interacted with the boy and it was alleged that he even taught the child to read.

In another case, I was investigating an old theater that was said to be haunted by a former actor who had once worked there. The man had committed suicide in May 1955 and had been reportedly haunting the building ever since. Over the years, there had been dozens of reliable accounts of strange happenings, all connected to this ghost. During my investigation, I was overwhelmed in an abandoned dressing room by a strong and peculiar medicine smell. I left the room, not knowing that I had apparently just encountered the ghost.

Several hours later, during interviews with the actors and theater staff, I was told that the ghost who haunted the building had a distinctive smell. It seemed that when the actor in question was alive, he was plagued by frequent rashes on his legs. To ease his problem, he often coated his legs with medicine and thus, walked about in a "cloud" of the smell. According to the staff, the medical balm was banned from the building in the early 1960's because it was realized that the actor's ghost had somehow retained this part of his physical make-up in death. Any unearthly appearances or encounters were always accompanied by the smell, including my own experience.

While debunkers are bound to have a field day with such a subjective report, the encounter confirmed the presence of the ghost for me because the smell could not have been my imagination. I simply did not have the information to "create" such a distinctive odor in that particular location. I never even knew of the "ghostly smell" until hours after I first noticed it. I also could not have picked up a stray odor, as the balm had not been used in the theater for more than 30 years at the time of my investigation.

While this may not be concrete evidence for some, it was very convincing to me and I felt strongly that an interactive spirit was present at the site.

THE RESIDUAL HAUNTING

Of all of the types of hauntings discussed here, the Residual haunting is likely the most common. Certainly, it is much more common than most people think and I would go as far as to say that a large percentage of ghostly activity falls into this category. When investigating strange phenomena, we have to be careful not to confuse this type of activity with that of the "Intelligent" spirit. The main reason for this is that it's possible that Residual hauntings may have little or nothing to do with actual ghosts.

The simplest way to explain this kind of activity is to compare it to an old film loop or a recording. By that I mean it can be a scene or image that plays over and over through the years. Many of the locations where these hauntings take place experience an event (or a series of events) that imprints itself on the atmosphere of the place. This event can suddenly discharge and play itself at various times, just as a recording would. The events are not always visual either. They are often replayed as smells, sounds and noises that have no apparent explanation. The famed "phantom footsteps" that are reported at many haunted locations are a perfect example of this.

Often, the mysterious sounds or images that are recorded relate to traumatic events that have taken place and that have caused some sort of disturbance (or "impression") to occur there. This is the reason why so many battlefields, crime scenes and areas related to violence have become famous for their hauntings.

But this is not always the case. In other situations, the images have been created by a series of events that have been repeated over and over again. These frequent and repetitive releases of energy also seem to be capable of leaving a lasting impression. A good example of this can be realized from the large number of haunted staircases that have been reported over the years in homes and public buildings. It's possible that because of the number of times that people go up and down these sets of stairs, the energy expended leaves a mark on the site.

These locations act like giant storage batteries, saving up impressions of sights and sounds from the past. Then, as the years go by, these impressions appear again as if a film projector has started to run. As mentioned, much of this activity can be experienced as apparitions but sounds and smells are common too. Many of them will be associated with the past history of the location and can be distinctive to that certain place. I have been fortunate to experience two very different kinds of Residual hauntings at Gettysburg, Pennsylvania. During one trip, I encountered an unexplained scent that I was later to learn was associated with a ghostly event that I was completely unaware of. At another time, I was accompanied by a historian onto the battlefield at night, where we experienced the renowned "Guns of Gettysburg". These thundering sounds of cannons and gunfire have been reported for many years and are believed to be the "ghostly" echo of the artillery from the battle in 1863. A few years back, I had another encounter while on the battlefield in the evening with a fellow investigator. We had simultaneous "experiences" with the sound of a horse snorting, the jingle of reins and even the smell of a sweat-soaked animal. The sounds and smell came from directly behind us but there were no horses on the field at the time.

But how is it possible that such events could be left behind?

No one really knows for sure, but there are many theories. Some believe that the building materials of the structure may absorb the energy to replay again later. In Europe, fellow researchers have suggested that the porous stones of the castle walls may soak up the events that occur, explaining why so many haunted old buildings are located there. This may be the case, although it does not explain why we have numerous Residual haunts in America as well. There is relevance to this theory though. Researchers have discovered that most buildings where Residual hauntings take place are older structures. Could older building materials play a part in this? Possibly, but I think that it's more likely that the age of the building itself is the largest contributing factor. The number of people that pass through an old structure over time, and the tapestry of history played out in it, seems to be the main reason why these hauntings occur.

There may be other reasons as well. One idea that I suggested in the past connected underground water sources and Residual hauntings. I have only conducted a small survey of such sites, but I do know of a number of locations where Residual energy has been experienced and which also have a water source below the ground. One site, where I conducted a number of investigations and experiments, was the old gymnasium at Millikin University in Illinois. Around 1900, when the college was being built, the future site of the gym was actually a small lake. The lake was drained and the water was forced underground, where it remains today. The building was used as a venue for athletic events for many years and then was given to the school's theater department to be used as a scene shop. Since that time, students and staff members have reported the continuing sounds of sporting events from the past, including clapping, cheering, whistles and basketballs bouncing on the floor. These events usually occur when the building is dark and empty and few people are around.

SIGNS OF A RESIDUAL HAUNTING

This type of case is the investigator's best chance to see a ghost. It is more common to visibly spot an apparition when investigating this type of case and traditionally, have provided the best opportunity to do so.

- The ghosts reported will be like moving pictures and will be unaware of the living people around them. Such cases do not have any interaction between the ghost and the witnesses.

- Strange sounds are common, like footsteps, voices, knocking, rappings, etc.

- Residual hauntings will not involve missing or vanished items, as there is no consciousness present. While windows or doors may be opened and closed, it is because of energy expending itself, not because it is physically being manipulated by spirits.

During the course of my investigations, I had several experiences of my own and managed to collect enough evidence to lead me to believe that a lot of energy was present at the site. In addition to the first-hand accounts I collected, I also heard voices in the building that should not have been there and also was on the scene during a bizarre power surge that activated a light, even though the light was not plugged in. This connection between lights and the odd energy in the gym is present in most accounts of strange activity here. In many cases, witnesses have reported the anomalous sounds but when a light (or other electrical appliance) is switched on, the sounds always stop.

Some theories have also connected atmospheric conditions to Residual hauntings. It has been suggested that perhaps barometric pressure or even temperature may have something to do with hauntings becoming repeatedly active. I have personally noticed an increase in some paranormal activity in the winter months, when there is more static electricity in the air. It's possible that the phases of the moon may play a part as well. One moon-related haunting that I investigated a number of years ago involved a house that seemed to "become haunted" whenever the moon was full. Each month, the sounds of footsteps would echo in an attic turret of the house --- a room that was never used and was completely empty. The owners tore apart the floors of the room looking for a solution to the phantom steps but the history of the house actually revealed the answer. It was learned that the original owner of the house had kept his library in the room and had a habit of walking back and forth as he read. His ghost was not present but he had apparently left behind a presence that would "replay" itself when the energy of the full moon was at its peak.

With ghostly figures, smells and strange sounds, how can we tell the difference between the Traditional haunting and Residual energy? In some cases, the two very different types of activity can manifest in similar ways. This is true, but the most important signs will be different.

Mainly, any ghosts that are seen in a Residual haunting (and in this case, they will be a mere "image") will not interact with the witnesses at the location. An apparition that is seen will be little more than a moving picture or it may appear to be completely solid, but will vanish when approached or confronted. As mentioned, it's possible that the images and activity may be atmospheric in nature. The haunting may be influenced by storms, temperature, artificial energy sources or even the proximity of living persons. These factors may determine when activity occurs and often anything that happens will seem to be random. However, it might not be and it is especially important that the witnesses keep a log of activity. In this way, a pattern can be developed as to when activity occurs and the researcher has a much better chance of experiencing it for himself.

Remember also that most things that occur do so because of energy expending itself and not because of spirit activity. In some cases, the things that occur may seem to be connected to the Traditional haunt, but there will be no interaction or consciousness behind them. Commonly reported in these cases are the sounds of footsteps, voices and odd, usually repetitive sounds.

Another way to know that you are most likely dealing with a Residual haunting is the presence of apparitions or visible spirits. As they rarely appear in any other type of case, a this is your best opportunity to actually see a ghost. However, these apparitions will be unaware of the people around them and will usually repeat the same actions over and over again. Sadly, you may as well be watching an old movie, as the ghost you might see will not be looking back at you.

POLTERGEIST-LIKE ACTIVITY

As mentioned already in the section about Traditional hauntings, poltergeists ("noisy ghosts") have commonly been blamed for any violent or destructive activity in a haunting. In the past, researchers believed that all such activity at a haunted location was the work of the spirits, or an outside force, but today, most investigators don't think so. While interactive spirits may be the culprits in some cases, many cases have a force behind them that is much closer to home.

In a poltergeist case, there can be a variety of phenomena taking place. There are reports of knocking and tapping noises, sounds with no visible cause, disturbance of stationary objects like household items and furniture, doors slamming, lights turning on and off, fires breaking out and much, much more. In some cases, this activity can be connected to ghosts, but in other cases it probably isn't. It certainly remains paranormal though and because of this, it is also unexplained and very controversial.

The current theory behind this Poltergeist-like phenomena is that the activity is caused by a person in the household, known as the "human agent". The agent is usually an adolescent girl and normally one that is troubled emotionally. It is believed that she unconsciously manipulates physical objects in the house by psychokinesis (PK), the power to move things by energy generated in the brain. This kinetic type of energy remains unexplained, but even some mainstream scientists are starting to explore the idea that it does exist.

It is unknown why this energy seems to appear in females around the age of puberty, but documentation of its existence is starting to appear as more and more case studies have become public. It seems that when the activity begins to manifest, the girl is usually in the midst of some emotional or sexual turmoil. The presence of the energy is almost always an unconscious one and it is rare when any of the agents actually realize that they are the source of the destruction around them. They do not comprehend that they are the reason that objects in the home have become displaced and are usually of the impression that a ghost (or some sort of other supernatural entity) is present instead. The bursts of PK come and go and most poltergeist-like cases will peak early and then slowly fade away.

It should be noted that while most cases such as this manifest around young women, it is possible for puberty age boys (and even older adults) to show this same unknowing ability. As with the young women, the vast majority will have no idea that they are causing the activity and will be surprised to find there is even a possibility that strange things are happening because of them.

In most cases like this, an excellent chance can be provided to the researcher to document strange activity. Unfortunately though, the case will have nothing to do with ghosts and there is really no way to help the home owners. It is usually better to refer the family to a good counselor or mental health care provider, rather than try to act as a paranormal investigator. A counselor is usually the best person to provide assistance under these circumstances because PK normally manifests because of an emotional disturbance. Luckily for the home owners, poltergeist cases of this nature usually come and go very quickly.

One famous poltergeist-like case involved a disturbed young woman named Wanet McNeill. In 1948, she went to live with her father on a farm near Macomb, Illinois. Despondent and depressed about her parent's recent (and messy) divorce, she began to unconsciously cause fires to start on the farm. Over a period of a few weeks, literally hundreds of mysterious fires sprang up, causing thousands of dollars in damage and

SIGNS OF A PK HAUNTING (HUMAN AGENT POLTERGEIST)

In cases like this, the movement of physical objects can be sudden and violent and occur more frequently than in cases involving actual, inter-active spirits.

- Reports will often escalate as time goes by but will peak early and then fade away.

- Keep an eye out for a young female or an adolescent to be present in the house. Usually the activity will be centered around this person in par-ticular. This person can be isolated or removed from the house to rule out connected activity.

- Always try to rule out human involvement (including fraud) before assuming that the phenomenon has anything to do with ghosts.

destroying two houses and several outbuild-ings. Startled witnesses saw fires suddenly appear on furniture, curtains and even on bare walls and ceilings. Investigations were launched by the Macomb Fire Department, the state fire marshal, the U.S. Air Force, Underwriters Laboratory and others, but the cause of the fires remained undetermined. Only the removal of Wanet from the farm, when she went to live with a relative, brought an end to the problem. Prior to that, the girl had been accused of starting the fires with kitchen matches, a feat that would have been impossible given the number of witnesses who were present at the farm. Only the work of researchers and reporters who were present, and a better understanding of paranormal events, has brought about a possible solution to the case in the person of Wanet McNeill. Those who accused her had the right suspect, but certainly the wrong method for starting the fires!

But not all such cases involve disturbed individuals. We have already discussed that not all hauntings can be easily categorized and we must be careful not to jump to conclusions in any case. In some cases, what appears to be the work of a human agent may actually be that of the spirits, and vice versa. In addition, some genuinely haunted spots seem to be so filled with energy that witnesses at the loca-tion can manifest their own phenomena (i.e. Marianne Foyster at Borley Rectory).

My own personal experiences with poltergeist cases have been varied and often frus-trating. As time passed, and I became more involved in paranormal investigations, I received many phone calls from people who believed their homes were haunted. It's quite possible that some of them may have been, although as any ghost researcher knows, not every house is active all the time. Despite the many false alarms and natural explanations that I investigated, there were also the cases where I truly believed the accounts of the witnesses, even though I experienced nothing at the location for myself. There were many cases where the occupants of the house simply had no reason to lie. They did not want publicity. They did not want their story to appear in a book with their names attached to it. They simply feared their house was haunted and called me to con-firm, or to debunk, the activity they believed they were experiencing.

Many of the cases seemed to point toward poltergeist-like activity, but this was very hard to confirm and as mentioned, frustrating as well. My frustration with these cases is mostly because I almost always seem to come into such cases after the fact. There has only been one case where I was actually present when the strange events were still occurring. At other times, I have arrived as the outbreak was coming to an end.

In 1999, I was contacted about an apartment that was shared by four female college students at a small Illinois university. They explained to me that weird events had been occurring for several months but by the time I arrived, had become less frequent. After interviewing the young women, we deduced that the height of the outbreak had occurred during the most stressful time of the year, semester exams, and had actually started at the same time that one of them was going through a bad breakup with a boyfriend. By the time we were finished talking, even the young women were theorizing that it had been their own stress that was responsible for the activity. This did not make the phenomena any less unnerving though, as they told of breaking glasses, slamming doors and cabinets and shower items that were constantly flying around the bathroom. As with other cases of this type, it did not last long.

I have looked into other such cases over the years but out of all of them, there was only one case that occurred when I was present as the weird activity was taking place. Even in this instance though, I found myself wishing that I had done things differently than I did --- but that's for later in the book.

In 1997, I got involved in the case of a young woman that I have since referred to as "Christine M.". The home where she and her mother lived became the first, and possibly most active, human agent poltergeist case that I ever got involved with. In the case of "Christine M.", I believe that the outbreak in the home was not only genuine, but I believe I really did experience phenomena that cannot be explained by natural means.

This case could almost be described as "textbook" when compared to many of the other cases that I have read about. Remember that, at the time, my only knowledge of cases like this were from what I had been able to glean from the writings of researchers like Dr. William Roll, Loyd Auerbach and D. Scott Rogo. My information was all second hand but I went into the case with my eyes wide open. I discovered then what I would find repeated in cases in the future --- that human agents in such a situation usually suspect their house is haunted before they suspect that they might be the cause of the activity they experience. This is what occurred in Christine's case. She contacted me because she believed her house was haunted. She told me of a wide variety of weird phenomena that was taking place like knocking sounds, lights turning on and off, doors slamming, cabinets opening and closing, windows breaking and other destructive happenings. Because she was under 18 at the time, I contacted her mother about the location and she assured me that the events described were actually taking place. She also agreed that an investigation might be in order.

During this initial interview, I asked her about the history of the location and if she had any thoughts on why the phenomenon was occurring? I also asked how long it had been going on? Her answer surprised me. She explained the phenomena had started just two years before, when Christine had gotten pregnant at age 15. She was very upset at the time and became depressed and anxious enough that her mother had taken her to see a therapist. She stopped going however and the weird activity began a short time later. While Christine believed that the house was haunted, her mother that her daughter was somehow causing these things to happen.

With the home owner's permission, I began a series of five in-depth investigations of the house. My interviews with Christine and her family collected numerous accounts of the activity that was taking place. The events began one night when Christine was laying on the living room floor watching television. The living room was the largest room on the first floor and when I visited the house, it contained a couch, some chairs, a table and a large piano. There were three doors leading into the room, which led to a spare room, a screened porch and to the kitchen. As she and her mother were watching television, the piano began to loudly play by itself. Not long after that, things began to escalate. Soon, doors began to open and close by themselves, windows broke inside of empty rooms and the sounds of knocking and footsteps began to be heard, usually on the upper floor of the house when no one was present. Lights and radios turned on and off and the volume of the television would often raise and lower without assistance. The knockings and noises from the second floor of the house became so bad that Christine insisted that her mother put a padlock on the door leading upstairs. She remained convinced, even after my initial visit and after her mother's insistence otherwise, that the house was haunted by ghosts.

Not surprisingly, the events in the house did not convince her otherwise either. The strangest event that reportedly occurred (and I did not witness this for myself) was when Christine's sister ended up with a horrible bite mark on the back side of her upper arm. There were no pets in the house and no way that the girl could have managed to bite herself in such an area of her body. I don't think that it was any coincidence that the bite mark appeared just shortly after she and her sister had an argument.

As you can imagine, I was having some reservations about the house being infested by spirits at this point, especially since her mother again told me that she was convinced that the activity centered around Christine. However, the young woman insisted that the house was haunted and would only agree to the investigations that I had planned if we would proceed as if the house were actually haunted. I reluctantly agreed and the five investigations began. Most of the time, things were fairly quiet, including the two uneventful investigations that were conducted with Christine removed from the house. Not a single trace of any sort of activity was detected when she was not present. However, on two occasions, I was present when violent phenomena occurred and I was also present when one of the other investigators snapped a photograph of a bright ball of light in the downstairs hallway. According to his account, the light was actually coming down the hallway, literally following Christine's little boy, who was two years-old at the time. I was in the kitchen with Christine when this occurred but I did see the resulting photograph, which shows a glowing light (apparently in motion), just a foot or two behind the boy as he is running into the living room.

On one evening, Christine, her mother, three other investigators and myself clearly heard what seemed to be someone banging loudly on the walls of the second floor of the house. There was no one else present at the time but the sounds really seemed to be made by a person upstairs, walking down the hallway and hitting the walls with his fists. Christine's mother told me that these were exactly the sorts of sounds that they had become used to over the past number of months. Unsure of what else to do, I ran up the stairs to see if anyone else was there. The downstairs door, as mentioned, had been padlocked, so Mrs. M. had to open it for me and I hurried up the staircase with another one of the investigators in tow. The pounding noises had stopped by the time we reached the upper floor, but if anyone had been there, we would have found them. Instead, we discovered the hallway and the rooms to be dark, quiet and empty.

During another investigation, on a separate night, I saw two cabinet doors actually slam shut under their own power. The incident occurred while I was in the living room with Christine, her mother and one other investigator. As we were sitting and talking, we began to hear a repeated rapping sound coming from the kitchen. It began to increase in volume until it started to sound like someone rapidly hammering on a wooden surface. The first sound was joined by a second and then a third. Each of the sounds was identical and my first thought was that it sounded just like someone slamming a cabinet door closed. Just as I had done when we heard mysterious sounds upstairs, I ran for the kitchen as quickly as possible. The two rooms were separated by an open doorway, a little wider than usual, and curved into an arch. Hurrying from the carpeted floor and onto the linoleum floor of the kitchen, I slipped just as I was going under the archway. I stumbled but didn't fall and was able to look up quickly enough to see two of the cabinet doors waving back and forth and cracking against the wooden frame. The movement ceased almost immediately as I came into the room but it was certainly the first time that I had ever seen "paranormal movement" during an investigation.

Over the next several weeks, the activity in the house continued but it did begin to decrease after two months. Thanks to the relentless and intrusive interviews that I conducted with Christine and the fact that we conducted the two completely uneventful investigations with the girl removed from the house, I felt that we could determine that the cause of the haunting was indeed Christine. Eventually, her mother and I were able to get her to agree with these findings and she returned to the therapist. Not surprisingly, the phenomena ceased completely soon after and to this date, nothing else has occurred at her home. She is now happily married and no longer bothered by any strange activity.

PORTAL HAUNTINGS

Without a doubt, Portal hauntings will be the most controversial of the hauntings discussed here. The problem is that this type of haunting is the least understood and least traditional of the forms of activity that we know of. In fact, one review of a past edition of this book called the idea that Portals might exist "silly" and stated that such things were "simply not possible" and that "serious researchers have abandoned such an idea". As I have already stated, few paranormal investigators ever completely agree on anything and everyone is entitled to his own opinion.

My initial interest in "portals" began because of an interest that I had in haunted cemeteries. I have always been fascinated with the ghost stories and weird legends that are often associated with burial grounds. And while this fascination continues, my paranormal research into cemeteries has led me in some strange and rather unusual directions. One of the things that I have learned over the years is that cemeteries are rarely haunted in the traditional way. In spite of this though, weird activity, hauntings, bizarre photographs and reports continue to come from graveyards all over the country. How and why can this be?

The theory behind some cemetery phenomena has been linked to what a few researchers call "portals" or "doorways". Dismissed by some and embraced by others, the idea of a portal is still mostly theory and conjecture but in my opinion, the idea explains a lot of things about cemetery hauntings and even some short-lived paranormal flaps or outbreaks.

The idea of a "portal" to another dimension is not a new one. It has been suggested that there exist places all over the world that serve as "doorways" from our world to another. These doorways may provide access for entities to come into our world. They may be the spirits of people who have lived before, or they may be something else altogether. Some researchers even believe that they could be otherworldly beings from some dimension that we cannot even comprehend. In famous cases like the "Mothman" or the "Mad Gasser" of Mattoon, Illinois, it may even be possible that such a portal opened for a short time in a specific area, allowing these figures to wreak havoc for a brief period, only to later vanish without a trace. Many of the readers of this book may have also read the book that I wrote about the infamous Bell Witch of Tennessee (Season of the Witch). If so, then the reader may be familiar with the theory that I have in that case about the haunting at the John Bell farm being a non-human entity that came through one of these doorways.

I know this all sounds far-fetched, but it may not be as strange as it seems. The entities that have been sighted, reported and even photographed around what many believe to be portals could be the spirits of the dead or perhaps something stranger. If locations like this do exist and they are some sort of doorway, it's possible that these spots may have been labeled as being "haunted" over the years by people who saw something near them that they couldn't explain, isn't it? I think it's possible that this has happened many times. In fact, I would even suggest that these places did not "become" haunted as traditional locations do (through death or tragic events), but had been "haunted" for many, many years already. This fits in well with the theories about haunted cemeteries that are not haunted in any traditional manner.

Many locations where groups of strange things happen seem to be "glitch" areas. An example of this would be Archer Avenue on the South Side of Chicago, Illinois. There are a number of haunted sites along this one roadway and many would consider it to be the most ghost-infested region of Chicagoland. There have been a variety of ideas that have been suggested as to why so many odd things happen here, from the fact that it was once an old Native American trail to the fact that Archer Avenue is almost completely surrounded by water. Some have also suggested that areas like Archer Avenue, or the portals in question, may be connected to what are called "ley lines".

The idea that a number of unusual spots are often located in a particular area, or along a straight line, was suggested by Alfred Watkins in 1925. The idea came to him when he was examining a map of Herefordshire, England and noticed an alignment of ancient sites. He gave such alignments the name of "ley", a Saxon word that meant "a clearing in the woodland". The lines (if they exist) are believed to be alignments or patterns of powerful earth energy that connect sacred sites such as churches, temples, stone circles, megaliths, burial sites and other locations of spiritual importance. The true age and purpose of such lines remain a mystery. Watkins suggested that all holy sites and places of antiquity were connected by ley lines and using an old Ordnance Survey, he claimed that the leys were the "old straight tracks" that crossed the landscape of prehistoric Britain and represented sites that were built from the very dawn of human settlement there.

After Watkins' theory was published, fascination with ley lines remained high until the 1940's, when it began to decline. Interest was revived two decades later and the idea of such lines remains a subject of speculation and debate to this day. Not surprisingly, most mainstream archaeologists and scientists dispute the existence of ley lines and say that Watkins contrived the whole thing using sacred sites from different periods in history. This would be true if the idea of such lines only dated back to the 1920's. As it stands, there should be sites that date from different periods in history if the lines had been there all along. Many contend that the ley lines mark paths of earth energy, which can often be detected by dowsing and which may have been sensed by early humans. For this reason, they chose to locate their sacred sites along the pathways and especially at points where the lines cross one another.

Points where the ley line paths intersect are believed to be prone to anomalies such as earth lights, hauntings and even UFO sightings. It is believed that the energy here is at its greatest and some might even describe such sites as portals.

SIGNS OF A PORTAL HAUNTING

The majority of events that might fit into a "Portal Haunting" category seem to come from cemeteries, although no location can be ruled out. With cemeteries, the best way to watch for them is to be on the lookout for graveyards that are rumored to be haunted. Be aware of stores (from cemeteries and other spots) that involve glowing balls of light, odd creatures, strange shapes or unexplained images.

With a home or building, these doorways can be harder to ascertain. In this type of haunting though, the spirits that are present may be more numerous than in a Traditional Haunting and are always unconnected to the history of the building. The site is nothing more than a crossover point, which can be confusing to those doing research.

Some of the most common sites alleged to be portals have been cemeteries. For years, ghost hunters and researchers have collected not only strange stories of haunted cemeteries, but dozens of anomalous photographs from them as well. In many cases, there seems to be no reason why the cemetery might be haunted unless it might somehow provide access for spirits, or entities, to pass from one world to the next. For this reason, some researchers, like my friend Barb Huyser, have started referring to these locations as "crossover points". In almost every case, there seems to be none of the historical reasons for the graveyard to be haunted -- no unmarked graves, natural disasters or desecration -- and yet ghostly phenomena is frequently reported.

Of course, some of the cemeteries are haunted in the traditional manner, but it's the ones that aren't that cause such a puzzle. Going back to what was mentioned earlier, it's possible that these sites were "haunted" long before the cemetery was ever located there. Might it be possible that some sort of "psychic draw" to the area was what caused our ancestors to locate a cemetery there in the first place? Perhaps they felt there was something "sacred" or "spiritual" about the place and without realizing why, placed a burial ground on the location and made it a protected spot. This would fit in well with the theories that many have about ley lines and their intersection points. They believe that the ancient inhabitants (in this case, our ancestors) felt the pull of the area and built their sacred sites along these "leylines" or "crossover points".

According to American Indian lore, the early inhabitants of this country chose their burial grounds in a conscious manner, looking for a place to bury the dead that was more closely connected to the next world. Many of these locations, including many disturbed sites, are now considered "haunted" or at least inhabited by spirits. They consciously chose these locations, again following the psychic draw of the spot.

So why not our own cemeteries? Could our own burial grounds have been chosen in the same way, although perhaps unknowingly? These sites could now mark doorways between this world and the next. In American culture, what more sacred sites exist than churches and cemeteries? Our ancestors may have placed their burial grounds on these spots as a way of protecting the location -- or perhaps because of something else that they sensed here. Is it possible that the settlers deduced that something was not quite right about the site and perhaps even believed that these strange feelings were of an evil or demonic nature? There has been a long tradition in this country about haunted or mysterious places being dubbed with "devil names" as a way of warning people away from something the discoverers did not understand. It's possible that superstitious settlers also felt that many of these portal locations were "evil" in some way, or of the Devil. Because of this, they attempted to "exorcise" the location by placing a holy or religious site upon it. This might explain the myriad of haunted churches that exist in this country and might also explain many of our seemingly spirit-infested graveyards as well.

Of course, the fear is that perhaps our ancestors may not have been as superstitious, or as mistaken, as we might first think. The strange entities that have been photographed around such sites could be the traveling spirits of the dead -- or they could be something far worse.

Cemeteries are not the only places to find these portals. I believe they may exist in other places too, including in places where we would least expect them. These "glitch" areas might be found anywhere, even under a home or building. In fact, these doorways, and the unknown entities that pass through them, might be the explanation for some of the strange sightings that have plagued paranormal research for years. For some time, investigators have attempted to dispel the myths that "ghosts are evil" and that they "hurt people", but what if we are wrong? Or perhaps even partially wrong?

Normally, I don't believe that ghosts hurt people. By that I mean that people involved in a haunting are not injured by the discarnate spirits of the dead. There are certainly instances of people being hurt though, but usually because they are struck by an object in a poltergeist outbreak or trip over a shifted piece of furniture. In fact, you are more likely to be hurt running away from a haunted place than by the haunting that is taking place there.

But what about people who get hurt in other ways? These are the cases that worry everyone and the cases that give rise to the stories of "evil spirits" and dangerous ghosts. In some of these cases, we hear accounts of violent acts, terrifying visions and even strange beings that may have never been human at all. Can we always take such stories seriously? Perhaps not, but they are out there and what if these cases involve entities who are not ghosts at all? Could they be strange spirits who have passed into this world by way of the "portals" that we have been discussing?

This is interesting to think about. If this might be true, such a theory would certainly provide answers for puzzling cases when traditional methods of ghost investigations have not worked. It might also provide a solution as to how stories of "evil spirits", "demons" and even "negative ghosts" have gotten started.

Research into the idea of non-human entities is a subject of great controversy. For centuries, there have been tales of nature spirits and elementals who spring from the earth. They have never been human but choose to interact and to communicate with us. In more modern times, researchers have theorized that such spirits may actually be beings that pass between dimensions. They use the portals and doorways to pass back and forth and such spirits have a reputation for being kind and benign, as well as dangerous and violent. As already mentioned, the passage of such beings between this world and another could provide an explanation for cases that are as far apart from one another as the infamous Mad Gasser, vanishing creatures and even haunted graveyards.

Who can say for sure at this point as to who or what these mysterious spirits may be and why places that should not be haunted, actually are? My interest in the possibility of portals began back in the middle 1990's and continues today.

In 1996, I became involved in a series of investigations at a small cemetery in a remote and isolated part of the Midwest. From the beginning, I theorized that this might be a portal location, thanks to not only our own investigations, but also based on the witness accounts and photographs that had been taken here.

During one particular experiment that was carried out in 1997, we worked with a sophisticated computer system that could measure a variety of different activity. In addition, we also tested one of the most basic forms of "spirit communication", an actual séance. This part of the experiment was conducted using three people who had absolutely no knowledge of the background or history of the graveyard. During their efforts, they managed to make contact (we believe) with a spirit who was present. According to the messages that came through, the spirit claimed to be that of a small child who could not spell her name, did not know her age, but yet claimed that she was not at the location alone. Strangely, the first burial that had taken place at the cemetery had been that of a young girl who was described (according to historical records) in just such a manner. The most curious thing about this whole incident was that I was the only person present who knew this piece of information and I had not been directly involved in the attempts at communication.

Could the spirit making contact have actually been that of the young girl? Or could there have been other spirits (as claimed by the "ghostly little girl") who passed along information they thought we wanted to hear? Or could the entities have been something far stranger, and so alien to us, that they pretended to be something familiar to us and something that we could understand. This is an option that we may just want to consider because there remains little doubt to me that the area of the cemetery where the séance was being held was a portal area. In fact, I would even go as far as to say that all of the activity in the graveyard was centered around this spot.

This seemed important to me because it not only seemed to indicate that the planners of the cemetery chose the location because of the psychical importance of it but that they also unconsciously highlighted the areas where the activity was the strongest. Following with my theory, I noted that these more active parts of the cemetery had been decorated with distinctive gravestones and architecture that set them apart from the rest of the graveyard.

So what does all of this mean? Unfortunately, I have to leave that up to the reader to decide. Are portals real and do they actually connect with another world, or even another dimension? For now, the theory involves a lot of speculation but I do believe that it has merit and should not be dismissed without much more study and research. All that we can do right now is speculate, theorize and try to gather as much evidence as possible to show that something unexplained is out there.

And in some cases, that something may be even stranger than we think!

OTHER TYPES OF GHOSTLY PHENOMENA

When we are dealing with ghosts and haunting phenomena, it is worthwhile for us to take a look at what may be related anomalies as well. It's hard to say for sure whether or not any of these things actually pertain to ghosts, but all of them have been perceived as hauntings at various times over the years. Descriptions of these types of events, or even the combination of such paranormal activity during an actual haunting, can be very confusing for the investigator, no matter what their level of experience. For this reason, it's good to have a general working knowledge of all sorts of strange happenings.

CRISIS APPARITIONS & WAKING DREAMS

While this phenomena may or may not have anything to do with ghosts, it has been reported since the beginning of time and may be the most frequently talked about type of paranormal experience.

Crisis apparitions are believed to be the spirits of those who have died and who appear in the moments after death to say farewell to a friend or a family member. On some occasions, these ghosts have been referred to as "spirits of the living" because they have also been reported as looking like people who are not dead. These apparitions normally are of people who are in some sort of danger or in dire circumstances and perhaps should be thought of as an "out of body experience".

These types of visions are usually meant to carry a message of some kind (normally that this person has died) and can occur in a dream state or when the witness has actually been awakened from sleep. The apparitions reportedly appear and then move on, leaving the witness to discover the next day that the subject who appeared to them has died. Most of the visions seem to be cloaked in light or appear slightly unreal.

While critics often state that such encounters are nothing more than a trick of the imagination, many researchers believe that this might actually be a form of telepathy between the dying and the living. In the case of living apparitions, they might be a psychic cry for help.

While many such cases have been verified over the years, the whole phenomena remains in question because of an event called a "waking dream". When such an event occurs, it is possible for a person to be having a dream and think that they have awakened from it, although actually they didn't. The terrifying visions that sometimes accompany such a state often lead to encounters with faceless phantoms standing at the end of the bed, demonic creatures that steal a victim's breath ("old hag syndrome") and even apparitions of dying relatives enveloped in bright light.

Like many of the readers, I have also experienced "waking dreams". Just prior to this writing, I spent the night aboard the U.S.S. Hornet, a reportedly haunted aircraft carrier that is docked in Alameda, California, near Oakland. While asleep that night, I dreamed that I had awakened and was on a bed in the Chief Petty Officer's bunk room, which is a short distance from where I was actually bedding down for the night. The dream was so vividly real that I could see every detail of the well-lighted room and for a moment, wondered how I had been spirited away to this part of the ship. Moments later, I actually woke up in the darkened room where I had gone to sleep. The dream stayed with me after it happened and again, was so real that I could understand how someone might believe that they had had an out of body experience. Instead, I knew that it was merely a "waking dream".

This sort of phenomenon can certainly have you questioning what may be a legitimate Crisis apparition and so would-be investigators are well advised to not base an entire investigation on an account of a person being awakened at night by a ghost.

GHOST LIGHTS

This type of luminous phenomena remains unexplained but it's unlikely that it has anything to do with actual ghosts. These balls of light (also called "Spook Lights") are known to appear in remote locations all over the country and have been observed for many years. Often elusive, they sometimes react to noise and other lights and will appear in the same location on a regular basis. Most of the lights can be explained naturally as "earth lights" that appear near earthquake faults, water sources and railroad tracks.

They are fascinating to observe and offer researchers a chance to investigate a fairly reliable form of strange phenomena. Some of the most famous locations for ghost lights are near Marfa, Texas.. Brown Mountain in North Carolina.. Silver Cliff, Colorado.. the Hornet Spook Light in southwestern Missouri and others.

These mysterious lights have long been tied to ghosts and hauntings because of the legends that usually surround them. In almost every case, a long-appearing light has a story told about it that involves a person who was somehow beheaded in an accident (this is especially popular for railroad ghost lights). The ghost of this person then returns, waving a lantern, and searching for his missing head. Such tales have long been a part of supernatural lore and in such a way, spook lights are "explained" as a ghostly phenomenon.

MAN-MADE GHOSTS

One of the strangest types of related phenomena is undoubtedly the "Man-Made Ghost". While uncommon, the idea of creating your own ghost came about in the early 1970's in Canada. During this period, much experimentation was being done into PK, including work by Dr. A.R.G. Owen, who started the "Phillip" experiments in 1972.

The experiment began in Toronto with a small group of researchers, who imagined the idea of a ghost named "Phillip". They gave the ghost a personality and a complete background, even drawing his portrait to make him seem more real. He was given a biography that was filled with historical errors and he had to be someone that the entire group knew had never existed in real life. The eight members of the circle memorized the fictitious biography, studied the period in which Phillip was supposed to have lived and even acquired photographs of an English manor called Diddington Hall. In his story, Phillip was supposed to have lived here but he bore no resemblance to the real-life inhabitants of Diddington.

After reinforcing their belief in him, the group attempted to make him manifest. For months on end, the group of five women and three men did their best to conjure up the fake spirit, even placing a drawing of what they imagined he would look like in the center of the table and concentrating on it. The initial séances produced no results but then in 1973, Phillip began to communicate. This began to occur only after the group "stopped trying so hard" and began to adopt a "relaxed and jolly" attitude. He first came through as a solid rap to the table. It was initially as a vibration to the wood. Next came a number of knocks, which the participants at first believed they had inadvertently caused. But then as the table began to move around the floor in an irregular manner, they began questioning one another. Finally, someone asked aloud "I wonder if Phillip is doing this?" and in response, there was a very loud knock. The imaginary ghost, it appeared, had finally arrived.

In the months to come, the sitters discovered that by asking questions and accepting one knock for "yes" and two for "no", they could enjoy a relatively rapid dialogue with the entity they had somehow conjured up. The experiment quickly escalated as one room in the house was set aside for Phillip and the ghostly personality was accepted as a distinct spirit that exhibited likes and dislikes and had strong views on many subjects. Occasionally, the table would shoot across the room at amazing speed during séances. Phillip even communicated in front of television cameras in 1974.

The experiment came to a strange end. One member of the group (who up to this point had strongly believed in the "ghost") broke ranks and stated aloud one day in a reply to Phillip that "we only made you up, you know." The rapping sounds stopped, as did all other communications. Once he denied belief that Phillip was real, the "ghost" apparently ceased to exist. He was later "re-born" after a new group of researchers learned to believe in him.

So what was Phillip? He was certainly not a ghost but some sort of manifestation of the human mind. In my opinion, I would say that he was not far off from some poltergeist-like cases. In fact, the late D. Scott Rogo theorized that some poltergeist-like activity could be created from stress, but not manifested by a living agent. He stated that the agent was able to literally "create" a presence to carry out the activity. The form could be totally separate from the person and act on its own, again unconsciously manipulating physical objects, but doing so in a way that was detached from the body. The agent could actually "give birth" to a ghost, just as the Canadian group did with Phillip.

Later in the book, in the chapter for "spirit communications", we will discuss the methods of "table tipping" and how experimenters can actually create their own "ghost".

WHERE TO FIND GHOSTS

One thing that I have learned over the past ten years is **that haun**ted places are more common than a lot of people think. Another thing that I **have learned** is that you have to go looking for these spots, because they aren't going to **come to you.** It is possible to let people know that you are looking for ghosts and interesting **cases by** making that information known (we'll talk about that in a later chapter).

One thing to remember is that you should never go where you aren't wanted. Some people don't want to be told that they have a ghost and others simply don't want to talk about it, or don't want the attention or the publicity. Ethical ghost researchers are a lot like any other profession. The ones who bother and pursue witnesses and owners of haunted places are a lot like lawyers who chase ambulances -- the reputable ones don't do it and they dislike and make bad jokes about the ones who do. This can be compared to ghost hunters who claim they are going to haunted places purely for research and then charge the owners for an investigation. There isn't anything much more disreputable than that.

There is little that can damage your reputation as quickly as being pushy or demanding in an investigation. You just have to face it; some people just don't want you hunting ghosts in their house or on their property.

THE TROUBLE WITH GHOSTLORE

Of course that's not to say that private locations are the only places to find ghosts. An alleged haunted place that is open to the public can provide hours of research and the history of the spot may give good leads toward finding the resident ghost. Many times, the folklore and legends of the location are a great place to start. These stories may just have a root in genuine phenomena. The lesson here is to not ignore the stories that sound too good to be true because there may be more to them than meets the eye.

The problem is however, knowing how to separate the "ghostlore" from the ghosts. What I mean when I say "ghostlore" is the practice that society has of trying to explain strange events by attaching a legend to them. In many cases, stories of a "lady in white" or a "headless railroad brakeman" (and think about how many of those are out there!) have been invented to try and add understanding to sightings of ghostly white mists and mysterious glowing lights. Without these chilling stories, the weird locations might never be explained. To put it simply, people just have a need to try and explain things. They crave a reason for everything, supernatural or not.

In many (perhaps most) cases, these locations truly are what we would consider haunted. Unfortunately though, the true facts behind the haunting may not have anything to do with the legend that is associated with it. There may be another reason entirely for the strange phenomena reported but what often occurred was that, many years ago, local residents felt the need to attach an explanation to events they could not understand. A witness may have glimpsed some sort of pale apparition that looked like a flowing dress, and thus, the legend of a "lady in white" was born.

In other cases, a story may have gotten started at some point in the past and then was embellished and enhanced to the point that it soon bears little resemblance to real events. In some cases, the owners or caretakers of the property may even know the truth but don't bother with it, feeling that the fanciful story is better than the real thing.

A good example of this is the famous Myrtles Plantation in St. Francisville, Louisiana. Although the house is genuinely haunted, which can be attested to by generations of owners, guests and ghost hunters, it is not haunted for any of the reasons that have been claimed in the publicity surrounding the house. Many readers may be familiar with this story, which tells of a plantation house that becomes haunted after a slave named Chloe accidentally poisoned the lady of the house and her two children. Chloe had been having an affair with the home's owner and when he tired of her, she feared that she would be forced out of the house and back to the fields. By putting poison into a birthday cake, she could nurse the family back to health and prove her worth to her owner. However, her plan goes badly awry and the woman and her children die from the poison. Fearing retribution, the other slaves hang Chloe in the nearby woods. Since that time, her ghost, along with those of the woman and her children, has haunted the house and grounds of the Myrtles.

It's a classic ghost story and one that has been featured in books, in magazines and on television literally dozens of times. The problem is that not a word of it is true!

The owner of the house during the period in question was Clark Woodrooff and there has been no evidence to say that he ever carried on an affair with any of his slaves. Even if he had, it would not have been with Chloe because a check through the plantation's records shows that no slave named "Chloe" ever lived there. In addition, Woodrooff's wife died from yellow fever, not from poison, in 1823 and one year later, in the summer of 1824, her son also died from the disease, as did another daughter in September 1824. And there were many other tragedies in the history of the house to explain why it might be so haunted -- although none of them were apparently so dramatic as the one that has been concocted to include the fictitious Chloe.

As has been said more than once - "when the legend is better than the truth, print the legend". This is an adage that has been closely followed by the Myrtles, misleading hundreds of ghost hunters and enthusiasts over the years.

In spite of this, we still need to pay close attention to the local legends and folklore of a location. Many people might have never come to the Myrtles if not for the legends that have been created and if they had not, they might have missed out on the genuine phenomena that is present. Just remember that the real activity just may be there -- but it might be hiding beneath the hemline of the local "lady in white".

WHERE THE GHOSTS ARE

Here are some of the places where others and myself have had good luck in finding ghosts, hauntings and weird phenomena.

HOMES

Many private residences, and not just old ones, have a tainted past that might include murder, suicide or some other tragic event. Many times, these events cause a place to become haunted. The location can also become haunted because of a spirit being drawn there by these events or because one has stayed behind on account of them. These spirits can be positive or negative and haunted houses boast all kinds of different phenomena. These are places where the ghost hunter can expect to find many residual effects also, so be aware of that.

In some cases, the history of the house itself may not reveal the reason the location is haunted. Many new homes can also be the site of unexplained events and hauntings. Most of the time, the reason for this can be discovered in the history of the property itself. The land may have once been occupied by another house, a building, a farm or perhaps even an old cemetery. This type of history is very important in determining the cause of a haunting in a newer home.

Note: Private homes can often be more difficult for a ghost hunter to gain access to than public buildings but can be very rewarding if you can get an invitation.

CEMETERIES

Cemeteries seem to offer the ghost hunter an excellent chance for strange phenomena and spirit photos, perhaps because of the theory involving "spirit portals" and "doorways" in many burial grounds. Cemeteries with unmarked graves, where desecration has taken place or where tragic events have occurred often become haunted. A search through historical records can often point a researcher to a haunted graveyard.

One thing to be careful of however, is to check into your state and local laws about entering cemeteries after dark. Some areas expressly forbid it while others allow it as long as the cemetery is not posted against trespassing. Be very careful to make sure that you are not breaking the law.

Another problem that has come about with cemetery research is the tendency for inexperienced ghost hunters to simply roam about random cemeteries, snapping photographs and hoping to take pictures of ghosts. A paranormal investigation requires time and planning and locations should be chosen with care. The sites for investigation should be where history and research indicates something supernatural may be going on, or at least has the potential to be going on. (See a later chapter on the best way to conduct cemetery investigations)

THEATERS

The entire range of the human emotion is expressed inside of a theater and this seems to attract spirits who use this energy. The theater also stirs a great love from numerous people who work there and many have returned after their deaths. The saying goes that "every good theater has a ghost" and many theaters are prime locations for all kinds of spirits.

You can normally expect two very different types of hauntings at these locations; both traditional haunts and residual ones. Thanks to the massive expending of energy inside of the buildings, you can expect to hear reports of ghostly footsteps, phantom applause, voices and laughter, and more. All of this phenomena normally signals that residual energy is present. You should also take note that there are hundreds of stories about haunted theaters where the ghosts of former actors and staff members have stayed behind, which makes them a favorite spot for many ghost hunters.

One note of caution though, theaters are prime locations for the creation of ghostlore as the actors are known for their dramatizations and imagination. However, they also tend to be more sensitive and more aware than the average person off the street, so don't disregard the eyewitness accounts, just be careful to separate the actual events from the wishful thinking.

CHURCHES

A church also contains a lot of spent human emotion and can attract ghosts. It is also possible that some churches could have been built on the site of a place that many considered "evil". This would be to drive away the so-called "evil spirits", although it is possible that the place was simply a haunted one. Many ghost hunters are often surprised to learn that a great many churches are haunted. It is rare though to actually find a church that admits to being inhabited by ghosts.

Researchers will also be able to make comparisons between the types of hauntings found in theaters to those found in churches. A wide range of human emotion is expended inside of a church also and for this reason, residual, or memory, hauntings are not uncommon. It's also not unusual to find those who were closely attached to the church and who have remained behind to watch over the place after death. Many churches have stories about phantom nuns, priests and ministers and rather than being a frightening type of ghost, they are a comforting one and good works are often attributed to them.

SCHOOLS AND COLLEGES

Many schools have had tragic events that attract ghosts, either from former students, staff members or perhaps attracted by all of the energy given off by having so many young people all clustered together. The best way to pursue ghosts at a college is to pass the word to a student or two that you are interested in hearing their stories (they almost always have them) or by talking to someone on the security or maintenance staff. Talk to a teacher or a custodian at the local high school or elementary school, but I don't recommend hanging around the playground and asking the students.

Again, ghostlore plays a big part on the college campus and nearly every school has stories that have been tainted by urban legend and campus rumor. For example, ever notice just how many colleges seem to have a murdered co-ed that has come back to haunt her dorm? I have personally heard such a story literally dozens of times and yet have only discovered two incidents (at least that I can verify) where such a thing has actually taken place. Such legends make great stories to repeat during late night parties or around the campfire, but bear little resemblance to reality.

However, do not toss aside these stories completely. They may still have some element of the truth as perhaps a genuine haunting really is taking place. What better way to describe a haunted dorm room than to suggest that a former resident was murdered there.

And maybe, just maybe, the story might be true. I met my wife because of a haunted college dorm where she was living at the time and it was a place where the ghost was a very real one.

HOTELS

Thousands of people pass through your local hotels and motels each year, so it isn't a far reach to think there might be a ghost or two around. You can do a little investigating into the history of older hotels and even find that a suicide or murder could have taken place there. Even newer hotels often have events that occur, including murders, rapes, assaults and mysterious deaths, that might lead to the place becoming haunted. Some people state that such memory ghosts are like "leaving a little piece of ourselves behind" and hotels are the perfect place for such a thing to occur.

However, unless the location happens to be a historical bed and breakfast or an old hotel that advertises its ghosts, asking at the front desk won't do you much good in securing a haunted room for the night. The best way to find out about stories which are not so well known, and which room might have an otherworldly occupant, is to ask one of the maintenance staff or the housekeeping workers. You just might discover they have a good story to tell.

Be prepared to spend some money though. You can't investigate a haunted hotel without spending the night there.

BATTLEFIELDS AND CRIME SCENES

These two types of locations are linked because of the tragedy that has taken place at both of them. These locations deal with a sudden loss of life and this can sometimes cause a spirit to linger behind in confusion. There have been many cases over the years of spirits who reportedly did not realize they were dead or whose life ended so abruptly they did not cross over.

The tragedy and the trauma involved can also lead towards a residual haunting as the terrible events replay themselves over and over again. There are many reports from battlefields (places such as Gettysburg) where witnesses report seeing lines of Civil War troops still marching to battle or where they hear the sounds of guns, screams and cries from long ago.

HOSPITALS AND NURSING HOMES

These are places often overlooked by ghost hunters and I will guarantee these places will be the hardest ones to get into for an investigation. It will even be tough to hear the stories and anecdotes from the people who work there. I personally know of nearly a dozen hospitals and nursing homes that have resident ghosts (from phantom nuns to spectral patients) but it is unlikely if any of these cases will ever be brought to light.

On some occasions however, such buildings can still offer hours of research after they have closed down. There are many cases of these abandoned buildings where the spirits still linger. Some would say that the former residents have left an impression behind, especially in cases of mental disturbance or extreme tragedy, when both residual impressions and conscious entities can leave an indelible mark.

4. FREQUENTLY ASKED QUESTIONS ABOUT GHOSTS

For centuries, man has been fascinated by tales of haunted houses: houses in which ghostly figures walk, eerie voices cry out, and in which furniture levitates in the air and floats to and fro. Many people don't believe that such things really exist - but they are wrong!

D. SCOTT ROGO

Even though very few clear-cut answers actually exist when it comes to ghosts and the paranormal, there seem to be scores of questions about all of the related topics. In this chapter, we'll take a look at a few of the most commonly asked questions and a possible answer to each of them.

Remember though, I do not claim that any of the answers listed here are meant to be the final word on the subject. As I have mentioned before, the reader should consider any of these replies as possible but should also consider each one of them with skepticism and an open mind.

1. Do ordinary people believe in ghosts?

The answer to that is yes. Ordinary, average people do believe in ghosts. Fascination with the unexplained is not limited to merely ghost hunters and enthusiasts. In fact, according to one poll, more than 70% of Americans believe in the possibility of ghosts and out of that percentage, nearly 80% of those polled believe that they had experienced something paranormal. Just about everyone has a story to tell about an encounter that they cannot explain. If it did not happen to them, then it happened to a friend, a neighbor or a relative.

2. Is there any scientific evidence that we become spirits?

There have been a number of scientific attempts to prove the existence of the human soul by the comparing body of a person just before and after death. One famous experiment involved the weight of the soul, believing that there would be change in mass when the soul departed the body. In 1907, a researcher named Duncan McDougall attempted to measure the soul by weighing five patients as they died. In two of the patients, there was a sudden weight loss of a half-ounce, followed by another sudden one-ounce weight loss within three minutes of the time of death. A third patient's weight fluctuated just after their death. It first dropped a bit , then gained several ounces, only to drop once more. There were no changes in the other patients though, making the results of the research inconclusive.

3. Are ghosts evil?

Despite the teachings of some religious faiths, traditional ghosts are not evil or harmful. Over the years, some have come to believe that a study of the paranormal is linked to the occult arts. This has prompted many people to think that ghosts and "demons" are one in the same. Many faiths teach that "communing with spirits" is wrong and this has led the followers of these faiths to assume that because it is considered wrong, the spirits themselves must be evil.

In addition, I have spoken with people who feel that ghosts are not the benign spirits of the dead at all, but demons who pretend to be ghosts in order to kill, maim and terrify the living. Needless to say, there is absolutely no evidence whatsoever to suggest that this is the truth... which leads us to our next question.

4. Do ghosts hurt people?

There have been instances of people being hurt by ghosts and by paranormal activity in their homes. However, it should be stressed that this is not the normal state of affairs and that instances of injury (caused directly by spirits) are very, very rare. As mentioned previously in this book, injuries have been reported because of displaced objects in a haunting and people have also been injured in accidents, usually caused by a fear of the activity. I have often stated and have written that more people are injured running away from a haunted house than by anything going on there.

In fact (despite what Hollywood tends to portray), cases involving injury are so rare that we tend to focus on them for years afterward. Many readers may be familiar with the story of the Bell Witch of Tennessee, a ghost that purportedly not only injured the occupants of the location but also took credit for killing one of them. This event happened nearly two centuries ago and we are still talking about it today. That's how seldom that people are ever really hurt by ghosts.

5. Do ghosts follow people from place to place?

Although it doesn't happen very often, yes, ghosts can follow people to different locations. However, this does not mean that by going on an investigation to a haunted location, a ghost will decide to go home with you at the end of the evening. Ghosts who do follow people only do so for a very good reason, not because they suddenly take a liking to someone.

Ghosts inhabit certain locations for a variety of reasons and, in most situations, are tied to that particular spot. This seems to be either because of choice or because the spirit is "trapped", due to the fact that his life ended suddenly and left him in confusion.

Because of this, a ghost would have to make a conscious choice to leave that location and move to another. I believe that this could only happen if the spirit was in some way "connected" to the living person.

Case histories of hauntings tell of people who inhabited haunted spots for extended periods of time, only to have the ghosts that haunted these locations move to new homes with them. There are also accounts of family members who have ghosts that move from place to place with them. Regardless, it is not something that occurs at the spur of the moment or without a very good explanation.

6. Do objects become haunted?

Yes -- there are many accounts of what some researchers have dubbed "possessed possessions", which simply means physical items to which ghost have become attached. In most cases, these objects (which seem to largely be antiques)are usually connected to Residual hauntings but there have been instances of traditional spirits attaching themselves to important or beloved items as well.

One account that I collected for my own files came from a woman who purchased an old ironing board at an antique store. She soon began to report seeing a young lady standing in her living room, seemingly ironing clothing. The apparition remained in the house as long as the antique did. I have also collected accounts of haunted books, haunted furniture and even a haunted stamp collection.

7. Can ghosts communicate with the living?

Yes, in some cases they can, but only in hauntings that involve Traditional or interactive spirits. Residual hauntings have no real presence behind them and this activity is without thought and without any ability to communicate.

Later in the book, we'll talk more about spirit communication but in short, ghosts don't usually speak and they don't usually make their wishes and messages conveniently known. Yes, voices, whispers and cries are sometimes reported but spirits seem to most commonly communicate through sounds like knocking and rapping or by simply trying to get the attention of the people present. This might occur through missing and vanishing items or even through visible apparitions.

This isn't always the case though. Some ghosts seem to be unable, or perhaps unwilling, to communicate with investigators and witnesses. So there don't seem to be any concrete answers to this question, other than to say that it's possible based on past evidence.

8. Are animals and children more sensitive to ghosts?

I would have to say that I believe that they are. In my own experience, animals (especially cats and dogs) seem to be much more aware of things that humans cannot see or hear. Are they aware of ghosts? That's hard to say, but it has long been reported that dogs brought into allegedly haunted locations react to presences that no one else can detect. They often bark, whine or merely seem fascinated by what appear to be empty hallways and staircases to us.

Several years ago, I lived in a house that was a constant source of amazement to my cat. We had one upstairs bedroom that no matter what we did, we could never heat. Summer or winter, it was always ice cold and for this reason, we seldom used it. Our cat, however, was intrigued by this room and would sit for hours at a time in the hallway outside of it, always staring inside. She would never actually go into it, but would always sit just outside of the doorway, as if watching or looking at something inside. Was the room haunted? I have no idea, but she could certainly sense something inside of it that we could not.

In addition, I once conducted an experiment using a dog at a cemetery that was believed to be haunted. Over a span of several years, I had documented a lot of strange stories and photographs from the place. I was curious to see what would happen when a dog was brought inside. As soon as we brought the dog to the gates of the cemetery though, he immediately began barking and pulling at his leash. No matter how much we prodded him, he refused to go inside and reacted in a way that was not consistent with this normally calm animal's usual behavior. He obviously sensed something inside.

I also think that children might be more sensitive to spirits and hauntings. There are a number of reasons for why this might be, but perhaps the most persuasive one is that a child's belief system is not as developed as that of an adult's. He has not yet "learned" that ghosts cannot exist and his screening process does not shut out the unexplained as an adult's might. For this reason, I think that children often develop "imaginary friends" that might not be so imaginary at all. That's not to say that all so-called "imaginary friends" are ghosts. I feel that the vast majority of them are really just elaborate creations that seem very real to the child in question. There have been instances and accounts in which the invisible being is more real than just a friendly playmate though. This leads me to believe that sometimes a child can be much more aware of things than we can.

9. Are haunted places only active after dark?

No, and despite what movies and some books might tell you, there is no time of day that is more active than another. It has always been my thought that if a place is haunted at night, then it is haunted in the daytime as well. This has become a common misconception and for this reason, most of us schedule our investigations of haunted sites after darkness has fallen. To be honest, I don't really think it's necessary but I always urge ghost hunters to conduct investigations at a time that is most comfortable for them. If this is in the middle of the afternoon or at the stroke of midnight, I don't think it really matters.

10. Why do some ghosts wear clothes?

This is probably one of the most interesting dilemmas to contemplate when it comes to ghost research. No one really knows (or can agree on) why ghosts are seen the way that they are but I have proposed this theory in the past and it still continues to generate questions and feedback from all sorts of people interested in the paranormal.

In the previous chapter, we pondered what ghosts really are. Are they discarnate spirits of the dead? Are they simply bundles of energy, let loose into the air when the human body ceases to function? Are they merely residual images left on the atmosphere of a place like an old film? As most readers probably agree, I think ghosts fit into all of these categories. Despite all of the labeling and categorizing though, many questions still remain. One of the most nagging is why would ghosts need clothing?

It cannot be denied that a huge number of ghost reports include sightings of ghosts wearing some sort of clothing, be it a flowing robe, a military uniform or even a plaid suit. No matter what it is, the clothing seems to be the thing which makes the spirit recognizable as human and even dates it to a certain period. But why clothing? If you're dead, what could you possibly need it for?

Now, as I have already stated in this book, I believe that ghosts are a natural part of our world. I believe that ghosts, whether they are spirits of the dead or residual images, have an explanation that is only considered paranormal because we don't understand it yet. I have explained that I don't much go in for metaphysical theories and new age stuff when a natural explanation, even a mysterious one, will do just fine. So, bear that in mind as you proceed with this section.

The first type of haunting linked to ghosts wearing clothing is the Residual Haunting. This haunting compares to an old film loop, meaning that it is a scene or image that is played over and over again through the years. Regardless of how or why these hauntings exist, all of the visual ghost sightings in these places seem to have one thing in common and it's that all of the ghosts that are seen are wearing clothing. Most of them are fully dressed, some transparent and some not, but all of them appear to be human and are recognizable as people.

The reason behind this is fairly basic as these ghosts are mere images or imprints of time on the location and yet they appear to be the spirits of the dead wearing clothing. But what about the ghosts that are not? What about those which are true, traditional spirits of those who have died and who have stayed behind? If these ghosts, personalities that are freed from the human form, are actually masses of energy then why do nearly all ghost sightings describe ghosts as looking like people who were once alive?

If we rule out residual images in many sightings, as we can do since many sightings occur to people who actually knew the spirit when the spirit was among the living, then we are still left with a large number of unexplained encounters.

Throughout the history of ghostlore, we have heard stories of everyday people's encounters with the spirits of the dead. In most of these stories, witnesses report coming face-to-face with ghosts who look, more or less, like real people. In many cases, the ghosts are even recognizable as a person who the living witness once knew. These spirits often have an intelligence and interact with the witness, making it impossible for them to be merely a residual image. But what are these witnesses seeing? How can an intelligent spirit appear as anything other than just energy?

Many researchers feel that ghosts are made up of electromagnetic energy. This energy, inside of the body, forms what we call our spirit, soul, or personality. Now, science cannot prove this energy, or personality, actually exists, yet we know it does. If it can exist inside of our bodies, in spite of the fact there is no proof that it exists, then why can't it exist outside of the body, once the body itself stops functioning. It's possible that it does and that this electromagnetic energy contains our personality and is what we think of as our spirit.

However, this still does not explain how this energy can appear looking like it did when it was contained by the human body but I do have a suggestion as to how this might work. It has been shown through scientific experiments that exposure to high levels of electromagnetic energy can cause people to have vivid dreams, nightmares and even hallucinations. In other words, people are seeing things as a result of exposure to this energy.

Does that mean that ghosts are all in our heads?

In a way, I guess that it does. If the spirits have any sort of control over the energy they are now comprised of (or even if their personalities are somehow manifested in the energy), then I would think it possible for the witness to see the spirit as the spirit sees itself. If the personality really does remain, the spirit would visualize itself as it was when alive, appearing as a living person and wearing clothing. This could be a totally unconscious effect of the energy on the living person, or it could be a manipulation on the part of the spirit itself, perhaps causing the person to see what it wants them to.

To understand this, I suggest that you close your eyes for a moment and then visualize yourself in your mind. How do you appear to yourself? Most likely, you were wearing clothing in your imagination and as with most people, you did not even visualize yourself all the way down to your feet. With the idea in mind that a ghost appears looking in the same way that he sees himself, this might explain why so many ghosts that are seen are not only wearing clothing but also tend to fade away below the knees.

Is this the answer to explain ghost sightings? Perhaps, or perhaps not. There is a lot out there that we still do not understand but we need to challenge the ideas that have been stagnating about ghosts for so long. Whether ghosts have a natural explanation or not, it is time to take the horror film mentality out of ghost research because these natural explanations might be more puzzling than the supernatural ones which already exist.

11. How do some ghosts manifest as smells?

There have been many accounts of ghosts that manifest as odors in various locations. Many ghost hunters have investigated, and have even experienced, locations where ghostly odors are present. Ghosts sometimes make themselves known through smells of flowers, perfume, cigar smoke and more. These are just a few examples though, for the varieties of smells seem to be endless. In every case of this, the odors have a connection to smells attached to the ghost in life.

For instance, I have investigated and have written extensively about the Mineral Springs Hotel in Alton, Illinois. One of the most prominent ghosts here is that of a woman who was killed years ago on the hotel's main staircase. Since that time, her ghost has manifested here as an overpowering jasmine perfume, which was reportedly her favorite scent in life. While I have never encountered her myself, I have interviewed a number of people who have, including those who never knew about the smell or even that the building was haunted at all.

A closer encounter with an intelligent spirit, who also manifests by a smell, was referred to in an earlier chapter. I came face to face with this ghost (so to speak) in an old theater that he haunted. He made his presence known by the distinctive odor of Noxzema cold cream, a smell that was associated with him in life. I had no idea that the ghost was known by this smell until later and while this was quite a mystery to me, the mechanics behind the encounter is an even greater puzzle. Regardless of the fact that encounters with "olfactory ghosts" had been taking place for years, I still had to wonder how I could have come into contact with a smell that was associated with a person when he was alive -- even though he was now a ghost.

Let's begin with the idea that I think we have compiled enough evidence to logically assume that this actor is the resident ghost of the theater. I think that it's safe to base this on the history of the place, the documentation that exists showing that he was a real person and that he died in the manner that is part of the theater's lore. It's also based on more than 25 independent accounts of the smell of Noxzema that accompanies paranormal activity. Needless to say, I became strongly convinced of the reality of the haunting after my own inexplicable encounter with the smell. Not knowing about the sign of the presence in advance ruled out (in my mind) any chance of imagination.

Now that we have established this however, I still have to question how I could have actually come into contact with a smell. And this is why I wonder about it - the smell that is associated with Joe's ghost should not be attached to his spirit. If we accept the idea that a spirit is the personality of someone who once lived and now remains behind as energy, then we can accept the idea that certain attributes of that person may remain behind as well. One such attribute might be the smell of that person. It's possible that someone could have a distinctive odor about them, perhaps a problem with body odor even, who knows?

In the actor's case, he also had a distinctive odor; however, it was not a part of his actual makeup. It was an artificial odor of something that he applied to his body. How then could this odor exist as part of his energy after death? That's a good question and my only guess on that could be that perhaps the spirit has more control over the energy attached to it than we ever imagined.

In the past, I have theorized about the various reasons why ghosts are reported wearing clothing. Outside of residual hauntings (where the ghosts are nothing more than imprints or memories), there are still many accounts of ghosts looking just as they did when alive, right down to the clothing they are wearing. I have come to feel that this occurs when the energy of the ghost interacts with the mind of the person seeing it. As the personality and attributes of the person remain within the energy that the spirit is now made up of, the affected mind now sees the spirit the way that it either once existed, or perhaps in the way that the spirit sees itself.

Could it work this same way with an artificial smell? Could the odor of Noxzema be such a part of the personality makeup of this actor that his spirit exudes the smell just as he once did? It's certainly a possibility and I have no other way to explain just what I experienced that day at the theater.

5. THE GHOST HUNTER'S KIT

ESSENTIAL TOOLS FOR GHOST RESEARCH & INVESTIGATION

The most beautiful thing we can experience is the mysterious. It is the source of all true art and science.

ALBERT EINSTEIN

Even though it has been mentioned in this book already, I can't help but do it again in a chapter about tools to detect ghosts --- the most important tool in any investigation is the ghost hunter himself. With that said, let me add that if anyone ever plans to be successful as a ghost hunter or paranormal investigator, he should first fine-tune his own skills and his own knowledge before ever attempting to conduct an investigation.

In order to do this, the ghost hunter must possess an open mind. Investigations that are launched with a negative attitude, or with a pre-supposition of the facts, are doomed to fail. It is essential that a fine balance is struck and that investigations are conducted with open-minded skepticism. That's not as hard as it sounds. It really just means that an investigation should be approached with the idea that anything is possible. This includes the possibility, or even the likelihood, that the location being investigated is not haunted.

In the majority of cases, natural explanations can be found, but a good ghost hunter should be prepared for anything. Of course, "anything" might even include an outright hoax. Believe it or not, instances of this are fairly rare, but they do happen. A researcher can be prepared for this by doing his homework ahead of time and knowing what to look for. In addition, he might also encounter individuals who have invented the phenomena in their minds as a desperate plea for attention. Or they may have misinterpreted natural events as being ghost-related, convinced that a spirit is haunting their house. Researchers have to be able to handle these possibilities as well.

All of this will be discussed more completely later on, but for now, let's take a look at the essential (and not so essential) items that a ghost hunter should be equipped with for an investigation.

BASIC ITEMS FOR AN INVESTIGATION

In the 1930's, during his investigation of England's Borley Rectory, ghost hunter Harry Price compiled a list of items that he always carried in his ghost hunter's kit. As far as I can tell, he was the first to put together such an assortment of items and they included:

- A Pair of soft, felt overshoes (for creeping about in silence)
- A steel measuring tape
- screw eyes, lead seals, a sealing tool, white tape, a tool pad and nails and small, electric bells (for the construction of motion detecting devices)
- dry batteries and switches (for secret electrical contacts)
- camera, film and flash-bulbs
- notebook, red, blue and black marking pens, sketching pad and drawing instruments (for maps and diagrams)
- ball of string & a stick of chalk (to mark movement of objects)
- bandages, iodine, surgical tape and a flask of brandy (for injuries)
- Electric torch, matches and candles
- bowl of mercury to detect tremors in a room or passage
- Cinematograph camera with electrical release

While the tool kits of the early ghost hunters undoubtedly sound very "quaint" to modern readers, it will soon be revealed that the essential list of basic items today is not all that different from what was being used years ago. In fact, some of the items are updated versions of tools from Price's original kit as some recommended items have not changed at all.

In addition to the basic items, the ghost hunter of today can be more prepared than ever with an ever-growing array of affordable devices that have been adapted for use in ghost research. Many of the items that will be discussed in this chapter are not the most complex (or even the most sensitive), but they do fall into a range of devices that are affordable to the average person. The items in this "essential tool kit" can be purchased by anyone but all of the equipment takes practice and knowledge to use correctly. Never --- and this cannot be stressed enough --- go out on an investigation if you do not know how to properly use your equipment. There is nothing that can destroy your credibility faster than compiling what amounts to false data that is collected from a location that may not be haunted at all.

Also, don't ignore the basic items on this list in an attempt to impress your friends with your technical expertise. Ghost hunters operated for many years, and got good results, using nothing more than basic items, good instincts and a camera. I have often been accused of being old-fashioned and a part of the "old school" of ghost hunting, ignoring the opportunities that exist from using the "gee whiz" technology that many feel is so necessary today. While I would never suggest that anyone stop using whatever technology is available to try and document ghosts, I would also remind the reader that nothing replaces good detective work either.

THE LIST

Here is the list of items that a ghost hunter should never be without while conducting paranormal investigations. You never know when they might be needed and many of them will compliment other items that will be discussed in the book. I also recommend buying large tool boxes or padded cases in which to carry your basic tools and your equipment.

Here is the list of basic items:

1. Notebook and pen (recording notes and diagrams)
2. Sketch pad and drawing pencils (maps of location)
3. Measuring tape (checking distance and witness accounts)
4. Extra Batteries (you never know when they might fail)
5. Flashlight (this requires no explanation)
6. Extra Film and Recording Tapes
7. Small Tool Kit (some electronic devices require screwdrivers)
8. Camera (see later chapter for more details)
9. Video Camera (see later chapter for more details)
10. Portable Motion Detectors (great for securing locations)

I firmly believe that these items are the most essential to have when conducting an investigation. If a ghost hunter properly uses his own investigative skills and techniques, then these items will aid him greatly in the research and documentation of authentic paranormal phenomena.

Another useful item, although not one that I would consider to be absolutely essential, is a set of two-way radios, which are very useful for teams who are conducting investigations. They allow the group to stay in constant contact with one another, which is invaluable when investigating infrequent phenomena or when working in large or outdoor locations.

GHOST DETECTION DEVICES

Despite what some researchers may claim, I believe that electronic devices, while excellent to use and work with, are simply items to further document phenomena. They should not be used alone to establish a genuine haunting, as we are still too unsure of how exactly these devices work to detect paranormal activity. They are best used in conjunction with eyewitness accounts, monitoring locations and with other investigative techniques. No single piece of evidence can stand on its own. Each piece of evidence is only as good as the corresponding pieces of evidence. In other words, anomalous readings on an EMF detector can only be seen as evidence of a ghost if the readings can be backed up by something else, like a cold spot, a witness account or even readings on other equipment at the same time.

In the chapter to follow, we'll take a look at using detection equipment in an investigation, the myths and mysteries behind the equipment and how best to use it. There have been many devices used over the years to hunt for ghosts, from the most basic to the incredibly complex. My focus here will be on devices that are accessible to everyone, from modern electronics to some of the oldest devices known to man.

THE COMPASS

For those who may not be able to afford an electronic device (or may want to practice with something else first), a compass can be purchased in just about any sporting goods store in your area. I cannot guarantee the validity of the results that you might obtain with this simple device, but other ghost hunters have used them in the past and often with successful results.

The best way to use the compass is to carry it into an allegedly haunted location, leaving the compass open and flat out on the palm of your hand. Your arm should be bent at the elbow and level, extended at an angle from your body so that the compass is directly in front of you. The needle on the compass will move each time that you change direction and according to reports, it will begin to spin when it encounters a ghost or some sort of anomalous energy field.

Even though the compass is a very basic item, the reported behavior of the device in a situation involving paranormal energy is actually quite consistent with much higher-tech devices. The theory (which we will discuss more in a moment) is that the device reacts to abrupt changes or fluctuations in the energy field of the location. A spinning compass needle would certainly show that something unusual is going on.

DOWSING RODS

The art of dowsing has been around for centuries, perhaps even thousands of years. It is the oldest form of divination known to man and has been used for a variety of different reasons, including searches for underground water, discovering the location of unmarked graves, determining the sex of unborn children and even locating ghosts.

How dowsing actually works remains a mystery, but it has proven to be uncannily accurate over the years. Even the American Society of Dowsers admits that "the reasons the procedures work are entirely unknown."

The standard practice of dowsing is to search for underground water sources. Many cities, counties and corporations keep a dowser on the payroll. In most cases, a dowser searches an area with either a Y-shaped rod or two L-shaped rods in his hands. He concentrates on what he is looking for and when he finds the right spot, the rods will either bend downwards or will cross over one another. No one knows how this works -- it simply does.

To use dowsing rods to find ghosts, most dowsers recommend using two L-shaped rods that have been made from brass or some lightweight metal. Some dowsers even use metal coat hangers, so there is really no standard material. The rods should be about two-foot long and bent into an L-shape, which fits into your hand. Then, hold the short end of the rod so that the longer piece points outward, away from your body. The rods should be held loosely so that they have room to swing easily back and forth.

After that, begin searching the building or location. It has been suggested that it's possible that by searching, and by concentrating on what you are looking for, you can find ghosts, anomalous energy and some say even dimensional portals using dowsing rods.

Walk about the location and follow where the rods lead you. They are supposed to point in the direction of any energy they detect. Once you have discovered the energy source, the rods will cross, signaling that the area in question has been found.

USING PARANORMAL DETECTION EQUIPMENT

GEIGER COUNTERS

In years past, ghost researchers had little or no electronic equipment that could be used to monitor locations or to search for anomalous activity that might be present in anarea. In recent times, new theories have been developed which seem to suggest that many haunted locations have high levels of electromagnetic energy present in them. Debunkers have pointed to these energy fields, which have been discovered to cause headaches, dizziness and even hallucinations, as an artificial explanation for all ghost sightings but this is unlikely to be the case. This pat answer, while compelling, does not explain away all of the hauntings that exist, no matter what the debunkers might like everyone to believe.

What is more likely is that the ghosts themselves may be electromagnetic in origin or perhaps that the ghosts actually use this energy to manifest. The magnetic energy might also explain how Residual hauntings occur as well, causing events and images to impress on the atmosphere of the location.

Whatever the answer, researchers began adapting electronic devices as a way to detect the energy that was not visible to the human eye. There are theories that exist to say that the energy a ghost gives off, or uses, whether it is a conscious spirit or residual energy, causes a disruption in the magnetic field of the location and thus, becomes detectable using measuring devices.

One of the first devices to be used for such a purpose was the Geiger counter. This device was first invented back in 1928 by H. Geiger and E.W. Mueller as a way to measure and detect radioactivity. Used to check materials and environments for radioactive energy, the device increases its count if there is anything present that climbs beyond what is called the "normal background" radiation of a place.

Radioactivity is the spontaneous emission of energy from the nucleus of certain elements, most notable uranium. There are three forms of energy associated with radioactivity: alpha, beta and gamma radiation.

Alpha particles are very weak when it comes to penetrating anything and a couple of inches of air, two sheets of paper or even human skin can act as an effective shield. They are really only dangerous if they get inside of you. If they do, they can accumulate and slowly cause damage over a long period of time. While alpha particles carry a positive charge, beta particles carry a negative charge and are slightly more penetrating than their counterpart. Gamma rays, the most well-known radioactive energy to the general public, are high energy photons. They have the greatest penetrating power of all forms of radiation and can pass through several centimeters of lead and still be detectable. Most Geiger counters will pick up all three types of radiation and inform the user of any changes in the surrounding field.

Geiger counters were really first acknowledged as useful in the paranormal field in 1974, when the "Entity" case began. Researchers Barry Taff and Kerry Gaynor from the now defunct Department of Parapsychology at UCLA, became involved in a haunting that would go on to be the basis for a book and film, as well as for years of study and speculation.

According to the woman who was embroiled at the center of the case, her home was haunted and she was being repeatedly attacked and raped by the spirits that were present. Taff and Gaynor spent many hours documenting the reported events and speaking to witnesses who had seen apparitions in the house but became concerned that "Doris", as she was dubbed, was either crazy or making things up. They did not plan to pursue the case at all.

However, a few days later, Doris called and informed them that five individuals outside of her family had now seen the apparitions. So Taff and Gaynor decided to return to the house with cameras and tape recorders. They immediately noticed something odd when they entered Doris' bedroom. Even though it was a hot, August night and the windows were closed, the temperature was unusually low when compared to the rest of the house. The cold spots faded in and out irregularly, sometimes completely disappearing. They could find no source for the cold areas, but these anomalies would not be the only methods through which the phenomena would make itself known.

The first of many inexplicable happenings occurred while Gaynor was talking to Doris' oldest son in the kitchen. He was standing a short distance from a lower kitchen cabinet when the cabinet door suddenly swung open and a pan jumped out of it, landing about three feet away.

After examining the cabinet, Taff and Gaynor went into the bedroom again with Doris and her friend, Candy, who had joined them for the evening and who purported to be psychic. Taff took a photograph of the bedroom with a Polaroid SX-70 camera and it came out perfectly. After they were in the room for about 15 minutes, Candy shouted that she sensed something in the corner. Taff ran back into the room with the camera and immediately aimed and fired it at the corner.

The photograph that resulted was bleached completely white, as if it had been exposed to some sort of intense energy or radiation. The same thing happened a few minutes later when Candy again directed their attention to the corner. This time, the photo still bleached out, but not as badly as the first time. Puzzled, Taff took another photo (thinking that something might be wrong with the camera) but this time in the living room. This photo came out fine, as did subsequent photos taken by Kerry Gaynor in the bedroom. The only difference was that these photos were not taken while Candy "sensed" something else in the room with them.

A short time later, Taff took another photo, this time because of a cold breeze that came from the closed bedroom door. This photo turned out to be the strangest of the night, showing a ball of light that was about one foot in diameter. It hovered a few inches from the door in the photo, but no one had actually seen the light appear.

Moments later, while the investigators were poring over the photo, Taff happened to glance over toward the bedroom's east window. In a flash, he spotted several rapidly moving, blue balls of light. He immediately raised the Polaroid camera and took a picture in the direction of the curtains. The resulting photo was blurred and badly bleached but the blue lights that Taff had seen were nowhere to be found.

A few minutes later, Candy again warned about the presence of an entity in the room, this time standing directly in front of her. Taff fired the Polaroid in her direction and he obtained an odd photo of Candy. Her face was completely bleached out, yet her dress and the room behind and around her was totally clear and distinct. Another photo, this time taken by Kerry Gaynor under the same conditions, again captured Candy with bleaching about her face while the rest of the photograph was very clear.

At this point, they became convinced that something out of the ordinary was occurring in the house.

Over the course of the next ten weeks, a team from UCLA was almost always present in the house. They returned many times for investigations, bringing dozens of eyewitnesses, researchers and photographers with them. Initially, most of the researchers were skeptical of the events reported by Taff and Gaynor but soon, more of them began to share their belief of the happenings after witnessing them for themselves.

One night, what can only be described as a "light show" took place in the house in front of 20 startled onlookers. Most of the photos that were taken of them though, were disappointing. The light was so bright that most of them came out overexposed. One photo did manage to show what the investigators saw that night. The frame was filled with reverse arcs of light. The reason this photo was so important is that the arc on the wall, if it were really on the wall, would be bent because the two walls are perpendicular to each other. In the photo however, the arc is not bent, which means that it was floating in space at the time and signifies that it was dimensional and not just a flashlight being aimed at the wall.

One of the witnesses present that night was Frank De Felitta, an author who would go on to write the book based on the case. De Felitta would later vividly recall the light as it moved into the center of the room and the shouts from those present. He said that Doris started screaming as the light moved toward her, cursing and daring the entity to show itself, instead of just a light. At that point, it started to appear and witnesses would later claim to see a part of an arm, a neck and what looked like a bald head. Everyone present saw the same thing at the same time, ruling out any individual's hallucinations.

Another interesting event of the evening involved an extremely sensitive Geiger counter that had been brought along to record any activity in the radiation field of the house. The instrument began behaving very oddly when the lights were the most active as the previously constant background radiation registering on the device dropped off to zero. When the light activity began to dwindle and then fade away, the Geiger counter's meter returned to its normal level of ambient background radiation. Barry Taff believed that it was possible that the strange activity either used the background radiation as an energy source or that the energy given off by the lights scattered the ambient energy field in such a way that it could no longer be registered.

Over the next few weeks, the activity continued but that strange night seemed to be the climax of the events. The phenomena began to diminish little by little and although there were more violent episodes, even after Doris and her family left the house, they were never as strong as they had once been.

This case offers one of the first, and best, examples of how Geiger counters can be used for paranormal investigation. Unfortunately though, their use is not as simple as it appears. In this investigation, the researchers found that the ambient radiation in the house seemed to be drained when the ghost / energy began to manifest. This is not always the case though. In other investigations, researchers like Dr. William Roll have been able to find signs of increased radioactivity in the presence of ghosts.

Regardless of the contradictions in what they can or cannot do, the evidence is in favor of the use of Geiger counters as an additional measuring tool for thorough investigations. While I might avoid them as the only tool that is used to measure energy fluctuations, they can present some worthwhile information when putting together a complete research package. The evidence that they ultimately provide may still be elusive but it is well worth exploring further.

ELECTROMAGNETIC FIELD METERS

Electromagnetic Field Meters (EMF Meters) are the most commonly used devices for ghost hunters today. Largely, they are also the most reliable. In this section, we'll discuss what they are and how they work and then we'll take a look at some quality, recommended devices and instructions on how best to use them.

These devices, like the previously mentioned Geiger counters, have been adapted for use in paranormal investigations and are used primarily to record and document disruptions in the electromagnetic field of a location, which is not something that we can do with our human senses alone. Being able to use such devices not only gives us credibility as investigators, but they also provide us with evidence that we can present to witnesses and observers. They also allow us to rely on more than just a "hunch" while we are in the midst of an investigation. That's not to say that sensitive feelings, or just plain intuition, is bad, but EMF meters can provide a confirmation of these instincts.

These devices also free us from having to depend on psychics for our investigations. Again, that isn't to say that all psychics are bad, or cannot be helpful in some cases. It's just that even the good ones can sometimes be unreliable or be influenced by something outside of the specific case. The other problem with psychics is that they really cannot provide tangible evidence in a case. The psychic may be a truly gifted person, who encounters a number of a spirits at a location, but unfortunately, that's the problem. The psychic becomes the only person who sees the ghost. However, using technology, cameras and detection devices, we can also collect real evidence that will be useful once the investigation is over.

I should also add though that the equipment is not perfect. These things were not designed to detect ghosts, but to be used in the building and scientific trades to detect energy leaks and problem fields. They can certainly (and were designed to) be influenced by things that are not paranormal. Because of this, you have to learn what the readings mean and how to tell if your sudden spikes of energy are paranormal or artificial. Still to come, we will delve into what to watch out for but it still takes practice to use these devices effectively. I stress again --- never go out on an investigation if you don't know how to use and read your equipment properly.

The other thing to beware of is the "crutch" that technology seems to provide for the inexperienced ghost hunter. It's easy for a person to get lured in by how easy it seems to let fancy devices and cameras do all of the work for them. Many ghost hunters have come into the field in recent years and have been introduced to the popular electronic devices that are being used. This person is soon under the mistaken impression that there is little more to ghost research than just wandering around with an EMF meter in his hand, waving it madly about in someone's home. A ghost hunter like this does not stay in the field for very long, as he quickly become bored with such things. Such an example just reinforces the idea that electronic equipment is meant to compliment the other tools that we use and the other research that we do.

For electronic devices to be useful in an investigation, the researcher must search for corresponding activity (evidence) to go along with the anomalies the EMF meter says is present. Such evidence can be gleaned from witness accounts, photographs, temperature changes or whatever else may occur. In this way, we can truly use this information to document a haunting. As mentioned already, no single piece of evidence can stand on its own to establish proof, especially nothing more than readings that might turn up with your EMF meter.

But just what are we looking for when we use these meters?

In the past, many of us were under the impression that "ghostly" readings that we might pick up with an EMF detector have to fall at a certain level (usually between 2.0 and 8.0 milligauss). A couple of years ago though, I began some research that convinced me that we had very little to base this theory on.

From what I could discover, the idea that this was the "ideal" reading for paranormal activity came about because we were trying to rule out artificial activity in a location, such as would come from power outlets, lines and appliances. We knew that if the devices registered higher than 2-8 milligauss, then we were most likely picking up some sort of artificial field. What this theory did not take into account was that experienced (or even slightly savvy) researchers would immediately begin to search for a source for the reading. By ruling out any high readings that came from an artificial source, we could safely assume that we were not dealing with a ghost.

Soon, we began accepting the idea that only readings that fell into the "ideal" range could be paranormal. That's where I have come to believe we began making mistakes. Soon, we had no explanation for abnormally high readings that could not be explained or for "buried" needles on meters in outdoor locations and graveyards with no sources of power. We had some glaring problems with our once convenient theory and no way to overcome them.

That's when I began to look into my own past research and some of the work being done by others in the field. I soon learned that there seemed to be no hard rules when it came to the use of detection equipment in the paranormal field. Honestly, I began to wonder why I had never looked into this before.

Here's what I found. Take a look and the reader will see that the use of equipment in the field is confusing and often quite contradictory.

- The majority of EMF detectors have been designed to read in the 30 to 500 Hz range. They are calibrated at 60 Hz, which is the standard setting for most household fields. What most meters are designed to gauge are the currents induced inside of the location by artificial fields. Most common fields are around 60 Hz. The problems occur because we really don't know whether or not ghosts and paranormal energy are above or below this standard setting. This remains a complete mystery and because of this, we had to re-think what we have previously thought about detection devices.

- Another contradiction is that we assume ghosts are made up of electromagnetic energy and also that they use it to manifest, drawing energy from the area around them. While these are very different scenarios, evidence suggests that both theories may be correct, depending on the case and the situation. This again shows that there are no set rules for the use of the meters.

- It should also be noted that reliable case histories and investigation reports show that in some situations, EMF meters and other devices can show either a huge surge or an unexplained drain of energy from the location. For instance, during the famous "Entity" case, Barry Taff's Geiger counter went from measuring a normal, low level amount of radiation in the house to suddenly registering none at all. He surmised (and probably correctly) that the entity present was using the natural energy of the house to manifest. This goes to show that we have to be careful about thinking that we have all of the answers when it comes to the effects that ghosts might have on our equipment.

Consider these examples from my own files:

I was involved in the investigation of an allegedly haunted house that had been abandoned. It had no electricity, no running water, no gas lines and basically nothing artificial that could interfere with the detection equipment and produce false readings. In one corner of an upstairs room, my EMF meter suddenly began picking up a very strong energy field that I could not explain. The field was so strong that the needle on the meter was literally "buried", detecting readings that were completely off the scale. At first glance, it would seem that the meter was picking up some sort of artificial field, like a power line in the wall perhaps. The problem was, there was no power in the house.

While such an event would be unexplainable based on the already mentioned theory of "ideal" readings, I felt strongly that I was dealing with a ghost. The reason for this is that I had something to base this feeling on. You see, at the same time that I was working with the meter, other investigators were recording a light fixture that was hanging in the hallway just outside the room. They were recording it because the light had suddenly starting moving by itself and it happened at the same time I began measuring the energy field. In addition, other investigators, outside of the house, took a number of photos that managed to catch some sort of activity around the outside of this upper level.

Later, I would also discover that at this spot in the room, near a window, was where historical accounts had it that a ghostly woman had been seen over a period of many years, by many different witnesses.

We couldn't have asked for better corresponding evidence and yet the theory of "ideal readings" had to be discarded in this case!

On another occasion, I was involved in an investigation of a cemetery that I already believed was haunted. Previously, other researchers and myself had been able to document strange happenings and had obtained a number of photographs here that could not be explained, even by commercial photographers. During this particular investigation, we set up detection equipment, motion detectors and an infrared video camera around a particularly active part of the graveyard. We began documenting the next several hours, keeping a close watch on the video monitor and noting any changes in the EMF detectors.

During the course of the evening, we managed to record what we felt were legitimate anomalies with the video camera (we also later learned that the still camera picked up activity too, but we didn't know this until the film was developed). These included small lights that moved on their own and in the opposite direction of any wind that may have been present and some odd flashes of light that we were unable to explain. But the strangest activity seemed to center on the EMF detectors. With chilling accuracy, we were able to show that the surrounding electromagnetic field actually dipped down each time one of the odd lights appeared on camera. They were not causing surges of energy, but seemed to be using the energy present at the location to appear.

So, what do we make of all this? Are we back to knowing even less about using detection equipment than we were when we started? No, I don't think that we are. I think that it just serves as a warning that we should not get too confident about what we do and what we don't really know.

I continue to believe that EMF meters and other electronic detection devices are instrumental in the furthering of ghost research. We just have to be careful about how we use them and careful about how much of our research is based solely on their use. I stress once again that we must have corresponding evidence for every investigation because mere EMF readings are not enough. In some cases, ghosts seem to produce surges of energy and in other cases they drain them. Such a "paranormal paradox" is what keeps this field so intriguing but also keeps every good researcher on his toes.

USING AN EMF METER

The following section deals with some different EMF meters that I have used in my own investigations and also with ones that I recommend for use in your research. Again, these are not the most technical devices that you can buy (if you have an unlimited bank account) but they are affordable and can be used by anyone who takes the time to learn them properly.

I have also included usage instructions with each meter and the reader will notice that each is basically used in the same way. However, I have included information for each specific device and things to watch out for in order to use them correctly. I have also updated the settings and usage directions for several of the meters from previous editions of this guide.

GAUSSMASTER / DR. GAUSS EMF METER

This model is probably one of the best types of meter for people just starting out in the paranormal field. I have recommended it for some time, even though less expensive devices like this one are not very sensitive and have a hard time picking up anything outside of the immediate range of the investigator. This meter is easy to use though and measures energy fields in the range of 0 - 10 milligauss on a colored, analog scale.

This device should be held in your right hand, with your fingers wrapping around the bottom of the meter and your fingertips touching the left side. Do not place your hand over the end of the meter, as your body will interfere with the readings. Then, bend your elbow so that the meter is held out in front of you at a distance from your elbow to hand. Your arm can be extended for further reach, but do not bring the meter closer to your body.

When conducting a study of a location, gently move the meter from side-to-side as you walk. Moving it up and down too quickly can cause false readings and spikes to occur. As you walk, be on the lookout for sudden and extreme bursts of energy to be registered on the meter. If such an event does happen, try to pinpoint the source of the field. Always remember to use cameras and any other devices available to document anomalous fields that appear.

Remember though, strong readings and surges of energy may be signs that you are picking up an artificial energy source like an appliance, an electrical outlet or even a hidden line in the wall or the floor. Always try to find a natural source for the energy readings before you begin thinking that you have found a ghost. This device easily picks up artificial fields (that's what it was designed for, remember?) and should be used with caution. All readings should be thoroughly examined before being accepted as evidence.

And a word of warning about this particular device... it is activated by pressing a panel / button on the left side of the meter. Once it is activated, the meter will operate on its own and then will shut off automatically if it does not register anything within 10 minutes. Make sure that the meter continues to operate during investigations. In addition, if you continuously press the button, it will begin reading on a scale of 0 -1 milligauss and will seem to be surging all the time. This is an extremely low electromagnetic setting and as everything has a background radiation field, it will be constantly going off. You don't want to use this setting for paranormal investigations.

This meter is a beginning model and is very simple in design. Anyone who is searching for a more sophisticated device should try a more advanced model. However, don't discount this meter completely. While admittedly it is not as sensitive as other meters and can be hard to use in indoor investigations, it works quite well for those who investigate cemeteries, historic sites and other outdoor locations. As little in the way of interference exists at these sites, just about anything that you pick up with the meter will demand an explanation. With no artificial fields in evidence, this meter might be one of the best detectors to use in such circumstances.

OTHER BASIC METERS

The above mentioned "Gaussmaster" meter is far from the only basic meter that is being used for ghost hunting purposes. However, I do recommend it as one of the most reliable meters on the market.

Other meters should be used in the same basic way, holding them away from the body and in a sweeping pattern so that they will pass through any energy fields that might be present. It should be noted that basic meters like these do not have sensors on the sides of the meter, only in the front. This means that the energy fields must be approached from this direction only in order for them to be picked up. Moving the meter back and forth in a slow, sweeping motion will offer the best opportunity for them to pass through the often small areas where anomalous readings can be found. Just be sure that, as with all meters, the fields that are picked up are traced back to their source, if possible, and are ruled out as being any sort of artificial interference.

CELLSENSOR METER

This meter is another basic monitor that actually serves a dual function. It can be used as both a detector of cell phone signals and as a gauss meter as well. It's also a useful meter to use in the dark because it features both a red flashing light and an audible signal that lets the user know when the strength of the radiation field changes. Like the "Gaussmaster" meter, it can be carried in hand and the sensor should be moved slowly back and forth so that it can pass through any anomalous fields.

This meter is simple to use but it does have some guidelines that must be followed. In order to use this device as a gauss meter, it must be used with the remote probe sensor, which is plugged into the side. Otherwise, it functions as a cell signal senor only. Once the probe is plugged in, it has a flexible, two-foot extension that allows the sensor to be held away from the actual device. The analog scale, the red light and the audible signal are activated by the readings picked up by the remote sensor.

The main drawback to the meter is that, because of the remote sensor, it has to be used with two hands and does not free up the investigator for anything else. Some ghost hunters have worked around this by attaching the sensor to the back of their hand or sleeve, which then frees up their hand for other work. In addition, the meter is not highly sensitive and occasionally seems to have problems "zeroing out". As far as basic meters go though, it is still recommended, especially for working in the dark.

EMF FIELD TESTER 200A

This meter, manufactured by A.W. Sperry, is one of the best and most reliable of the basic EMF detectors on the market. It is well-liked because it is so easy to use and features an easy to read digital screen. It is equipped with a simple on/off switch and gives a constant reading of what kind of activity you may be encountering. The device measures from 0.1 milligauss up to 199.9 milligauss and has a bandwidth down to 30 hz, which makes it capable of picking up lower range fields than most basic meters.

To use this device, be sure to carry it in one hand and make sure that you hold the meter below the banner on the face of the meter that reads "EMF SENSOR". This meter has a single axis and this is where it is located. If you hold your hand so that it blocks any part of the sensor, it will not be able to give you reliable readings.

When conducting the survey of the location, hold the meter out in front of you from about the distance between your hand and your elbow. Gently sweep the device from side to side and try to keep it in a fairly constant motion. Once you pick up any higher readings, try and track down the source, always trying to rule out artificial interference in the location. This meter will pick up electrical sources and appliances, so be cautious about jumping to conclusions over your evidence. Also, try not to move the meter too rapidly up and down because this tends to skew the readings.

As with the other basic devices, watch for sudden and abrupt surges of energy to be detected. Once again, always rule out any possible artificial causes for the readings, especially when conducting indoor investigations. This meter also works very well in remote and outdoor locations where there is no possibility of interference. The only drawback comes when trying to use it in a dark place because the digital screen can be hard to read without a light. A more electronically inclined ghost hunter might consider customizing the meter with a small light source.

MULTIDETECTOR II PROFESSIONAL

This German-made device emerged on the American market a few years ago and I have always been surprised that it has not become more popular than it is. European sources call it "one of the best and most sensitive" meters available but it has been slow to catch on in the United States. The meter has an odd, egg-shaped look to it and has a number of switches and a scale made up of a series of colored (green, yellow and red) lights. Many consider this to be a pretty confusing meter but we have managed to simplify its use with some experimentation and research.

First of all, to use the meter, you simply have to hold it in your hand in the way that is most comfortable for you. I recommend using your right hand because it makes it easier to reach the power button with your thumb. This button is located on the face of the meter and slightly to the right. In order for the device to continuously monitor the area, you must keep this button pushed down at all times. Any readings that you get will appear in the colored LED lights (running from 0-10) and you will also have an audible whistle, which makes this meter ideal to use in dark locations.

To best use the meter, follow these instructions for your basic settings. As with any other equipment, be sure to experiment with the meter and find the settings that seem to work best for you. I think the following will make a great starting point for your research though:

- On the top right, put the first switch to the "H" setting. This is to register magnetic fields and this will keep you from getting too much interference from artificial sources. Investigators are encouraged to work with both this field and the "E" setting (which is electrical) in areas where interference is at a minimum.

- The Professional Model is also equipped with an integrated frequency filter (you won't find this on the other Multidetector models) that allows you to switch between "highpass" and "lowpass" energy detection, both above and below the 500 Hz level. I recommend the using the "ELF" setting for this particular meter.

- Just below the Power button are the Sensitivity settings. After much experimentation, I recommend switching your meter to the "x 100" setting. This setting allows for normal artificial interference, but does not drop so low that it picks up nothing but background fields. I think that you will find it works the best for paranormal investigation.

Once you have all of your settings in place, survey your location by holding the meter in your right hand (pressing the power button down) and gently moving it back and forth. Maintain a short distance from your body at all times and watch out for artificial power sources.

This is another excellent meter for use in darkened locations as the colored LED lights and audible signal make this a highly recommended device.

TRI-FIELD METER: MODEL 100XE

The Tri-Field Meters, which are manufactured by AlphaLab in Salt Lake City, Utah, are (without question) the finest EMF meters on the market. While this particular model would still fall into the realm of a standard meter, it is far and away more sensitive than any of the other meters already mentioned in this chapter. Perhaps more success has been obtained in paranormal investigations using this particular meter than with any other.

Once again, there has been some confusion over the best uses for this meter. After a lot of research, I have come to believe that the meter is best used on the "magnetic" setting for indoor investigations and on either the "magnetic" or the "electric" setting for outdoor investigations. In all honesty, I would prefer the "magnetic" setting for either type of research, but since there are no set rules for the use of the meters, experimentation is highly recommended.

For the best use of this meter, it should be held with the right or left hand curled underneath the device so that the fingertips wrap around the opposite edge. You should never hold the meter so that your hand blocks the top of it. This can block the detection of all electrical fields. Even though you cannot block magnetic fields this way, I suggest being safe at all times and holding it with your hand around the center.

After that, turn the meter on and set the knob to the "magnetic (1-100 range)" or the "electric" range, depending on your investigation. Then, hold the meter extended in front of your body, again using the distance from your hand to your elbow as a guide. Move the meter back and forth and watch for abrupt and sudden surges of energy. You should notice that you will be detecting a background radiation of the location that falls between 2-3 milligauss on the analog scale. This is normal. You will want to watch for sudden changes and fluctuations that drive the needle much higher on the scale. Once you find one, you will again want to try and rule out any artificial interference before accepting the readings as evidence of anything paranormal.

As stated, this is an excellent meter for paranormal research but it does have some minor drawbacks, such as the lack of a light source and no audible signal on the standard meter. This makes the meter difficult to use in a dark investigation without tying up your free hand with a light. However, recent models of this meter have been fitted with an audible switch so that changes to the field will register with a high-pitched sound. This updated meter does cost a little more but it is well worth the price if you plan to use it in the dark.

TRI-FIELD NATURAL EM METER

Also manufactured by AlphaLab, this meter is superior to even the previously mentioned model when it comes to sensitivity and usefulness in a paranormal investigation. What makes this meter so beneficial to our type of research is the fact that it only registers DC or "natural" electrical and magnetic fields. This is the type of field that is given off by humans and animals and possibly, by paranormal energy as well. It makes a great addition to any investigator's arsenal but it can also be very difficult to use and I seldom recommend it for people who are just starting out in ghost research.

But before we get into that, and the best uses of the meter, we should discuss what it was originally designed for and that will answer many of the questions that have come up about it.

The Natural EM Meter was designed to detect changes in extremely weak DC fields. It is equipped with both an analog scale and an audible signal that moves whenever a field changes from its previous level. The meter was also designed to ignore artificial (AC) fields that are generated by man-made power sources and this has made it a popular model with paranormal researchers.

Originally, the meter was used to do field experiments on the energy levels of geomagnetic storms, including unusual solar activity in the earth's ionosphere and the electrical activity of ordinary thunderstorms. (NOTE: This is why I do not recommend using this meter during high solar flare periods or during storms) The meter is very sensitive to changes of as little as 0.5% of the strength of the earth's magnetic fields. When set on "magnetic", the meter can detect the movement of any magnetic sources at the location. A tone will sound when the field increases or decreases. After the meter detects a change and then the field becomes stable for more than five seconds, the tone will end and the meter will return to a base reading. The meter will then remain at rest until the field changes again. The user can determine the amount of change that signals the audible tone by using a "squelch" knob on the side of the meter. Any changes in the strength of the magnetic field will register.

When the dial is set to "electric", the meter will become sensitive to electric fields that are as weak as 3 volts per meter. As an example of how sensitive the meter is, this is the equivalent of taking a 10-foot square room and filling it with enough energy to lift a single grain of salt. Typical electric fields will fluctuate at about 1 -2 volts per meter. Because of this, the minimum sensitivity on this model has been set to 3 V/m and has been designed to disregard "background noise". Regardless, the meter remains so powerful that it can pick up the electrical field of humans and animals, sometimes through a wall. You can actually see the changes for yourself by holding the meter in one hand

and moving your other hand across the top of it. For this reason, the meter can even function as a motion sensor. However, it isn't foolproof because some people do not give off an electric charge and are actually "invisible" to the meter. In addition, some people have such a charge to their bodies that they cannot use this meter without causing constant interference.

This particular meter also features a "sum" setting, which combines the readings from the electric and magnetic fields of the location. The meter will not differentiate between the two and the scale and signal will change whenever either field changes. This setting it so sensitive that it will detect the approach of a living person (or paranormal anomaly) from 5-10 feet away. This makes it especially useful for paranormal investigations, but only under certain conditions. (see the instructions to follow)

Sound complicated? Well, it can be and that's why this meter is best suited for those who have been working in the field for some time. Don't worry though, it can be learned by just about anyone as long as they have the time and the patience to experiment with it. And speaking of experiments, I have worked with this meter for several years and am constantly finding new uses for it. Below, I have listed what I feel are the best uses for the meter, although my findings are, of course, open to interpretation and I suggest that you work with the meter to find out how it best suits your own investigations.

For Indoor Investigations: This meter can be delicate to use as a hand-held device, but not impossible, despite what some investigators claim. However, you have to be very careful with it and for this reason, I have outlined some steps for you to take when using it. When conducting indoor investigations with this model, I recommend using the "magnetic" setting. This will detect any changes in the natural magnetic field of the location but remember, don't try to use it during storms.

When using the meter as a hand-held device, always hold the meter around the middle and always hold it very level. If the meter is rotated from north to south, you will see extreme changes in the readings and this is best avoided during your survey of the location. Watch for sudden and unexplained surges to signal the presence of anomalous fields and be sure to use other equipment to obtain corresponding evidence.

You can also use this meter as a stationary device to pick up transient fields and some researchers find their best results this way. Because of the meter's sensitivity to slight rotations while hand-held, some recommend only using it in this manner. I believe that it isn't necessary when placed on the "magnetic" setting, but I suggest that the individual researcher judge for himself. It might be best to use the meter as a stationary device in conjunction with the TriField 100 XE meter, which can be more easily used as a handheld instrument.

To use the "electric" or the "sum" setting for an indoor investigation, I recommend that the meter be used only as a stationary device. The meter is capable of detecting activity in an entire room and the device can be easily monitored by either a video feed or even by the researcher himself, as long as he remains quiet and relatively still during the investigation. This enables the ghost hunter to detect any unseen changes or fields in the location and it is very effective. To make the meter especially sensitive in the "electric" and "sum" settings, place it on a metal stand or surface.

For Outdoor Investigations: When using this meter outdoors, it can largely be used in the same manner as indoors, although I have found that the researcher is much freer to choose between settings and whether or not to use it hand-held or stationary. No matter how it is used though, the same rules apply as to thunderstorms and solar flares. Attempting to use the meter under these conditions will result in false readings and poor data. My suggestion is to experiment with the meter and find out which settings work best for you in an outdoor situation.

For myself, I tend to use the "sum" setting when working in outdoor locations, isolated spots and cemeteries. Despite what the makers of the meter claim, I still believe that some interference can take place indoors as magnetic energy (even natural DC energy) can travel along man-made wires. However, in an outdoor location, I feel that any of the settings will work properly in a hand-held position.

Even so, the best results can still be obtained by using the meter as a stationary device. Although outdoors, the meter can still be monitored in the most active areas of the location and thanks to the audio tone that it emits, it can even be used in the dark.

Hand-held Instructions: As mentioned, always hold the meter around the middle and do not place your hand over the top. While this will not interfere with magnetic readings, it will cause problems when searching for electrical fields. It is imperative that the meter is held very carefully and it should not be moved too rapidly. Also, avoid moving it up and down and too quickly in a north / south position. This will cause slight (and sometimes extreme) changes in your readings.

Stationary Instructions: To use as a monitoring device, place the meter on a stand or a level surface in the center of the active area, or the room that you wish to observe. When using in the "electric" or "sum" settings, consider placing it on something metal so that you can take advantage of added conductivity. The device will monitor a fairly large area and the researcher will undoubtedly be surprised at how well this works. This is an ideal situation for most investigations and if done the right way, a single investigator can cover several areas at once with multiple meters and cameras. Highly recommended!

Another added bonus for this device is that it can also be customized to the specifications of the individual researcher. For a small sum, the makers of the meter will add additional sensors, change the volume of the alarm and even add a light source. This just adds to the many highlights of the Natural EM meter and makes it one that no investigation team should be without.

While this list does not contain every electronic device that has been (or will be) adapted for use, it should work well for those who are getting involved in the field. If you have technical skills, you can build your own equipment using information from the Internet and from your local library. You can also purchase many other kinds of equipment to assist with your research.

Here are some other items that you might want to consider investing in.

IR MOTION DETECTOR

The reader may have noticed the inclusion of motion detectors in the list of basic items for a ghost hunting kit earlier in this chapter. After some research (and some good luck with them), I have come to feel that they are essential additions to an investigator's arsenal. An Infrared Motion Detector (and there are a number of good ones on the market) can be used to secure an area from intrusion and also to pick up energy fields that register a temperature change.

In years past, before the widespread availability of electronic equipment, researchers used string and tape to seal off rooms and doors that they were monitoring for ghostly activity. This insured that the locations remained uncontaminated and if the tape was broken on the door, the investigator had some idea that the room had been entered. Now, infrared motion detectors are available so that researchers can still seal off rooms and the meters serve the dual purpose of monitoring anomalous activity as well.

When searching for your own motion detector, look for a device that is not only triggered by motion but also by temperature changes. A meter that will monitor in the infrared range will be able to pick up light changes, the previously mentioned temperature changes and of course, what is not is seen by the human eye. By backing them up with a camera or video camera, a motion detector might become a vital piece of equipment when compiling evidence of a haunting.

As mentioned, there is more than one worthwhile use for a motion detector. When sealing off an area for investigation, simply place the meter outside of any door leading into the room that you want to remain closed. This can also work for larger areas by "closing" all of the access points with motion detectors. This will insure that your paranormal experiments or monitoring is not interrupted and provides good evidence that any anomalous readings that are collected were not caused by human interference.

In addition, because of its sensing capabilities, a motion detector may also be able to pick up "spirit energy" or at least unexplained activity. By spreading the motion sensors out through the area that is reportedly haunted, researchers should watch for them to be triggered by the activity. If the alarms on the meters are set off, be sure to first look for a natural or artificial explanation for the alert. It's possible that it may have been inadvertently set off by a household animal, another researcher or even an artificial surge in the electrical system of the site.

One of my first successful uses for motion detectors took place a few years ago, when I was monitoring a location for the entire night. I had collected numerous accounts of strange activity at the place but feared that it could still be a hoax. I was concerned that the owners might be looking for publicity, although they were quick to grant my request to spend the night at the site by myself. Before bunking down for the night in an upstairs room, I placed motion detectors at all of the access points and doorways to the second level. In this way, I could be sure that no one could slip into the building and try to fake any "ghostly" activity. After several hours of waiting (and finally drifting off to sleep), I was startled when one of the motion detectors, which was next to a door that led to an outside staircase, suddenly began beeping. A few moments later, another meter also began to blare. It had been placed in a separate room and nowhere close to either the first detector or my location. A few moments after that, another detector began to sound from over to my left. It was also in a separate room and it was almost as if the meters had been set off by someone who slowly jogged past them, setting off the array of meters in a counter-clockwise motion.

And while I could have suspected that this was exactly what had happened, I knew that it was not the case. The simple reason for this was that each of the locations where I had placed the motion detectors was separated from one another by solid walls. The only way that one person could have set them off was to enter each room individually and move on to the next one by passing the location where I was, which was directly at the top of the staircase leading to the first floor. A quick search revealed that there was no one else on the upper floor - or in the building at all!

From that point on, I came to the realization that motion detectors should be a basic part of any researcher's tool kit. I highly recommend their use and strongly feel that they are capable of providing excellent evidence of "things unseen", so to speak.

RELATIVE HUMIDITY GAUGE

This device is relatively inexpensive and can be used in conjunction with a thermometer to record the ambient conditions of an indoor or outdoor location. This will enable you to record what the conditions were at the time of the investigation and may also help to rule out any natural effects that may appear in photos that are taken.

ION PARTICLE COUNTER

This expensive device has not yet been implemented widely by research groups but may prove to be very useful in the future for ruling out natural interference in photographs. An ion particle counter is designed to number the particles in the air of the location where it is being used. If camera anomalies (often photographed, but rarely seen) actually have density to them, then they should register on the ion counter.

The best way to do this would probably be to get a base reading of particles in the area where the investigation is taking place. When meters or video cameras that are monitoring the area start to show some signs of activity, then a new reading should be taken with the particle counter to see if the readings have increased. If they do, this may prove that the ghostly energy we are researching does have some density to it.

THERMOMETERS
& TEMPERATURE SENSING DEVICES

When recommending equipment to any ghost hunter, I always suggest the inclusion of a temperature sensing device in his research tool kit. For a number of years, I have suggested the use of Infrared Non-Contact Thermometers for tracking down paranormal presences. These meters take instant temperature readings form a location and detect any changes that might be sudden or extreme. To state it simply, they pick up "cold spots" (unexplained temperature variances) that are believed to signal that a ghost is present. It is thought that a ghost uses the energy in a particular spot to manifest itself and by doing so, creates a cold mass. The energy may not be invisible to the eye but still detectable using one of these devices.

For this reason, we cannot deny that the measuring of temperature is essential to any investigation and I always include a device like an IR Thermometer as an important tool for a researcher to utilize. Through experimentation and further research though, some problems have arisen that seem to show that IR Probes, while still useful, might best be used as a back-up tool for measuring temperature changes rather than as the main piece of equipment.

IR Thermometers are an excellent tool and they are very accurate when used as intended. The devices were designed so that they can measure the surface temperature of an object. The problem comes however, when they are used to try and measure the ambient temperature of a location. Many ghost hunters (myself included) have been guilty of trying to do this, believing that the devices could sample the air temperature. I believed that the infrared beam of the device, because of its optic spread, could give me an accurate reading but I have since learned this was incorrect. Most basic devices have optics that balance out at 6-1. That means that at a distance of six feet, the device is testing an area of about one-foot in diameter. I was under the impression that by testing a distance of no more than 60 feet, which is about the reach of the device, I would be alerted if anything cold passed in front of the instrument. This is somewhat true but as a whole, not entirely accurate.

Many of the initial arguments about the use of these devices stated that it would not work for paranormal research because it had to come into contact with something solid in order to register temperature changes. This is not entirely accurate either because even the makers of the thermal probes will state that it can pick up readings from moisture in the air and from heat sources, like fire. The flames are undoubtedly not solid but still register a reading from the infrared beam. I have always maintained that the beam had to come into contact with something though. In my early research, I spoke to a technician who worked for Omega, the makers of one of the best IR probes on the market, and she explained to me how the device worked and that it had to make contact with something to register a reading. She explained that the thermometer reads the infrared energy of an object and converts that into a temperature. A basic hand-held IR Thermometer is set at a level of about 98% of the energy given off. The good news is that rock, bricks, trees and most natural objects are also at about this same level and so extreme cold temperatures are more easily picked up by the meters.

Is it some sort of "spirit energy"? Perhaps --- but no matter how we look at it, using these types of meters to track it down can be inaccurate and may call into question the evidence that we gather when using them. Even if we concede that we are picking up surface temperatures of some sort of paranormal mass, I believe that we may be able to get much further with other types of monitoring. Because the ambient temperature is one of the most important pieces of evidence to monitor in an investigation, we may be wasting a lot of our time with unnecessary work caused by the use of IR probes.

Ambient temperature (which cannot be picked up with an IR Thermometer) is basically the temperature of the surrounding air. We are aware of this in our daily lives, from the heat or cold outside and even from the weather forecast on the evening news. When a witness or researcher speaks of feeling a "cold spot" in a reportedly haunted place, it is in the ambient temperature of the location. This is where we need to focus our efforts when looking for temperature changes and abnormalities.

After researching the idea and speaking to other investigators (like David Betz) who have been pursuing these theories as well, I have tried to collect some investigation ideas that will not only measure temperature changes but also take very fast readings, which had always been one of the benefits of the IR Thermometers.

The first step is to make a record of the background, ambient temperature of the location. I recommend a basic thermometer for this. It does not have to be fast, merely accurate, and I would also suggest getting one that reads the humidity levels of the location as well. This may be important information for your records, especially when it comes to later analyzing your film and photographs. This temperature device should be separate and independent from all other temperature sensing devices, so there will be no confusion later about the accuracy of any readings.

Then, we move on to our second unit. The best device to measure rapid changes in the ambient temperature is a thermocouple based temperature measurement device. These devices are affordable and can be purchased from many electronic supply companies, like Omega. Most of them have a measuring unit of less than three centimeters, which is capable of measuring the rapid changes to the temperature needed when looking for cold spots. It is also feasible that a moving cold spot could be tracked with such a tool since it can react so quickly.

When looking for a device like this, it is suggested that you try and find one that is accurate, simple to use and comparable in price to an IR Thermometer. There are several digital thermocouple units on the market and I would recommend one that comes with a "T" type thermocouple, which has faster response times in the temperature ranges that a paranormal researcher would be concerned with. These devices also come with "K" type thermocouples but they are not as fast and read for higher temperatures. I also suggest using the standard sensor that comes with the meter, rather than any additional probes. The probes are exposed to the air, which might give a slightly quicker response time but the downside is that they are very delicate and easily broken.

Using a thermocouple device is no more complicated than using an IR Thermometer. Simply plug the thermocouple into the meter (polarity is an issue but the slots are clearly marked on the meter and the thermocouple) and then turn the unit on. It gives you a new and updated reading every one second. Most meters will also offer other options like high and low limits and will sound an alarm when these limits are reached. An effective way of using them would be to set up an array of thermocouple devices so that separate sections of the location can be monitored at the same time. By setting the alarms on the units to sound whenever a low temperature threshold is reached, we can easily focus on different parts of the location when needed. We can then have definitive temperature data from within the room, or at the exact location that we are monitoring, rather than at some unknown distance away, which is the best that the IR Thermometer can offer.

So should we stop using our IR thermal probes meter?

No, definitely not... while I have come to believe that a thermocouple device can offer more legitimate readings from within a more confined space, I also do not believe that this type of meter makes the IR Thermometer obsolete. As mentioned previously, IR probes do work and they work quite well. They measure any mass that has an extreme temperature reading between the optics on the device and a solid object. As long as that mass, invisible or not, crosses the infrared beam that the device emits, we can have a record of it. The problem is that there are a number of things besides ghosts - or paranormal energy - that can affect the device. We mentioned fire already but it can also measure anything that emits infrared radiation, like water, vapor, smoke, dust and more. All of these things can drastically affect the temperature measurements.

But this does still not negate its use. When an IR Thermometer is used in conjunction with a thermocouple unit, it can actually compliment your investigation, rather than be the focus of it. When both devices are used together, it can offer some very compelling evidence. If a thermocouple unit picks up a strong temperature drop in the ambient temperature, the IR Thermometer could be used to track the location and the degree of the temperature drop. When offered together, you now have two different devices that have measured the same drop in temperature. This would be significant data and it would be very difficult to discount by anyone trying to debunk your investigation.

Remember that because paranormal research is not an exact science, we have to check and double check and confirm and re-confirm any of the evidence that we collect in order for it to be seen as legitimate. In a field where "I heard a strange sound" or "I felt a cold spot" is too often collected as actual data, there is a need for us to find a way to measure these things. Although we should never, ever discount the feelings and experiences of witnesses and investigators, we should also make every effort to legitimately verify such claims with the most reliable equipment that we have at our disposal. I have long been in support of IR Thermometers for use during investigations but now urge the researcher to take one step further and back up the data you collect from them with an additional device. You will be glad that you did should your evidence ever be called into question.

6. SPIRIT COMMUNICATIONS

The nearest simile I can find to express the difficulties of sending a message - is that I appear to be standing behind a sheet of frosted glass - which blurs sight and deadens sounds - dictating feebly - to a reluctant and somewhat obtuse secretary. A feeling of terrible impotence burdens me - I am so powerless to tell what means so much - I cannot get into communication with those who would understand and believe me...

FREDERICK MYERS,

through the automatic writing of a medium in 1906... five years after his death

Since the beginning of recorded time, man has claimed to be able to communicate with the spirit world. However, it would not be until the heyday of the Spiritualist movement that he would begin claiming to do so as an everyday occurrence. That particular movement was founded by two young girls who established a way to communicate with a ghost. They used a series of knocks and raps that answered "yes" and "no" and eventually assigned a code for letters of the alphabet. In this way, they were able to spell out longer and more detailed messages.

As Spiritualism grew in popularity, those with an interest began to establish what were called "home circles", small groups of friends and family members who would gather around and attempt to communicate with spirits. The knockings and rappings of the early movement spread in other directions as ordinary people began experimenting with their own skills as mediums. Soon, the tiresome and time-consuming method of knocking began to fall out of fashion and so mediums began a new form of contact called "automatic writing". While practiced almost solely by spirit mediums, it still became very popular at séances as a direct line to the spirit world.

Automatic writing was defined as writing that was done while the medium was under the control of the spirits. It was believed these ghosts would guide the medium's hand and spell out messages for the sitters who were present. Most likely (ignoring cases of outright fraud), automatic writing actually consisted of material that was gathered in the unconscious mind of the medium and then put to paper as a message from the dead. However it may have worked, it soon replaced the slower methods of communication and soon mediums claimed to receive more complex messages from the beyond.

Obviously, many questions remain as to the authenticity of automatic writing, although in some rare cases, the messages received were eerily precise. Just like with the other facets of spirit communication still to come, a number of mysteries remain unsolved.

THE TALKING BOARD

While automatic writing was being embraced by mediums, those who satisfied their curiosity about the spirit world in the "home circles" were also searching for a more efficient way to reach the other side than by rapping on tables.

In 1853, a French Spiritualist named M. Planchette invented a device that could do much more than tap on the table. The "planchette" was a small, heart-shaped table with pencils attached to its legs. Those who used it claimed that it operated by spirit force and ghosts were able to write out messages from beyond. The invention was often used by the mediums as a more elaborate form of automatic writing, but it really did not hold wide appeal for the general public.

However, a short time later, another invention would come along that could be used by everyone. No experience was required and no real psychic skills were needed. This new device would revolutionize the Spiritualist movement and have an impact that still resounds today. The Ouija, or Talking, board was born.

Legend has it that shortly after the planchette came to America, a cabinet and coffin maker from Maryland named E.C. Reiche created a new method of communicating with the dead. He devised a wooden lap tray with the letters of the alphabet arranged in two lines across the center of the board. Below these letters, he placed the numbers 1-10 and the words YES and NO in each lower corner of the board. He used the planchette with his board but removed the pencil tips and placed wooden pegs on the bottom of it. In this way, the planchette was free to move about the board.

It was said that Reiche named his board the "Ouija" because the name represented the French and German words for "yes" (oui and ja) but other versions of the legend say that this was not the case. He named it that because he believed that the word "Ouija" was actually Egyptian for luck. Needless to say, it's not, but since he claimed to receive the word from a spirit on the board, the name allegedly stuck.

The real story behind the talking board is not as mysterious, although it does hold a number of unusual elements. It actually took seven men, from very different backgrounds, to create the first American talking boards. Those men were Charles Kennard, Harry Welles Rusk, Colonel Washington Bowie, Elijah J. Bond, William H. A. Maupin, William Fuld and the elusive E.C. Reiche (a man about whom almost nothing is known and who may not have existed at all!) These men pooled their assets, cash and resources to create the Kennard Novelty Co. of Baltimore, Maryland. All of the men had two things in common. Each of them was a wealthy entrepreneur who was not opposed to taking risks and all of them were Freemasons. It is believed that they met through their association with this secret society and they soon made a pact to start the company and to produce the first American talking boards.

Colonel Bowie initially handled most of the matters involving the company. Rusk was named as president, as he had the most experience with patent law and was able to file all of the necessary papers himself. Kennard had some land and buildings from a defunct fertilizer company and he offered the property, located at 220 South Charles Street in Baltimore, for use by the new firm. Because of this, his name was used on the masthead. Elijah Bond contributed little to the firm, save for some ideas, and shortly after the patents were filed, he disappeared. William Maupin remains a mystery to this day. He was gone before the company even got started and the only proof that he even existed at all was his name on the patent filings. The most active investor in the company was a young varnisher named William Fuld. He played a major role in the daily operations of the company, including in production, and had many ideas of his own. Due to his age and finances, when compared to the other investors, he had to work much harder to achieve success. It took him nearly a year to begin his climb to the top.

Historically, William Fuld has been acknowledged as the inventor of the Ouija Board, a fact that is confirmed by the remaining Fuld and Bowie families. At the time the company was created, Fuld had little money to invest but it is believed the idea for the board became his contribution, which is what earned him a partnership and his name on the patent papers. He remains the name most connected to the boards today, despite the apocryphal legends of E.C. Reiche.

By 1891, the Ouija Board was selling well and on November 10 of that year, Charles Kennard filed a patent that would improve the performance of the board's planchette. This turned out to be his last act as a member of the Kennard Novelty Co. and one day later, he was removed from the board. Although the company bore his name and used his land, Kennard was said to have been a poor businessman and so he was voted out of the company. Years later, his descendants would claim that William Fuld drove Kennard out of business but most likely, it was Colonel Bowie. By 1892, Kennard was no longer listed in connection with the company but Bowie was named as manager and Fuld as supervisor. The company was moved to 909 East Pratt Street and the name was changed to the Ouija Novelty Company.

Soon after, Kennard tried to sell another version of the talking board that he called the Volo. Bowie and Fuld answered this by purchasing the Espirito trademark from the well-known W.S. Reed Toy Company and they placed an exact copy of the Kennard's Volo design on the back of their Ouija. Consumers loved getting two boards for the price of one and soon, Kennard's business was destroyed. He had no trademark for the Volo, so he tried to advertise the "Igili - the marvelous talking board" instead. It also failed and Kennard would vanish from the scene until 1919.

In 1894, the Ouija Novelty Co. moved to larger quarters at 20 North High Street, thanks to the fact that they were turning out huge numbers of talking boards. Bowie remained in charge of the company with Fuld and Rusk as his side. A few years later, Bowie's other business interests caused him to sell out his share of the patents and he and Rusk both stepped into the background of the company. Production was turned over to Fuld, although Bowie would remain a financial part of the company for another 20 years.

Fuld now needed a partner. He was also a customs inspector and was unable to devote full time to the Ouija business. In 1898, he and his brother Isaac went into business together and they leased the rights to make the Ouija Board from Colonel Bowie. They split the proceeds from the talking board production and from other games. By April 1901 though, the partnership was over. William and Isaac had a falling out and Isaac was immediately fired. The two of them never spoke to one another again, except in court. Colonel Bowie employed his son, Washington Bowie Jr., to represent William

Fuld against his brother and the parties returned to court again and again over the years, bickering about money, rights and even who had the authority to open mail addressed to the company. This would be just one of the friendships and family relationships that was utterly destroyed over what most people claim is just a game.

Fuld soon changed the name of the company to the William Fuld Manufacturing Co. and moved the Ouija business to 1208 Federal Street. Business started to slow down and from 1905 to 1907, Fuld moved the company into his home at 1306 North Central Avenue. By 1908, business had improved once more and he relocated to 331 North Gay Street and then on to 1226-1228 North Central Avenue. This building would remain the home of the Ouija until an enormous sales boom in 1919.

Meanwhile, Isaac Fuld was breaking an injunction that had been filed against him in 1901 by sending out samples of a talking board that he had created called the Oriole Board. They were exact duplicates of the Ouija with stencils cut out to replace the "Ouija" logo with "Oriole". He named his toy business the Southern Toy Co. and operated it from his home.

At this same time, William decided to expand his company and issued press releases that stated that he was preparing for "big business". He took a risk and moved his company to an enormous, three-story building and opened his doors again. The gamble paid off and Ouija Board sales began to climb. This made 1919 perhaps the greatest year in the history of the company. Not only did William enjoy an income from national sales of the boards, he also began to see national acclaim, the remaining rights to the boards were assigned to him by Colonel Bowie and he finally sealed the ingoing feud with his brother.

In April of that year, William began mailing letters to stores who placed orders for Isaac's Oriole Board. He warned them that the boards violated his patents and anyone who bought the boards was also breaking the law. When Isaac found out about the letters, he filed suit against William. But William countered with the allegations that Isaac had violated the injunctions filed against him in 1901. Isaac's case was dismissed and the judge ruled that he had copied and distributed the Oriole Boards in violation of the injunction. A review of the trademark that he had filed revealed that it had nothing to do with talking boards but rather to pool tables. Isaac was ordered to pay all of the courts costs associated with the case and to never make another talking board.

Once the court battles were behind him, William continued to expand. He retired from his customs position to dedicate more of his time to the Ouija business. He later served in the General Assembly in 1924. Washington Bowie Jr. continued as his legal counsel and years later, Bowie's son would recall his father sitting he and his siblings down to look through toy catalogs. They were instructed to circle any boards that might infringe on the Ouija trademarks and he recalled finding many of them. Bowie aggressively pursued each of them and strangely, never accepted any payment for this service.

In 1920, another talking board company appeared in the news. The Baltimore Talking Board Co. was started by two men named Charles Cahn and Gilbert Michael and they had absolutely no contact with Fuld or his business. They did, however, pay a fee to call their boards Ouija. The Internal Revenue Service collected tax on their Ouija Boards in 1920 but the Baltimore Talking Board Co. resisted the tax payments, claiming that the boards were a spiritual tool, not a game, and should not be taxed. They took the I.R.S. to court and mysteriously, they were represented by Washington Bowie Jr. in the proceedings. They lost and Ouija Boards were considered taxable. They appealed the decision all of the way to the Supreme Court but the case was never heard. Talking boards are considered taxable - and legally not a tool to communicate with the spirits --- to this day.

From 1919 to 1927, William Fuld continued to expand his business, offering cheaper forms of his board in an effort to combat knock-offs, a line of Ouija jewelry and even a Ouija oil for rheumatism. He also trademarked the Ouija Board as the Egyptian Luck Board, the Mystifying Oracle and the Hindu Luck Board. Things didn't seem like they could get any better but then on February 24, 1927, disaster struck the Fuld family. William always supervised any work that was done on the factory and when a flagpole needed to be affixed to the top of the three-story building, Fuld joined the workmen. When an iron support that he was leaning on collapsed, he fell backwards off the structure. He caught himself for a moment on one of the factory windows but the force of the fall slammed the window shut and he plunged to his doom. Amazingly, the fall only left Fuld with a concussion and some minor broken bones but he received a fatal injury on the way to the hospital. One of his broken ribs pierced his heart and he died.

William Fuld's children took over the company. Catherine and William A. Fuld ran the company until the youngest brother, Hubert, became president in 1942. Sales sagged for years but the talking board industry saw a renewed interest in the 1940's, around the same time that the Spiritualist movement enjoyed a revival. Many companies introduced their own talking board designs, offering extravagant designs and colors, but eventually, disinterest and a declining market saw each of the companies collapse to the Fuld's.

The heirs maintained the company until 1966, when they sold out to Parker Brothers. Today, this company owns all of the rights and trademarks to the "talking board" and they still produce it in large numbers. In spite of the fact that it is now sold in toy stores, it remains an exact duplicate (albeit a more cheaply made one) of the talking board that was sold many years ago.

The Talking, or Ouija, Board is perhaps the most controversial method of spirit communication, mostly because it can be used by anyone and requires no special powers to navigate. This may be why most psychics discourage the use of the board. It enables the average person to produce "medium-like" effects without a psychic actually being present.

Regardless, the Ouija has been both condemned and praised in equal amounts as a way to communicate with the spirits and as a direct link to the dark side. Many people ask if these boards are dangerous, but I think that this depends on the person. In all honestly, I can't offer many clear-cut observations on the power of the Ouija because my own experimentations with it have been uneven, at best. When asked, I usually just tell people that they probably shouldn't mess with it unless they are prepared to handle whatever consequences may come up. However, I can offer instructions on the best way to use the board (should you wish to try it) and you can decide for yourself if you are actually talking to spirits or if you are merely taking part in an interesting experiment in psychic phenomena.

USING THE TALKING BOARD

The Talking Board should be used by at least two persons at a time and can be placed on the laps of the sitters, or on a small table within easy reach of everyone. The sitters place their fingers lightly on the edges of the planchette, being careful not to push down too hard. If you should ever take part in a talking board session, or witness one, where you can hear the sound of the planchette scraping on the board, or it seems to be unusually loud as it moves, there is probably something fishy afoot. What this means is that someone is accidentally, or willfully, guiding the pointer and the session should be stopped immediately. Any information received from the board is bound to be false.

Once the session begins, it is recommended that the sitters invite a spirit to come through and speak to them. The sitters are advised to add that they wish to communicate with a "willing" spirit. The reason for this is that it's been suggested that negative spirits will try to come through and confuse the sitters. For this reason, it's best to state up front what you are looking for from the session.

Then, the questions should be asked and repeated in a slow and deliberate manner. Only one question should be asked at a time, and by a single person, to avoid confusion. The answers to the questions will be theoretically spelled out using the planchette.

But how does it work? Many feel that the answers provided by the board are simply the unconscious movements made by the people touching the pointer. If this is true, then the Ouija is operated by nothing more than the power of suggestion. But how can we explain the accounts of the Ouija providing information that none of the sitters could possibly have known?

On that note, it has been suggested that the Ouija is actually powered by the psychic portions of the human mind, spelling out answers to questions either by precognition, telepathy or unknowing communication with spirits. By the latter, the board would be a mystical tool that is guided by the sitter's unconscious movements, which are in turn manipulated by the spirits. On the other side of the same coin, many researchers use the Ouija as a way to experiment with the effects of PK, noting the movement of the planchette as it is propelled by the human mind.

Some people believe that it isn't that complicated though. They believe that the planchette is actually moved by the direct force of spirits, guiding the hands of the sitters. The Spiritualists believed this, as do some ghost hunters today, feeling that the Ouija is an important tool in spirit contact, both good and bad. Those who believe in the authentic powers of the talking board to make contact with the spirit world will often recommend against its use by amateurs. Communication with spirits who might come through the board can be deceptive and at the very worst, dangerous. They say this because they believe that spirits that can be so easily contacted are "low spirits", which inhabit a plane that is close to the Earth. For this reason, they liken using a talking board to dialing up a random number of the telephone and asking the unknown person who answers for correct information.

And this brings us to the reputation of the Ouija, which has become pretty bad over the years, especially with parents and religious groups. They often cite the overwrought (and usually unsubstantiated) cases of so-called "spirit possession" that occur after teenagers use the Ouija. Apparently, malevolent forces, masquerading as good spirits, possess children and impressionable adults and cause emotional damage and suicide among those who dare to use the board. (cue the spooky music!)

But how common is this really? Not nearly as common (and I have yet to see an authentic case) as our society watchdogs would have you think. However, I will say that I think it is possible for people to become dependent upon, or even obsessed with, the Ouija. Of course, with that in mind, it's possible for people to become dependent on or obsessed with anything, like religion, for instance.

In the end, I am not going to say that it's impossible for spirits to come through the Ouija board and cause problems for the users. There is really no way that anyone can make a definitive statement on that. There are simply too many variables as to how the board even works, let alone if it is a doorway to the other side.

But what do you think as a well-rounded reader? Is the Ouija a harmless toy or a way to way to communicate with the dead? You will have to judge that one for yourself for now, but I do want to leave you with a couple of thoughts.

Frankly, I don't believe that the Ouija is as harmful as some would have you believe. I don't believe there is any inherent danger in its use, especially as it does seem to be a way to test and perhaps even generate PK. However, I don't recommend that it be used by teenagers, overly emotional people or anyone not equipped to handle what may occur as a result of the board's use. There are many accounts of people using the Ouija and then discovering that "things begin to happen". Some of these experiences are alleged voices and the movement of objects in their home. Those who believe the Ouija achieves spirit contact will say that the person used the board unprotected and thus attracted "lower entities". It's possible though that the Ouija induces PK effects and that the lingering activity has more to do with the generation of psychic activity than ghosts. For this reason, people who are overly excited should avoid the use of the board.

It's possible (and this is my own personal belief) that the Ouija works as a sort of "lightning rod" for activity. The forced concentration of the sitters incites a PK effect that possibly creates a directed energy, or perhaps even opens a sort-of "doorway" to the other side. I have seen the Ouija used as a way to stir up activity in a haunted location as the energies of the sitters are directed toward a common purpose.

So, yes, I do believe that a talking board can be a paranormal tool. However, I don't think that it works as a legitimate tool to be used in ghost investigations. Be cautious with it, but don't be afraid to try it out in your immediate circle of researchers. Keep careful notes of your sessions and you might be surprised what comes from them.

Just remember that the use of the Ouija will most likely not inspire confidence from anyone who contacts you about an investigation. With that in mind, I don't recommend (no matter what you do on your own time) showing up at their house with a Ouija board tucked under your arm.

TABLE TIPPING

During the early 1900's, when professional mediums all over the country were claiming to communicate with the spirits, ordinary people developed an interest in psychic phenomena. Most of these people had neither the means, nor the access, to professional mediums, so many of them developed "home circles". The home circles were simply small collections of family and friends who would get together and attempt to contact the spirit world. Many of the members of the circles quickly began to realize that what was causing the planchettes of talking boards to move, tables to tip and mysterious rappings sounds to be heard was not the work of ghosts, but rather the collective work of the human mind. The energy created by a group of people gathered together, intent on a single purpose, could produce some amazing results.

Outside of the talking board, one of the most popular methods of experimentation for home circles was table tipping. I confess that I have engaged in this many times myself and not only is it entertaining, it's a remarkable method of examining the psychic abilities of the average human mind. Although I have never claimed to be psychic in the least, I have been present for some very interesting events during table tipping sessions. I believe that all serious ghost hunters should explore this weird and wonderful past time and see what is possible to learn about others --- and ourselves.

Table tipping in the early days of the past century was really considered little more than a parlor game. The basic technique behind it is quite simple. The group of people simply sits around a table, with each person resting his hands flat on the top surface of it. If everyone is patient enough, and prepared to possibly do this for several sittings, they will almost always be rewarded with some sort of phenomena. When starting out, it's likely that the sitters will be startled by rapping and knocking noises but as the experiments continue, the table will likely vibrate and will eventually begin to move. As the number of sittings increase, the group will increase in power and the phenomena will increase along with it. An example of this type of thing was examined earlier in the book when we discussed the creation of "Phillip", the Canadian group's man-made ghost.

It's also possible that the table (as it did in the days of the home circles) will behave as with some intelligence. Once the group has begun to experience strange effects, it will be possible to ask questions and receive knocks, raps and even tilts in reply. When you experience this, it will be easy to understand why people believed the phenomenon was caused by ghosts during the days of Spiritualism. What you will actually have is an entire group that is focused on creating energy and the human mind can do some amazing things.

Although I have never personally experienced anything like this myself, it has been documented by some table tipping groups that they have literally experienced tables that are so charged with energy that the table moved about with all four members of the group sitting on top of it!

GUIDELINES FOR TABLE TIPPING

To start off with, you will need to select your group for the sessions. The best number to start with is usually 4-5 people. Make sure that all of the same members can be present for each session and also make sure that they are willing to continue with the experiments for an extended period of time, or at least until you have achieved the desired effects for your experiment.

2. Choose a location like one of the members' house for the experiments. It should be

a place where everyone can be comfortable and relaxed. You will also need to choose a table to use as well. I recommend a trip to an antique store to find a small wooden table that can seat everyone comfortably, but is not too big or too heavy. Experimenting with a gigantic, oak dining room table is not recommended if you want to see results any time soon.

3. Once you get ready to begin the sessions, consider having a video camera trained on the group the entire time. This will be worthwhile if you plan to document your experiments and you'll be able to see what sort of phenomena occurs later on.

4. The lighting in the room will also be important. Table tipping seems to work the best in near darkness, perhaps because the sitters are creating a "spooky" atmosphere, but who knows? With most ghost hunters, dark or nearly dark lighting will not be a problem as most video cameras used for research are equipped with night-vision and infrared technology.

5. Once you sit down to try and experiment with this, be sure to maintain a casual and relaxed atmosphere. Be sure to talk normally, make jokes and just try to relax. If you are too uptight about things happening, it's not going to work. Simply relax and try to avoid concentrating on getting the table to move at first.

6. Be sure to have everyone's hands on the table all the time. As things start to occur, it's liable to become exciting but no one should move their hands if at all possible.

7. While nothing at all may happen in the initial sitting, it is bound to get more interesting as time progresses. Just be sure that the group meets regularly, once or twice a week if possible. To succeed, the group needs to be dedicated and willing to sit through several uneventful sessions before phenomena actually occurs.

8. Make sure that the meetings are always free from interruption and do whatever it takes to prepare for this. Turn off the television and radios in the house and take the telephone off the hook if you need to.

9. It is almost unavoidable that someone in the group will become impatient with what's going on and will want to try and change things and experiment. If you do decide to change anything about your sessions though, only change one thing at a time. For example, if you want to try a different table, don't introduce a new member to the circle at the same time. If you want to try a different location, bring along the original table and so forth.

10. Interestingly, faking phenomena sometimes encourages real phenomena to appear. In one experiment, a sitter tried this and found that he was able to induce real rappings from the table after he faked rapping noises or moved the table. He was never seen doing this as the sittings were conducted in near darkness. His view of why this occurred is because people have an inherent disbelief in this type of phenomena. The

disbelief might be deeply buried but it is almost always there. Faking the phenomena seems to bypass the problem and allows the mind to work. In short, it seems that once people have been led to believe that something faked is true, then it actually occurs, possibly because their resistance to real activity has been broken down. This is something to consider in your own experiments and while I would never encourage anyone to fake anything during an investigation, this is merely an experiment and not designed to try and "contact the spirit world" anyway.

No one really knows what causes this to work, but its likely that a group can create PK effects more easily than a single individual can. By experimenting with this, it might give us a better understanding of what to expect from PK related cases, as opposed to cases that may involve actual ghosts.

TABLE TIPPING:
THE SEANCE VARIATION

The group might also try experimenting with investigations that go beyond PK effects and actively seek to communicate with ghosts who might be present at the location. Although most of us would concede that this is not exactly scientific, I believe that just about anything is worth trying as an experiment. Such investigations can be easily conducted so that they do embrace the scientific side of ghost research too, since the séance investigations should always be monitored by observers who are outside of the "circle" and by all of the various types of equipment at the ghost hunter's disposal.

1. Start off by selecting the location for your experiment. I would recommend a location that you reasonably feel is haunted. Try to find a spot where you have conducted successful investigations in the past and where activity is normally high. This will possibly help to achieve greater results for the experiment and might make it more likely that any events that occur are not created by the researchers themselves.

2. Next, select the team for the experiment. Try to find members of the group who are not blatantly skeptical of the idea, but are willing to maintain an open mind. Pick 4 to 5 people for an optimal sized group but steer clear of any investigators who believe they might be psychic or sensitive, except for one. This person should be the control person for the experiment.

3. Choose a spot in the location that is comfortable to all of the participants in the experiment. It does not have to be around a table (although this is preferable) but make sure that everyone is seated comfortably, as this may take some time.

4. The lighting in the room will be important here too. As with recreational table tipping, séances seem to work the best in near darkness, perhaps because the sitters are creating that "spooky" atmosphere. With most ghost hunters, dark or nearly dark lighting will not be a problem as most video cameras used for research are equipped with

night-vision and infrared technology.

5. Before the experiment begins, set up all of the equipment needed to carefully monitor the circle. I would recommend using at least two video cameras, an audio recorder and if possible, TriField Natural EM Meters, which can be used as stationary monitors for changes in the electromagnetic field of the area around the séance circle. Also, include a stationary thermometer (as well as a humidity gauge) and thermocouple devices that can measure the ambient temperature and check for temperature changes around the area as well. Another team member should be frequently photographing the circle while the experiment is taking place and another should be taking notes of the entire experiment.

6. To be able to use all of this equipment, it will be necessary to add more team members than you might consider for a single location. In addition to the 4 or 5 members needed for the séance circle, you will also need members for the following:

- video cameras (1 member)
- photographer (1 member)
- equipment monitors (2 members)
- notes (1 member)

7. Once the experiment begins, there are many different directions in which it can go. There are also a number of ways to try and "make contact" with whatever spirits might be present. This can include audio recording where the questions are asked and replies are waited for; working with a talking board to get information; table tipping or knocking; or perhaps even medium-type contact. To be honest, I recommend against the latter for scientific investigations though, as this type of experiment makes it nearly impossible to obtain any solid or authentic evidence.

8. My suggestion at this point is to record everything that takes place and to be sure that all of the equipment is monitored. Any changes in the temperature or EMF readings should be carefully noted. Good luck!

ELECTRONIC VOICE PHENOMENA

There is no question that a tape recorder is an essential piece of equipment in a paranormal investigation. It can be effectively used to keep notes for the researcher and also as a way to record interviews with witnesses. There have also been many instances when paranormal phenomena has been captured on tape and this activity includes strange voices and bizarre sounds that cannot be explained. Many claim that these strange anomalies, captured on ordinary tape, are communications from spirits.

But are they really the voices of the dead? And most importantly, if they are, can we prove it?

The practice of attempting to record ghosts is called Electronic Voice Phenomena

(EVP). The sounds that make up EVP are apparently sonic events of unknown origin, which can be heard, and sometimes captured in recordings, on various types of electronic apparatus, including tape recorders and even radio equipment.

The voices on the tapes take on diverse forms, sometimes seeming to speak in tongues, singing or speaking in gibberish. The messages often make a sort of backward sense as though communication is difficult. They can also apparently call by name and speak directly to researchers. They can be heard over telephones and as anomalous interference on tape recordings. Some of them seem to enjoy engaging in dialogue, answering questions or supplying personal information about the researchers, possibly as a way of achieving credibility.

Of course, with all science (both conventional and paranormal), there are those investigators who are so keen on finding evidence to support the validity of their field that they will impose meaning on what might otherwise be random sounds or noise. This tendency seems especially prevalent when it comes to the recording and research of EVP.

HISTORY OF EVP

In the early days of the Spiritualist movement, communication with the dead was limited to Ouija boards and automatic writing. As the new century dawned, the ability to speak with the dead became an obsession for one of the greatest scientists of all time, Thomas Edison.

Edison was a self-taught genius who began experimenting with scientific theories as a child. Throughout his life, he maintained that it was possible to build anything if the right components were available. Edison was not a believer in the supernatural however, nor a proponent of the popular Spiritualist movement. He had always been an agnostic and although he did not dispute the philosophies of religion, he didn't necessarily believe in their truth either. He believed that when a person died, the body decayed but the intelligence the man possessed lived on. He thought that the so-called "spirit world" was simply a limbo where disembodied intelligence waited to move on.

He took these paranormal theories one step further by announcing that he intended to devise a machine that could communicate with this "limbo". In the October 1920 issue of *American Magazine*, an article appeared that was entitled "Edison Working to Communicate with the Next World". The news of the invention made headlines around the world.

According to journals and papers, Edison began working on the apparatus. The famous magician and friend of Edison's, Joseph Dunninger, claimed that he was shown a prototype of the machine but few others ever say they saw it. Edison reportedly continued working on it until his death in October 1931. Did Edison's machine actually exist? And if so, would it have worked? In the years following his death, curators at both of the Edison museums in Florida and New Jersey have searched extensively for the components, the prototype or even the plans for the machine to communicate with the dead. So far, they have found nothing, making Edison's device the greatest mystery of his complex and intriguing life.

The first recording of a spirit voice on tape was achieved by Rev. Drayton Thomas who, during his investigations of the spirit medium Gladys Osborne Leonard in the 1940's, captured an audible, disembodied voice during a séance. He later came to believe that the voice was that of his dead father.

The psychic Attila von Szalay, who often claimed to hear disembodied voices in the air around him, started researching EVP with Raymond Bayless in the early 1950's. Their initial attempts with a 78 rpm record cutter and player were disappointing. Regardless, they continued their efforts using a device that Bayless invented. It consisted of a box with an interior microphone resting inside of an old-fashioned speaking trumpet. The microphone cord led out of the box and connected to a tape recorder. Almost immediately, the researchers began to hear whispers originating from inside of the box, which they managed to record. Von Szalay carried on taping for many years using an open microphone connected to a reel-to-reel recorder.

Around 1959, Friederich Jurgenson, a retired Swedish opera singer, film producer and bird watcher, was recording bird songs in the woods near his home. When he played back his tapes, he discovered that strange and garbled fragments of human speech had somehow made its way onto the recording. This was in spite of the fact that he was sure that he had been completely alone when the recording was made. He allegedly recognized one of the voices as that of his dead mother, calling his name. As he listened to the tapes, he found that the voices spoke in different languages. Also, he noted that longer phrases spoken by the mysterious voices often had improper structure and bad grammar and in some cases, the syllables were stretched or compressed in a way that made it hard to understand what was being said. The strangest aspect of all was the eerie way that the voices seemed to reply to comments that Jurgenson inadvertently made. He began to hold conversations with the voices by recording questions and then later searching the tapes for answers. In 1963, after four years of recording, he gave a press conference of his findings and published a book called *Roesterna Fraen Rymden* (Voices from the Universe). His conclusion was that the tape recorder acted as a form of electronic communication link to the realm of the dead.

In the later part of the 1960's, a student of Jurgenson named Dr. Konstantin Raudive began cataloguing thousands of EVP recordings. Some of the recordings were made available in book and record form and were later released as *Breakthrough: An Amazing Experiment in Electronic Communication with the Dead*.

There came another resurgence in EVP study in the 1970's and 1980's, especially after the publication of the book *Voices of Eternity* by Sarah Estep. In addition to her more than 15 years of research in the field, Estep also founded the American Association of Electronic Voice Phenomena, which still exists today.

HOW REAL IS EVP?

After the experiments of Friederich Jorgenson, EVP began to be accepted as a legitimate form of paranormal research, but it has remained controversial ever since. The problems come because of the way that messages are normally recorded. They are rarely simple messages but often are fragments and sounds that require hours of listening to understand. This often opens the research up to criticism, but by using detailed, restricted and well-monitored techniques to achieve EVP recordings, much of the room for error can be eliminated from your experiments.

Many of us have heard dozens of recordings of what might be voices and the sounds of ghosts on tape. But we often have to ask ourselves just what we are hearing? Are they accidental recordings of the researchers themselves? Sounds that have no meaning? Or real ghosts?

Many researchers make the valid point that there is a natural human inclination to project meaning onto otherwise innocent phenomena. Many tend to do this with EVP. It is an attempt to make the messages simpler or to appear more mysterious than they really are. The human imagination will try to impose meaning on what appear to be intelligent sounds on the tapes. If no sense can be made of them, then an idea will be invented and/or introduced to support what we want to hear. The human mind has a tendency to "fill in the blanks", which can be a problem with EVP. It has been suggested that if you listen to something enough times, you can hear anything that you want to hear. This problem is most apparent when the researcher announces to anyone who will be listening to his recordings, just what they should be listening for. The power of suggestion can easily take over and destroy whatever credibility this experiment may have had.

In past editions of this Guidebook, and in other places, I have maintained that the authenticity of a recording is almost impossible to prove. I have stated many times that there is no way that a researcher can absolutely prove that the sounds recorded on his tapes are not the result of a hoax, or a result of some natural interference. All that a non-believer (or a debunker) had in the way of evidence is the word of the researcher and unfortunately, that has never been enough to make it qualify as the evidence that many believe it to be.

Further research and experimentation on my part has caused me to change my mind about this but let me first explain why I came to believe that EVP was impossible to authenticate:

Prior to an investigation that I conducted in 1996, I was very interested in EVP and often experimented with trying to record voices on tape. One evening, while working with a particularly haunted location, my group decided that we would try and conduct a séance that would be monitored with high-tech gear, recorders and cameras. The first portion of our evening was spent setting up cameras and recorders that would monitor the events that we hoped would come. Once we had everything prepared, we shut down the lights and took up positions in a circle of chairs. One of the team members stayed outside of the circle to monitor the cameras and to snap photos of the proceedings.

The rest of the group was seated and then one of the members began to try and make contact with the spirits in the room. Whether or not this was successful is open to debate, especially in light of what later happened. Anyway, nearly an hour passed with the one team member speaking aloud, hoping that the ghosts in the room might do something to let us know they were present. At the end of this period, we called the séance to a halt and began to review the tapes and video that we had obtained.

A short time later, one of the group members became very excited over what he heard on the large, reel-to-reel recorder that we had been using. As he played back the tape, he heard an eerie exchange and I have to admit that when I listened to it, I felt the hair on the back of my neck stand on end! He played the tape again for me:

"Can anyone hear us?" the voice of the group member who had been presiding over the séance intoned on the tape. "Is anyone there? Will you make some sign so that we know you are with us?"
<silence>
"Are there spirits present in this room?"
<silence - then the sound of someone shifting in their chair>
<more silence>
"Is anyone here with us?"
Another voice then cuts into the conversation, although it was definitely no one in the room and none of us heard the voice during the séance. It spoke with a very eerie, moaning sort of sound.
"Hellooooo", the voice groaned.

After that, the voice of the group member continued on but the playback of the tape got the attention of everyone in the room. All of the investigators abandoned their tasks and came over to hear the recording again. It seemed that we had actual evidence of ghosts in the building and we had captured them on tape. We marked the spot on the recording and then played the rest of the reel but there was nothing else out of the ordinary on it.

In the weeks that followed, we played the recording over and over again. I listened to it carefully, speeding it up and slowing it down. I knew that no one had spoken during this moment of the séance because there had been nothing on the video recordings of the event. I watched those closely as well and heard absolutely nothing. The only explanation for that was that we had been using a very sensitive microphone with the audio recorder. Could this have picked up something that nothing else did?

After all of this, I could find nothing to dispute the fact that we had captured the sound of a ghost, or at least had captured something paranormal, on the tape. I played the recording for dozens of researchers and ghost enthusiasts and even announced its existence at a meeting and played it for an assembled group of about 50 people. Imagine my embarrassment the next day when I discovered that the "ghost" on the tape was likely nothing more than a bowl of chili!

Let me explain... After the meeting that night, one of the team members who had been present at the investigation came over and explained that he needed to talk to me. He felt terrible about something and hadn't known how to tell me about it. What he told me was that the sound on the tape was definitely not a ghost! According to this team member, he had eaten dinner just before the investigation and by the time that the séance began, his stomach was starting to bother him. At the point in the recording where the "voice" was allegedly taped, his stomach had gurgled and churned, emitting a sound that (on the tape) sounded just like someone moaning the word "hello". It happened that he had been sitting the closest to the sensitive microphone and the quiet sound had somehow been picked up on tape, even though none of us present had heard it and neither had the microphones on the video cameras.

Boy, was my face red! The team member felt terrible (although apparently not terrible enough to come forward with his explanation a little sooner) and I quickly began explaining to people that the recording was not exactly as it seemed to be. It was an embarrassing lesson to learn and it was one that jaded me to EVP recording for several years afterward.

EXPERIMENTING WITH EVP

Even at during my most cynical moments in regards to EVP, I have never outright condemned it. I have only condemned the results of many of the experiments that have been conducted. The reason for this is that I don't believe in claiming evidence to be genuine if there is no way to back up those claims. Unfortunately, EVP is one of the biggest culprits in this field when it comes to unverifiable evidence. This happens because many ghost researchers are not willing to take the time to verify their results by simply using some standard safeguards that can actually prove their recordings are authentic.

During the 1970's and early '80's, EVP was tremendously popular among paranormal researchers and it has caught on again in recent years. You can find websites all over the Internet, maintained by very reputable (and some not so reputable) ghost hunters, that feature clips of recorded phenomena. While the researchers themselves are usually very credible, the problem remains that most of them have not verified and authenticated their research. Far too many "ghost hunters" believe that simply leaving a tape recorder running and walking away from it is enough to prove that there are real ghosts recorded on their tapes. Unfortunately, this is not the case.

So, how can we do it? How can we show even the most hardened non-believer that whatever we captured on tape has no logical explanation? Here are some guidelines to follow:

1. Buy a tape recorder with an external microphone that can be placed away from the machine. Do not (under any circumstances) try to record EVP using a small, hand-held tape recorder. This type of recorder only works in the range of the human voice and in addition, the recording can be polluted by all sorts of ambient noises at your location. The sounds of the motors and gears in the recorder, as well as incomprehensible background noises, can be recorded on the tape and can be mistaken for strange phenomena.

2. If you are using a digital recorder, you should avoid using a handheld device as well. They have the same problems as a standard, handheld tape recorder with ambient noise. My recommendation would be to use a digital recorder that records directly to a CR-ROM but be sure to record as "write-only". You should also be sure to record at settings that do not compress the recording. Since we are not sure what part of the data actually contains paranormal artifacts, we have to be careful not to destroy that material with compressions for a digital media player.

In the last edition of the Guidebook, I recommended against the use of digital recording but further research has shown that it should work just as well as magnetic tape. It appears that any anomalous sounds or voices that are recorded are being picked up through the microphone and with digital, it records sounds exactly as they are heard. There have been some arguments in the past that perhaps the mysterious voices are recorded directly onto the magnetic tape in some mysterious manner but this seems unlikely. It's more likely that the sounds are recorded at the point of the microphone itself. Most external microphones for voice recorders are dynamic, which means that they use an electromagnetic effect to create a small current that in turn moves when sound waves strike its internal diaphragm. This means that the microphone uses a magnet in order to pick up sounds. For this reason, it is believed that the phenomenon is recorded here. It's possible that we don't hear "ghosts" until the recording is played back because their "voice" is recorded directly through the microphone's magnet. As long as you are using an external microphone for your recording process, it should give you good results, no matter what type of recorder you are using.

3. When recording, random locations are not recommended. It is best to take the recorder to a location that you have good reason to feel is haunted. In addition, your EVP experiments should be conducted in the most active spot in the location. This obviously increases your chances for good results.

4. When you arrive, make handwritten notes of the weather and any natural or artificial sounds that can be heard where you plan to do your recording.

5. If you are using a standard tape recorder, use only a brand new tape that comes right out of the factory-sealed package. Never try to record on a tape that has already been used.

6. When you put the recorder into place, be sure to extend the external microphone away from it about three feet or so. It is not recommended to walk around with the recorder. This creates a lot of sounds pollution and takes the experiment away from a controlled environment (more about that in a moment). It is recommended that you place the recorder and the microphone in a secure spot, on the floor or on a table, and preferably on a rubber mat, which would reduce any sound traveling though material to the recorder.

And finally, the most important step to take when attempting to provide solid and incontrovertible evidence that anything that is recorded on your tape is genuine:

7. After setting up the recorder, you will also want to set up three video cameras in the vicinity of the machine. One of the cameras should be aimed directly at the recorder, one should be aimed at the recorder and offer a wider view of the entire room or location and the third should be focused on the recorder and the following array of equipment, which should surround the machine:

- A noiseless, digital clock that should be placed next to the recorder
- A Geiger Counter (if possible)

- Two TriField Natural EM Meters (one set on Magnetic / other set on Electric)
- A Standard Thermometer and Humidity Gauge
- A Thermocouple device to monitor temperature changes

8. One of the most crucial aspects of the experiment is to stick to the question-answer format of attempting to record. Selected questions should be asked with at least a 30 second span between them to allow time for replies. It is best to that the questions be prepared in a way that they can be answered by yes or no, or at least words of one syllable.

9. Once the taping begins, the recorder should be monitored by at least two people and absolute silence must be maintained. It is imperative that verbal notes be made on the recording whenever any outside sounds are heard by those monitoring the tape. If one of the researchers makes a sound (aside from the asked questions) it should be noted on the recording. The same direction goes for automobiles passing outside, noises in the house, etc.

10. When reviewing the tape, if any sort of EVP is identified, go to the video record and see if the equipment detected anything. A check of the wide view of the room will reveal if any of the participants might be responsible for the sounds.

11. If you should capture something on your tape, have others listen to it to provide a confirmation of the sounds. Do not tell them what to listen for. They should discover anything strange on their own. This has always been another of the drawbacks to EVP. It is often presented to people and, as mentioned before, listeners will natural hear what they are told to listen for. This occurs in spite of the fact that what they are actually hearing is nothing more than gibberish.

Good luck with this and I believe that if you follow these guidelines (or at least your own version of them), you can not only be successful at experimenting with EVP but can actually offer some authentic evidence that the voices of the dead can, and do, communicate with the living.

7. GHOSTS ON FILM

USING A CAMERA TO GATHER EVIDENCE OF GHOSTS

One of the greatest potential tools was given to us when photography was invented: for if we could photograph the dead under conditions that carefully exclude trickery, we would surely be so much wiser - and the argument for survival would indeed be stronger.

HANS HOLZER

The camera has become one of the most important tools used by the ghost hunter to collect evidence of ghosts and strange phenomena. Since the days when investigators were debunking mediums and ghost hunters like Harry Price were prowling Borley Rectory, the camera has been an essential part of paranormal investigations.

THE HISTORY OF SPIRIT PHOTOGRAPHY

The actual practice of attempting to capture ghosts on film dates back about 150 years to around 1861. Not surprisingly, this type of photography has been controversial and the subject of much debate ever since. While much has changed in regards to photographic equipment since then, even today, many so-called "spirit photographs" can be explained as flaws on film, mistakes in developing, tricks of light and even outright hoaxes.

The very first spirit photograph has been credited to a Boston engraver named William Mumler. In 1861, he took a photograph of himself and to his surprise (or that's what he claimed anyway), he discovered that a ghost has managed to appear in the photo as well. The discovery of this spirit "extra" came during the expansion of the Spiritualist movement and soon other photographers (now billing themselves as "mediums") claimed they had psychic powers and could make dead relatives appear in photographs taken of their grieving loved ones.

Spirit photography soon became a popular pastime and literally thousands of dollars were made from those who came to have their portraits taken. One photographer,

William Hope, claimed to take more than 2,500 spirit photographs during a period of about two decades. Few of these photos appear to be in the least bit authentic.

Typically in the photographs, ghostly faces appear, floating above and behind the living subjects. In others, fully formed spirits would appear, usually draped in white sheets. Unfortunately, the methods of producing such images were simple. The fraudulent photographers became adept at doctoring their work, superimposing images on plates with living sitters and adding ghostly apparitions and double exposures. The appearance of the fully formed apparition was even easier. Old types of cameras usually demanded that the subject of the photo remain absolutely still for periods of up to one minute, all the while, the shutter of the camera remains open. During this time, it was very simple for the photographer's assistant to quietly appear behind the sitter, dressed in appropriate "spirit attire". The assistant remained in place for a few moments and then ducked back out of the photo again. On the finished plate, it would seem that a transparent "figure" had made an appearance.

While nearly every one of the old spirit photographs looks laughably fake to the modern researcher, those who were duped by the photos at the time they were taken did not have the information needed to properly distinguish real photos from fraudulent ones. In those days, trick photography was something totally new. Even the camera itself had not been around for very long and people did not yet realize just what it was capable of.

There was also the problem of those who so badly wished for the photographs to be real that they were willing to be convinced by anything. Unfortunately, this has not changed much since then and you will still find people today who are more than willing to trust in the latest fads. A good example of this is someone who so desperately wants to believe that they have captured something called a "vortex" on film that they refuse to admit that their camera has a strap on it. It boils down to the fact that some people have such a fragile belief system that they would rather not know something than to be confronted with the truth. A good investigator cannot be this way and has to consider all options, whether he wants to or not.

As time passed and photographic techniques and equipment became more advanced, researchers began to discover that some of the photographs being taken in allegedly haunted locations could not be explained away as film flaws and tricks of light. There have been many "classic" photos that have been taken over the years that have survived the efforts to debunk them and remain enigmatic to researchers and debunkers alike. In the pages ahead, we will hopefully reveal the answers to questions the reader might have on how they might collect mysterious and authentic photographs of their own.

GHOSTS ON FILM

Far removed from its namesake during the Victorian era, Spirit Photography today involves many kinds of advanced techniques. Despite the gains in technology though, it is still (and should be) subjected to the same kind of scrutiny now as it was then. It is imperative that a good ghost researcher knows all that he can about his camera and how it works because one of the most important parts of your investigation will be the photographs that are taken and later examined for evidence of the paranormal. For this reason, it is vital that your entire team is well aware of your "protocols" for using cameras in your investigations. Spirit photography involves many kinds of advanced, and several basic, techniques that can be used to try and capture ghosts and "spirit energy" on film. The following is some information for best using your camera for your investigations and also some methods and ways to be sure that what you are getting on film is actually something paranormal.

To start with, it shouldn't matter what sort of technology you are using to try and obtain spirit photos if the photos themselves cannot stand up to the scrutiny of a practiced eye. In other words, just because someone claims that they have a photo of a ghost, does not necessarily mean that they do. Often, anyone with any experience with photography at all can spot the claims of those who want to "believe" they have a ghost photo. There are many problems that can occur, even with the most simple cameras, from double exposures, tricks of light, camera straps, lens refractions and even obvious hoaxes.

But how does taking photographs of ghosts actually work? How do ghosts end up on film when they cannot be seen with the human eye?

Unfortunately, no one really knows just how ghosts end up on film. Some believe that it has something to do with the camera's ability to freeze a moment of time and space in a way that the human eye cannot do. This may also combine with the intense energy pattern of the ghost, which somehow imprints itself through emulsion onto the film itself. This is the reason why many researchers recommend that the ghost hunter does not load his film into his camera until he actually reaches the place that he plans to investigate.

In addition to those theories, it has also been suggested that ghosts, or paranormal energy, may be at a different spectrum of light than we are used to. This light spectrum may be one that is not visible to the human eye and yet the camera manages to sometimes pick it up. This may be the reason that infrared film is often suggested as the best film to use when hunting ghosts.

Once again, these are only theories. It may be a combination of any of these methods and for all we know, every one of them is correct -- or perhaps none of them are. As with anything else to do with the paranormal, few researchers are ever in complete agreement as to how something works. Most ghost hunters simply find a method for producing ghost photographs and then adapt it to work in their own research. Most often though, ghosts are captured quite by accident, leaving no clues as to why a particular photo was successful.

Each photo that is taken and is displayed should be under intense scrutiny by the researcher before he presents it to the public. There are hundreds of terrible photos out there that claim to be authentic. Most of them are not and this sort of shoddy ghost research is damaging to every ghost investigator who is trying to provide legitimate evidence that ghosts exist.

In order to be sure that your own photos are genuine, it's important for you to have a good working knowledge of cameras, films and natural lens effects. I encourage anyone to go out and purchase standard books on photography. You should know your camera, your shutter speeds and what can happen with lens refractions, light reflections and arcs. By doing this, you have protected yourself from the arguments of the debunkers and perhaps have spared yourself some embarrassment by finding your own flaws in some of your photos. Once you understand the natural effects that can occur, you will be confident about the photos you are taking.

I also recommend that you try experimenting with what fake photos look like. Try bouncing your camera flash off of a reflective surface and see if you can make "orbs" appear. Try taking photos in the rain and in poor weather conditions. Also, drop various things like flour, dust and water in front of your lens and try photographing your camera strap to simulate many of the photos that are out there. I think that you will be amazed to find that you have debunked a number of photos that you may have previously thought were genuine.

But what kind of photos can you expect to get when using your camera during an investigation? I have made some references here to paranormal energy and "orbs", but what are they and are they really evidence of ghosts?

THE TROUBLE WITH "ORBS"

There are a number of different types of photographic anomalies that turn up on film during investigations. Many researchers believe that these types of activity portray actual ghosts, but I cautiously refer to it as "paranormal energy" on film, simply because there are so many unknown variables when it comes to paranormal photography. Some of the strange images on photos that turn up include eerie rays of light, floating objects, mists and shapes and even apparitions that appear to be human, but perhaps the most common images are the so-called "orbs".

Many of the "orb photographs" that turn up on Internet websites or in books seem to come from cemeteries but they actually have an annoying habit of showing up almost anywhere. They have become the most commonly reported types of "paranormal photos" claimed by ghost hunters today. Despite what you might see and hear though, there is absolutely no hard evidence whatsoever to suggest that orbs are in any way related to ghosts. Yes, they do often turn up in photos that are taken at haunted locations, but as you'll soon see, many of these photos have been called into question. However, I do think that legitimate photos of image anomalies (or "orbs", if you prefer) exist. These photos do show a type of paranormal phenomena, but just what type that is remains to be seen.

As mentioned, orb photos are the most commonly seen "ghost photos" today and you will probably see more photos on the Internet of these purportedly "mysterious" balls of light than of anything else. While I do believe that genuine photographs of paranormal orbs exist, they are not as common as many people think. An "orb photograph" is usually one that is taken in an allegedly haunted place and somewhere within the photo is a hovering, round ball. Some of these "orbs" appear to be giving off light, while others appear to be transparent.

Despite the claims, the majority of "orb photos" are not paranormal at all, but merely refractions of light on the camera lens. This occurs when the camera flash bounces back from something reflective in the range of the camera. When this happens, it creates a perfectly round ball of light that appears to be within the parameters of the photo but is actually just an image on the lens itself. Many people often mistake these "orbs" for genuine evidence of ghosts. These false "orbs" can also be created by bright lights in an area where the photo is being taken, by angles of light and by many types of artificial lighting.

When looking at "orb" photos, you will note that most of them occur when the camera flash is used. Some of the photographers will insist that their flash was not on, which usuallymeans it was and they didn't know it. The automatic exposure control on most any standard 35 mm camera uses fill flash in all but the brightest light. It should also be noted that "orbs" were actually quite rare before digital cameras became common. In the early days of low-cost, cheap digital cameras, some "ghost hunters" actually proposed that digital cameras are "superior for orb photography". And since they were producing more "orb" photos, this was technically true. But the digital imaging chip is very different than traditional film photography and was far inferior until recent times. Some of the earlier, low-end digital cameras were made with CMOS chips and they would create "noise" in low-light photographs that would be mistaken for "orbs". It seemed that when they were used in darkness, or near darkness, the resulting images were plagued with spots that appeared white or light colored, which was where the digital pixels had not all filled in. In this manner, the cameras were creating "orbs", and they had no paranormal source at all.

If all of these problems exist with image anomalies --- "orbs" --- then is there any reason to believe that they might be paranormal at all? I believe that there are legitimate photos of what are anomalous, round balls of light that can be photographed and can sometimes be seen with the naked eye. But how do we tell a real "orb" photo from a false one?

There are a number of determining factors, not the least of which is corresponding activity. By this I mean photographing an "orb" just after recording a sharp temperature drop, or some other event that can be documented. In every aspect of paranormal research, corresponding activity(and documentation of the activity) is vital to the success of the investigation and to authenticating the activity, evidence and especially the photographs.

The investigator should also look at the photograph itself. In doing so, watch for image anomalies that are especially bright or are especially dense (in other words, you can't see through them). This is important in determining which anomalies are likely genuine because false "orbs" are readily identified by the fact that they are almost always very pale white or blue in color and are transparent. Also, watch for anomalies that appear to be in motion. This can be a very good sign that the image is genuine. I have seen a number of photos that are believed to be genuine in which the anomaly actually moved several feet during the time when the shutter of the camera was open. In situations like this, it's hard to believe that the anomalous object could be anything other than paranormal in origin.

As mentioned though, one of the things that I have noticed about "orb photos" is that the majority of them seem to be taken in cemeteries. I have often been openly critical of "ghost hunting" in cemeteries. When I mention this, I am referring to the habit that some of have just going out to cemeteries and shooting photographs and hoping to capture something on film. While this is great for the hobbyist, I don't feel that it's serious research. Needless to say, I have been harshly criticized for this view. In spite of this, I have not changed my mind about the fact that random "ghost hunting" is not an investigation. And if this isn't reason enough to discourage this kind of activity, I now have another reason for taking this view.

One of the problems that I have had with this type of "ghost hunting" involves the photos that often come back from it. Ghost hunters, with no idea of any corresponding evidence, often come back from cemeteries with copious numbers of "orbs" in their photos. Again, I do feel that some of these anomalies constitute paranormal energy, but most don't, so I decided to try something out on my own.

With three other researchers, I went out to a cemetery that we picked at random on a warm summer night and took several rolls of film. We had no readings, stories or reports to justify the decision, but just took photos anyway. After having them developed, we discovered a number of the photos were filled with semi-transparent "orbs".

On a hunch, we then went to a nearby football field that was roughly the same size as the cemetery we had already visited. We walked around for a few minutes and again shot a few rolls of film. I was unfortunately not surprised to find that these photos were also filled with orbs. Was the football field haunted? Of course not!

What we did was walk around both areas and stir up dust and pollen from the grass. When we took the photos, these particles in the air caught the reflection of the camera flash and appeared to be "orbs". We also discovered that such photos could be taken after walking or driving on a dusty road. The dust particles would reflect the light, just as moisture can do, and make it seem as though the air was filled was "orbs".

I can't help but feel that this might explain some of the photos that have been taken in cemeteries that have been thought to be paranormal in origin. Does it explain them all? No, it doesn't, but such tests and experiments beg all of us to be careful in our research. As I have always maintained, there exist no experts on ghosts or paranormal photography. My thoughts are that if we can discover the ways to rule out the false photos, we have a much better chance to discover which ones might be genuine.

MYSTERIOUS MIST-LIKE ACTIVITY

In the course of many paranormal investigations, photos have been taken in which strange mists, fogs and streaks appear. These images have no natural origin and were usually not visible to the human eye when the photos were taken. Whether or not these photos actually show ghosts or not has yet to be firmly determined but they are strange and many of them remain unexplained. I prefer to think of these photos as showing a kind of "paranormal energy", meaning that it is most likely paranormal in origin, although no explanation exists for it yet. These types of photos can be some of the most exciting for a ghost hunter to capture, basically because, unlike most "orb" photos, these images are much harder to explain away.

But the researcher still has to be very careful. He should note that when looking at many of the photos on display, the "strange" fogs seem to be very close to the faces of the ghost hunters in the photos. If the weather conditions of that particular investigation are checked, it's likely that it was cold that night. If this is the case, then the images could be vapor from the researcher's breath or some other moisture exuded from the ghost hunter's bodies or equipment. It's also possible that it might be fogging on the lens of the camera. This is usually noticeable by the way that everything in the photo is blurred or distorted.

Unfortunately, the best thing to do when searching for a genuine photo of this type is to take your own. In this way, you can be sure of the conditions under which the photos were taken, making sure that no natural fog is present and that temperatures were well above normal at the time of the investigation.

Another thing to beware of is the tendency that people often have to look for faces, shapes and forms in photos of this type. Don't be fooled into doing this! The human imagination wants to find an explanation for what it cannot interpret and in this way, we often create additional phenomena from what was already believable evidence. The energy that has been captured in the photo is already supportive of the paranormal. By trying to pick out shapes and images from the photo (without some sort of other corresponding evidence) we begin to stray towards the mindset of those who are willing to believe anything and will look, not for true facts, but for anything that might validate our own beliefs.

APPARITIONS ON FILM

This is, without a doubt, the smallest section of paranormal photographs that exist. This is due to the fact that such photos are rare and hard to find and that it is usually very difficult to prove whether or not the photos are hoaxes or double exposures.

Most photos that you see of actual apparitions seem to be "too good to be true" and they often are. However, we cannot be too quick to judge in some cases. I have been given hard copies and negatives of a well-known ghost photograph that depicts a ghostly woman. This photo has been criticized in print and in the media but what most readers and viewers don't know is that the critics and debunkers did not have all of the facts. What they do not know (or will not admit) is that the photo that is often seen is only a cropped portion of the entire photo. When the entire print is examined, the researcher can see that the woman in question casts no shadow. Also, I have given this photo (and a negative) to three different professional photographers for analysis. None of these men believed in ghosts and were anxious to tell me that the photo was a hoax. However, they could not and to this day, none of them have an explanation for the image.

In addition to this photo, there are a number of other possibly genuine ones as well. In most cases, researchers have come to believe that the full-bodied apparitions depicted in these photos are probably the result of Residual hauntings. These images can be very much like photographs themselves, repeating their actions over and over again in a constant film loop. Because the energy seems to imprint on the atmosphere of the location, it might be possible for the camera to pick this up. Unfortunately though, as with the other types of photos, no one is sure at this time as to exactly how this can work.

DIGITAL CAMERAS:
NO LONGER GHOST HUNTING AT ITS WORST!

When I first began writing about ghost hunting and published my first research manual on the subject in 1997, I was already speaking out against digital cameras and why they should not be used for paranormal research. However, one of the statements that I made was that perhaps someday, the technology of the digital camera would finally be adaptable to the sort of research that legitimate investigators would like to do. And, after all of this time, it looks as though that day has finally arrived. I still feel that standard cameras are essential for paranormal research but I also feel that digital cameras do have a place as well.

There are likely some readers of this guide who are amazed to see that I would actually write these words. It seems impossible to believe that I would ever endorse the use (even a limited one) of digital cameras in ghost research but hopefully, I can explain:

Since my first Guidebook was written years ago, I have been under constant and continued attack for my stance against digital cameras. Many of those who criticized my opinion misunderstood the point, believing that I had something against the cameras themselves. This was not the case. I have always understood the benefits of them. They provided instant images and there was no wasted film or development costs. In most cases, you could actually see the photo in a matter of seconds after it was taken. I understood the reasoning behind this. Digital cameras were saving ghost hunters a lot of money but I could never just accept the authenticity of the images that were photographed by them.

No matter what I ever said or wrote though, digital cameras continued to be used in ghost research. Thankfully, not all ghost hunters were using them incorrectly. These camerhave always been excellent for documenting a location and also as a secondary, back-up camera. The problem came when the digital cameras were the only cameras used in an investigation. This was (and still is) an incorrect use for the camera and it has led to some disastrous results for the credibility of paranormal investigations. Many ghost hunters are out snapping hundreds of digital photos at random, using nothing else for their "investigation" but the camera. They are presenting digital images as absolute proof of the paranormal and by doing so, are making a mockery out of the real investigations that are going on. Fortunately, these people are in the minority when it comes to paranormal investigators, but they are still out there, wreaking havoc with their cameras.

But why was I so concerned about digital cameras and why would I maintain for more than six years that they should not be used in paranormal research?

Earlier in this chapter, I mentioned the problem that the early digital cameras had when operating under low-light conditions. I have always referred to this as the "orb factor" and it was an ongoing problem with digital photography for years. There were a great number of ghost hunters who were out on "investigations" and discovering copious amounts of "orbs" in their photos. Unfortunately, they were nothing more than sections of the images where the pixels did not fill in completely. The good news is that time and advances in digital technology have all but eliminated this problem in the newer and better quality cameras. The lingering problems come from those who have not updated their cameras for newer models and we'll discuss that a little further in a moment.

Aside from the "orb" problems in the older digital cameras, the biggest problem that was being experienced was that there was no way to determine if an image was genuine or not. To be able to analyze a photo and to be able to determine the photo's authenticity, two things have always been needed --- a print of the photo and its negative. This was something that a digital camera could not provide and since electronic images taken with the older cameras could be easily altered and changed, it was impossible to prove they were authentic.

However, time, and technology, has changed and now it is not only possible to authenticate the images that have been taken with a digital camera but, depending on the camera, it can be used as the primary photographic instrument in an investigation.

What has changed my mind about digital cameras?

In addition to trying to rule out natural explanations for reported activity before considering that it might be haunting, one of my other research philosophies has always been to try and continue to update my theories of the paranormal. I do not believe that we will ever know all that there is to know about this field and I have never stopped searching for further information. There is much that we still have to learn and even when it comes to something that I have been as adamant about as digital cameras, I am the first to admit when I have changed my theories based on new technology and new information.

My theories have only recently changed and I would still maintain that, prior to recent times, digital cameras have not been suitable for paranormal investigation. At no time have the older cameras been capable of collecting authentic evidence and I base this on the problems with the false "orbs" that the makers of the cameras readily admitted to and also base it on the lack of a negative or any other method of examining a digital image in order to authenticate it. Until just recently, the verification of digital images was only possible with professional quality digital cameras, which were far out of the price range of the ordinary person. For this reason, only lower quality cameras were being used by investigators and strong evidence could not, and cannot, be collected using them.

But times have changed. It is now within the means of investigators to purchase 5 megapixel and greater cameras. These newer cameras not only offer clean and crisp images that do not have the problems with false "orbs" but some models also offer "Night Shot" technology and all of them offer a way to authenticate the images that is as trustworthy as a negative. One of the options of a higher quality camera is access to what are called Raw Data files. These files are uncompressed and unprocessed and an anomalous image that is examined using this option can actually be authenticated -- perhaps with even more detail than in a photographic negative. In addition, the newer cameras also offer access to the EXIF information about images that are photographed. EXIF is data that is embedded into the image once it is taken. It contains everything about the camera that took the image, including camera settings, date and time the image was taken, if flash was used, the ISO settings and more. If anyone attempts to manipulate the image, the EXIF data holds this information too. In this way, a person trying to analyze a digital image will be able to see if it has been manipulated or not. If anyone attempts to alter the EXIF data, it will destroy the image. In this way, it becomes a "digital negative" of every picture that is taken.

With this new technology now within reach of the average person, digital photography has reached a level where I believe it is finally acceptable in paranormal research. By using cameras that start at a level of no less than 5 megapixels and taking advantage of all of the options available to us, we can actually gather evidence with our digital camera that is comparable to that of a 35 mm camera.

With all of this said however, I do not want this to be misinterpreted as a blanket endorsement of the way that digital cameras have been used in the past. Neither the methods, nor the low quality cameras that have been used, have a place in our research. Even now, with all of the technology that we have available, no camera should be used as the single tool in an investigation. Reputable photographs should still be accompanied by good research and corresponding activity, whether the captured images can be authenticated or not.

PARANORMAL PHOTO HOW-TO GUIDE: USING 35 MM CAMERAS IN GHOST HUNTING

Often ghost hunters ask me to suggest cameras and film for ghost hunting but there really doesn't seem to be a definitive type of either one to use. I have seen remarkable photos that have been taken with everything from expensive 35mm cameras to instant cameras to even cheap, disposable cameras. Obviously, cost is almost always a determining factor in choosing a camera, but remember that while an $800 camera may be of a better quality than a $200 one, it is the person behind the lens who makes all the difference, unless you are dealing with a digital camera and then technology is almost as important as the person using the equipment.

There are many different kinds of cameras manufactured today but the most popular 35mm cameras are two basic types. One of them is the "point and shoot" camera, which is very simple and is completely automatic in its operation. The other camera type is the Single Lens Reflex camera (SLR). This type is larger and more complex to operate but is a favorite for most professional and amateur photographers. I usually recommend to people that they use a model of camera that is most comfortable for them, regardless of the type. When it comes to film, I usually suggest Kodak 400 ASA film (and sometimes higher speeds) for overnight, outdoor investigations, depending on the strength of your camera flash. There are three basic methods of photography to consider when photographing your investigations:

<u>COLOR FILM:</u> This is the simplest and most basic method of photography during both daytime and nighttime investigations. For interior locations, or daytime investigations, use a 200 ASA Kodak film. At night, I would recommend a 400 ASA speed Kodak film, along with your camera flash, to obtain results. This is a small grain film, so enlargements will not be difficult and it is fast enough to use under low light conditions.

You may want to experiment with your camera at night and make sure this is a high enough speed film for your particular model of camera.

BLACK & WHITE FILM (No Flash): If you prefer to try and experiment without the flash, thus eliminating the chance for false "orbs" and lens refractions, you will want to use a 400 ASA film made by Tri-X or Kodak. This film is ideal because it is more sensitive to ultraviolet light and so you have a better chance of possibly picking up something unseen by the human eye. In most cases, the Kodak film can be developed by just about any processor but it should be developed at the same settings as color film, so be sure that your processor is aware of this.

INFRARED FILM: One of the most reliable, but most difficult to use types of film and photography is infrared. There is a lot of experimentation and money involved with using it but this type of film is sensitized to light that we can see with the naked eye, as well as light that is of a different wavelength of radiation and is invisible to us. The film allows you to see, literally, what is beneath the surface, or what the human eye cannot see. Infrared does not detect heat, but rather sees and photographs radiation. It can actually "see" a level of radiation that is one spectrum below thermal radiation and this is illumination caused by electromagnetic fields. Because we believe that paranormal energy also lurks in this same "dead zone", infrared film becomes a very helpful tool in ghost hunting.

However, infrared film does require special filters to use, must always be kept refrigerated, requires special processing and must always be loaded and unloaded into the camera under conditions of absolute darkness. Also, most automatic cameras cannot be used with infrared film. There in an infrared sensor inside most models to make sure that the film advances properly. This sensor will badly cloud your film.

The Best Way to Use Infrared Film:

1. It has been suggested that if you are going to try infrared film, you should take along 2 different cameras on an investigation. One of them should be loaded with 400 (or higher) ASA film and one with infrared film. Your local camera shop should be able to order it for you, or you can order it directly from Kodak for about $12 per roll. Always ask for HIE 135 Black & White film. It comes in 36 exposure rolls.

Remember that you are going to have to experiment with this film. The first time that you use it may be a total bust! For each exposure that you take, make sure that you have notes about your camera settings so that you will know later what worked and what didn't. I suggest making your first trip out to a place where you don't expect activity, just so that you know how the film works best with your camera. There is always time for a solid investigation using infrared film later.

2. When the film arrives, it should have come in a box packed in dry ice to keep it cool. This is essential because infrared film is sensitive to heat and must be kept refrigerated before it is used. If you buy the film (already in stock) at the camera shop, make sure that it was kept cool. You should store the film inside of your refrigerator and not take it out until about one hour before you are going to load it into your camera. This

way, it warms to room temperature and you avoid any chance of fogging the film.

3. Also essential is the fact that this film must be loaded and unloaded in total darkness. Find a room or a closet with no outside light and stuff towels under the door or any other way that will make the room pitch dark. Then, you can safely load the film into your camera. Any light leaks at all can damage the film.

4. When using the film, some researchers recommend different filters to use when working with it, so experiment and see what works best for you. Deep red filter blocks (no. 25) will block out visible light if you want that. When shooting in the daylight, you will want to make sure that you have a filter, as UV rays and other spectrums of light can cloud or overexpose the film. Also, try not to use a flash because you can get some very weird light reflections from it. It's best to just open up your lens to the widest aperture and experiment with it. If you do use a flash, be sure that it has the same type of filter over it that your lens does.

5. After the film is exposed, unload the film in your "dark room" and place it back into the container that it came in. Tape the canister shut and do not allow it to be opened by anyone until it is ready to be processed.

PHOTOGRAPHY HINTS & TIPS

When conducting investigations, remember that photographing ghosts is not an easy process. Many investigators only use a camera when they encounter anomalous readings on their equipment and still others cover the location with their camera to document as much as they can. You just never know what might turn up on your developed film. Do plan to use a lot of film when you are ghost hunting. It is a common fact that it sometimes takes dozens (or even hundreds) of snapshots to come up with even one paranormal photo that you can feel is genuine. With this being the case, try not to get discouraged if every investigation fails to turn up a "ghost photo". Just because you don't get any results with your camera, doesn't mean the location is not haunted. The camera is just like any other tool in your ghost hunting kit. The results that you achieve with it do not stand alone and it's always possible that you won't find anything with your camera, even though your other equipment says that something is there.

And when the camera does work, you still have to be careful. Turning to the camera for proof of ghosts does not insure against mistakes and many ghost hunters are fooled into believing that some erroneous photos are real. We have all seen dozens of photos that supposedly show ghosts and paranormal energy but that actually do not. Be careful to do your research and know how to tell "accidental" photos from the real thing. Here are some things to be careful of when experimenting with ghost photographs:

1. Be careful that you have nothing protruding in front of the camera lens. Believe it or not, this can be anything from a finger to clothing, items around you like trees, clothing and even hair. People with long hair should make sure that it is pulled back tightly or tucked under a hat. Loose hair that ends up in front of the camera lens (which may

be unseen by the photographer) and which gets illuminated by the flash can look pretty eerie.

2. Be sure that your lens is clean and covered when not in use. Even a small drop of rain, dirt or moisture that ends up on the lens can show up on the developed print. This would not be seen through the viewfinder, so you would never know that it was there.

3. Make sure the weather is cooperating with your photographs. By this, I mean to make sure that it is not raining or snowing. Round balls of glowing light that are photographed during a rain storm are not exactly overwhelming proof of the supernatural.

4. Make sure that conditions are not damp, promoting moisture or fogging, on your camera lens. This is why I always mention bringing along temperature and humidity gauges to an investigation site. You can check and see if "fog-like" images that later turn up on film could have a natural explanation.

5. Be sure to point the camera away from reflective surfaces when using a flash. Avoid mirrors and windows in a house and bright or polished surfaces when working outdoors. The light from the flash bouncing off this surface can refract back onto your camera lens and create "orbs" that are not of paranormal origins. This can often happen in cemeteries with reflective tombstones, especially polished granite, which easily catches the light.

6. Make sure you know where your camera strap is at all times. Notice how many so-called "ghost photos" that you see look like camera straps? That's because most of them are! Observe how those "anomalous" images always come from the right side of the camera, where the strap is normally located. I suggest taking the strap off your camera or at least leaving it around your neck, where it belongs.

7. No matter where you are taking photographs, be sure to use a photographic log sheet to keep track of where the pictures were taken, who took them and whether or not they were taken randomly or because some strange activity was occurring at the time. This can be very important when it comes to analyzing the photos and looking for corresponding activity at the site.

USING VIDEO IN YOUR INVESTIGATIONS

There are many uses for video cameras during your paranormal investigations. Most ghost hunters have started taking and setting up video cameras for every investigation that they go on. Also, thanks to the fact that many of the newer cameras are now fitted with infrared (or as Sony calls it "Nightshot") capabilities, we can shoot at a 0 lux setting that allows us to film in total and complete darkness. This innovation has allowed us to overcome the problems of the past, when video cameras were not useful in dark locations.

One of the main uses for a video camera in an investigation is to record your witness interviews. You might be surprised by what turns up on video over what you might record on an ordinary audiotape. Just the expression on someone's face, or their mannerisms, can often speak volumes about an event and bring to light facts that you may not have even considered. The only problem with this is that many witnesses (in my experience) are ill at ease in front of a camera. This can often make for a disjointed and nervous accounting of events. You should try the video camera first and if this doesn't work, switch over to recording on audiotape instead.

Another advantage to the video camera is the ease with which you can document the location of the investigation. I always recommend that researchers draw up a map or chart of the location and note the various areas where phenomena have been reported. This is much easier to do if you have covered the entire area with your video camera too. Also, if you are writing the investigation up as a report, you can check your memory of the location by watching the video that you have recorded.

To most researchers though, the main reason to carry a video camera into an investigation is for the chance to capture some sort of paranormal phenomena on tape. Of course, the fact that video does seem to pick up anomalies may discredit some of the past theories that we have entertained about how still cameras manage to pick up ghosts. It is long been suggested that the camera will pick up paranormal energy because it is moving faster than we can actually see. If this is true, then how do we explain how video cameras manage to record strange images? The video camera acts more like the human eye, seeing things in real time and not frozen as they are with a still camera. Perhaps ghosts actually are in that other spectrum of light, who knows? Regardless, there have been a number of very authentic video tapes that have emerged showing strange shapes, mists and especially, speeding balls of light that don't seem to be explainable except as paranormal phenomena. They appear to be some of the same anomalies that have been captured by still cameras. This leads me to think that they are probably the same type of phenomena.

Many of these videotapes were shot under ordinary conditions while investigators were checking out reportedly haunted locations. Some were filmed randomly and others were done while certain areas were under surveillance, which is another great use for the video camera in your investigation. In fact, I always recommend the use of several video cameras for an investigation if possible. This allows us to monitor various sections of the location because we never know where activity might occur next. One of the cameras can be used to record the witness testimony, while the others can be used to thoroughly cover the location.

The grueling part of this will be that you have to be sure and watch everything that you have recorded. You never know when something might turn up. I would even suggest, if you have the capability, to watch the tape frame-by-frame. It is very possible that you might miss something on the general run-through. This will take a lot of extra time, but may be well worth it. In one case that I was involved in, the location seemed to be without activity until the films were watched one frame at a time. After that we realized that it was actually a very active place.

In the past, there have been many problems with using video cameras at dark investigation sites. In the case of older VHS cameras, it was pretty well impossible to film after the sun went down without the use of a lot of extra light sources. As times have changed though, better quality cameras have become available and in fact, it is now possible to use a standard, commercial camera and film in total darkness.

This type of camera has been manufactured in several models by Sony and is outfitted with what they call "Nightshot" capabilities. This means that it can film at O lux, in total darkness. The camera has the ability to convert infrared light to a part of the spectrum that the human eye can see. You can actually see the light being emitted by the camera and it literally "paints" the dark location and converts it to an inverted white and green color. It is an extremely effective device and for several years after it came on the market, it had better capabilities than most broadcast cameras that were being used by television and documentary crews.

As mentioned earlier, some of the best evidence captured on video has been the mysterious balls of light that are filmed at many haunted locations. The lights are normally round and often give off a faint glow. They move independent of their surroundings and dart between people and objects at the location. No one knows for sure what these lights may be. At this time, they have no explanation whatsoever.

If you happened to find something like this on your videotape, be careful to observe the object's movements and be sure that it is not some sort of dust particle or airborne pollen. There are several ways that assurances can be reached, including the fact that dust has a distinctive way of moving on camera and will usually drift rather aimlessly back and forth as it settles. Heavier natural objects will always fall straight down past the camera, following the laws of gravity. The anomalous lights will have a movement pattern all their own and will seem to have a purpose. They will not float side to side and may even interact with the investigators or the witnesses at the scene.

There are ways that you can be sure of what you have filmed though and as suggested by investigator Chris Moseley, all that is required is measuring every object that can be seen on camera with a measuring tape, using an inexpensive wind gauge and having a lot of patience.

When setting up a location to be monitored on video, you should first monitor the wind speed directly in front of any heating or air conditioning vents. After you have logged in the highest velocity speed from in front of the vent, you will be able to say, with certainty, that dust will not move faster than the air flow at the location unless someone walks in front of the video camera. Once this data is collected, measure the distance of everything that can be seen in front of the camera, including the size of the room. Log this information in your notes next to the wind current data from the wind gauge.

You can also adapt this to use in outdoor investigations as well. Most of us avoid trying to use video in the summer months because of the chance of picking up flying insects, but with the right calculations, you can even rule out natural explanations during this time of year as well. Simply follow the same steps of measuring items that in line of sight of the camera and then also place your wind gauge within view of the camera. That way, any changes in wind speed will be picked up in the video record and comparisons can be made next to any anomalies that are filmed.

Video moves at 30 frames per second and so if an object moves one inch between frames (this is why you need to know the distance of everything in the room in relation to the possible anomaly), then it's moving at 30 inches per second. When broken down, this would equate to about 1.7 miles per hour, which means that it could clearly be dust.

However, if it was moving one foot between frames, it would be traveling at 20.4 miles per hour, which means that, unless it is an insect, it is not dust. In many cases, investigators have filmed anomalies moving much faster than this, sometimes as quickly as 60 (or more) miles per hour. Even the world's fastest flying insect (the Australian Dragonfly at 35 miles per hour) does not move that quickly and by having measurement and wind speed data from your investigation site, you can obtain some very reliable and authentic evidence of the unknown.

Remember that using a video camera is just like using any other device in the pursuit of the paranormal. It takes practice to be good at it and experimentation is essential. To be able to obtain good, authentic evidence using a video camera, you have to use the same sort of caution that you use with anything else. Be sure that you carefully review any evidence that you might have before presenting it to the public and proclaiming it genuine. We have all seen examples, just like with still photos, of sloppy research that shows images that are far from paranormal in origin.

8. THE PARANORMAL INVESTIGATION

PUTTING YOUR GHOST RESEARCH INTO PRACTICE

In the pages of the earlier chapters, we have discussed at great length what you will need for a paranormal investigation, including what sort of equipment to have, cameras to use and methods to be concerned about when it comes to actually searching for evidence of ghosts. Now it is time to delve into the investigation itself. This is where the researcher gets the chance to put all of the information that he has gathered into practice.

WHAT TO DO BEFORE YOU GET THERE

One thing that every ghost researcher has to do is to get the word out and make it public knowledge that he is interested in hearing about strange events, haunted houses and ghost stories in his area. Once this is done (and we'll talk about how to do this in a later chapter), he is eventually going to get calls from people who want him to investigate their own personal haunted houses. One of the most important conversations that the ghost hunter will have with these people will be the first one. It is this conversation that will establish the nature of the situation. To do this, I have listed a few things that are very important to find out before getting involved with an in-depth investigation:

1. Determine, if you can do so over the telephone, if there could be some sort of normal explanation for the person's report. This will be hard to do in a telephone conversation but try suggesting some non-paranormal reasons for the activity and see how the witness replies. In one case, I actually had someone suddenly realize what was causing the "strange sounds" after I made one such suggestion. Everyone laughs a little in embarrassment but it saves you from going out on a "wild ghost chase". Just be sure to explain to the person that you are not asking because you don't believe them (they are already likely to start the conversation with... "I know you'll think I'm crazy, but...").

Simply explain that you have to be sure about the phenomena that they are describing.

2. Also, find out why the person called. Are they simply curious about a possible ghost? Do they expect you to make the activity stop?

3. Try to decide if there is a need for an on-site investigation. Find out how often the reported events occur, if there are other witnesses involved, and whether or not these witnesses might be available for you to talk with as well.

After talking to the witness, try and contact anyone else involved in the case who might be able to provide further information and then consider whether you plan to go to the location or not.

Most readers will not be surprised to learn that it isn't always necessary to visit the site. I often get calls from people whose "ghost" is easily solved over the telephone as a natural event, or perhaps the activity they are describing occurred only one time and has never been seen or heard since. In a situation like this, it is best for you to suggest that the witness keep a "journal" or a "logbook" of any activity. Then, leave it up to them to call you back and keep you updated about any new events. Often, during that time period, the witness will realize the one-time event had a natural explanation or that it was an isolated incident that will apparently not be repeated. What had once seemed so frightening will no longer be and it is unlikely that you will hear from them again. While this might seem discouraging, it will actually be quite helpful as there will always be other cases for you to investigate and you won't waste any time with this one.

On the other hand, if they do get back in touch with a list of additional activity, you will have an excellent timeline of events in the case and a written account of any incidents that took place before your hands-on involvement in the matter.

Always try to be an open-minded, but optimistically skeptical when dealing with witnesses. Depending on the person, they may be looking for reassurance that they are not "crazy" and that their experience has a logical explanation, even a strange one. You must start out by trying to prove that the situation is not a ghost, don't listen to their story and jump to the conclusion that it is. People who are scared will usually misinterpret natural events as supernatural ones and you have to be careful not to encourage the witness until you have actually investigated the location.

Another important thing to try and determine with this initial interview is whether or not the witness is "stable" or not. Believe me when I say that I am not trying to be cruel or humorous with this warning because I can speak from painful experience. Nearly every experienced investigator has run into a situation of being contacted by someone is not in complete control of their mental faculties. In fact, at one time I was being repeatedly contacted by someone who claimed that a "giant ghost with teeth the size of a shark's" was flying about his house and "biting the heads off other ghosts". Who was I to say this wasn't actually happening, but let's just say that I had some serious doubts.

Believe me, sometimes a little tact and diplomacy will serve you well. The best thing to do in a situation like this is to bow out gracefully and suggest they contact someone with more experience in dealing with cases of that nature.

WHEN IS IT OKAY TO CALL?

One of the things I often talk about in ghost research is being ethical about how we conduct our investigations. I have mentioned already that it isn't a good idea to go where you aren't wanted or to annoy and pester potential witnesses to paranormal events. On the other hand, many aspiring ghost hunters often ask me how to find cases, or haunted places, to investigate. I usually point them toward public records or books and articles about alleged haunted spots and remind them that while many of the stories they find seem to be folklore, that same folklore can often point us in the direction of authentic phenomena.

But what about when this method is all tapped out? Maybe there aren't any historic haunted places in your area (that's hard to believe, but let's pretend it's possible), what do you do then?

One of the first things to do is to check your local papers daily. Reports about ghosts, and especially poltergeist activity, always make great back page stories, especially in October. Make sure that your friends know of your interest too and that they keep their ears open for anything strange that comes along. When you do find a story though, it's unlikely that the address where something weird is happening will be printed, or that many details will appear. Normally though, the names of the property owners and the main witnesses will be listed and those are great leads to start with. From there, you can usually find the location of the house by checking the local telephone book or city directory.

There are a couple of different ways to approach things from here. You can try finding someone who knows the owners of the house so that you can secure an invitation. This is the preferred method of access to the investigation, but I admit, this may not work.

My next suggestion is to try and contact someone at the local police station. The reason for this is that one of the first things that comes to mind for many families is that someone has broken into their house and may be causing the reported activity. For this reason, they usually contact the police first. Police officers and investigators can be very useful to you and even fill you in on small details in the case, but only if you handle it correctly. You have to be able to convince them that you have a scientific interest in the case and that you aren't some kind of "nut". Play your cards right, and you might even get an introduction to the "haunted" family itself.

Finally, the last course of action is to contact the family directly. The best way to do this is by a phone call or a letter --- showing up on their doorstep with your "ghost hunter's kit" is not recommended. In this situation, it is okay to contact the family, even though I advise against it in most cases. In this instance, where the story has been publicized in the newspaper, most witnesses will not turn away your inquiry.

Be careful though! As most of you know, the media can be very intrusive and unfair when they want to be. Their reports may have brought unwanted attention to the case, or may have reported the facts inaccurately. For this reason, approach the witnesses with caution and make sure they know your interest in the case is not only scientific, but aimed at getting to the root of the problem too.

RULES TO FOLLOW IN AN INVESTIGATION

If you should decide to pursue the case and conduct an on-site investigation, there is a lot to know and consider before you even get to the location. You should start off by doing your research. Look into the books and journals that you might have, which might feature cases that are similar to the ones that the witness is reporting to you. Check and see what the outcomes of those cases were. Here is another place to be careful though! Don't jump to the conclusion that your case is an authentic one before investigating. Remember that what the witness is reporting may not be the only explanation for the activity.

Use this time to prepare for what to do when you arrive at the location. The following is a list of rules, or guidelines, that is worth looking over. These are hints, tips, ideas and suggestions for conducting your own paranormal investigations. There is a lot of information here and while I wouldn't expect each one to be worthwhile in every case, I am sure there are some valid points here that might help in any situation. They are listed below in no particular order:

1. Never go alone into an investigation unless you absolutely have to and then, always let someone know where you are going. This will give you someone to help out with the investigation, corroborate anything strange that happens and may be essential should you walk into a volatile domestic situation (which can happen!).

2. Try to make sure that all parties related to and who own the location have given their permission for the investigation (in writing if possible). You don't want anyone present to give you or the witnesses a hard time. This will make the investigation difficult, if not impossible.

3. Keep your perceptions clear prior to the investigation. Maybe this is an obvious one, but never drink or smoke during or prior to an investigation. Not only will this inhibit your photography results but your sense of smell and intuition also.

4. Arrive with skepticism. I have mentioned this before, but always remember to maintain your open mind and be aware that there may be a natural explanation for what is going on. Always know what to look for and remember to try and prove that the place is not haunted first, before accepting that it is a ghost.

5. Make sure that you bring along all of the items that you need to properly conduct your investigation. Make sure that you know how to use your equipment properly and always try to find a natural source for your EMF readings before assuming that the detected energy is paranormal in origin.

6. Avoid publicity and the media if possible when starting a case. You want to begin the case as unobtrusively as you can. Reporters, or people outside of your group, can add an unwanted dimension to the case. Media attention can also be disruptive with a witness who needs to be clear and coherent. Also, try to get the witnesses to refrain from

inviting their friends over to watch. Carefully explain that you would like only people directly related to the case to be present.

7. Keep out any would-be investigators from outside your own group, or those you have not worked with before. Unknown factors like this could be disastrous, especially if they start talking about "demons" or "exorcisms" and they could turn the whole investigation into a circus.

8. Interview the witnesses in depth, repeating questions if necessary. This will allow you to tell how consistent the experience account is and whether any of the witnesses may be embellishing their version of the story.

9. Look for a pattern in the accounts and try to see if the activity is related to only one person in the group.

10. Become a part of the location. Try to blend into the background as much as possible and don't let the investigation turn into a spectacle. Also, make sure that your equipment is out of the way and not the focus of the entire household.

11. Make sure that the witnesses are comfortable with the investigation and understand what you are doing. You do not need to be technical with your explanations but make sure that they understand what the equipment is for and why you are taking so many photos, etc. You will, at some point, run into a situation where the "haunting" has a natural explanation (like a banging water pipe or the wind) and you have to be careful how you explain this to a witness. Some people will be relieved there is an alternate explanation besides a ghost, but if this is not handled right, some could feel that you think they were lying about the whole thing. Always explain the reasons why you think the activity has a natural cause and if possible, demonstrate this for them.
On rare occasions, you will meet a witness who is actually lying, or has at least imagined that what they are telling you is the truth. This is also a situation to be handled delicately and I would suggest following the same procedures and explaining why you feel the "haunting" has a natural cause.

12. Remember that just because you want to study and research the activity (if it does prove to be genuine) the witnesses might not feel so inclined. In this case, the owner of the location must always take priority over the wishes of the ghost hunter and help must be provided if possible.

13. Try some field experiments to reconstruct the events. Let the witness walk you step-by-step through the encounter or experience and have them explain their feelings at the time.

14. Check with experts outside the paranormal field, like a plumber for explanation of water pipes, an architect about the design of the house, an electrician about strange events with lights turning on and off, or any other kind of expertise that you need. (more

about this later in the chapter)

15. In the course of the investigation, remember to write down everything that occurs as soon as you can, no matter how small or insignificant it might seem at the time.

16. Be careful not to let your own beliefs influence the witness accounts in any way. They could be seeking the rational explanation that you are overlooking.

17. If you should make public the information that you discover in your investigation, be sure that you have the permission of the people involved. Also, be careful of what you say and how you say it, because the manner in which you present the information could influence the way that others perceive it.

Keeping these guidelines in mind should assist you in pursuing an investigation. Obviously, these suggestions are not set in concrete, but they should help you in a manner that will allow your investigations to be conducted in a professional manner.

A STEP-BY-STEP GUIDE: STARTING & CONDUCTING A PARANORMAL INVESTIGATION

The following is a checklist guide of how I have conducted past investigations with members of the American Ghost Society. Obviously, this list will not work for everyone and I continue to suggest that you take the information that you can use from this book and adapt it to work for your own investigations. Whether you choose to follow this list or not is up to you, but if nothing else, I think that it may offer you some pretty valuable starting points.

I should start out by saying that I believe investigations are best conducted with teams made up of 5-6 people. This allows you to thoroughly investigate the entire location (without tripping all over a large group) and to interview the witness and record their statements without the person feeling overwhelmed. A small group will also allow you to avoid the distractions that arise and complicate the investigation for researchers who attempt to work alone or with only one other person. Remember that working alone in a research investigation is not recommended. You should always have someone else along, if not for safety's sake, then to at least be there to corroborate any strange things that might occur. On the other hand, a large group is merely pointless, especially in someone's home, where things quickly become awkward and congested.

Here are the steps to follow in an investigation:

1. Arrive with skepticism. I know that you are probably tired of reading this, but it can't be stressed enough. Don't go into a location looking for ghosts --- go in looking for a natural explanation and rule out everything until there is nothing left but ghosts.

2. Make sure that the witness understands what you are going to do at their house or location. Make sure that they realize this can be an intrusive process. The more comfortable that the witness is, the better the investigation will go.

3. Next, divide up the separate functions of the investigation among the team members. Decide who will be handling what aspects, who will be photographing, who will be video taping, who will be using what equipment, etc.

4. Interview the witness in a secluded location with all of the team members present except one. This excluded person should be simply walking through the house making a layout drawing of the rooms and getting a general impression of the place. This person should also note every location where he finds, or feels, something out of the ordinary. His perceptions will be essential to the findings of the investigation because he will not have any idea of the witness testimony or where previous encounters have taken place. A particularly sensitive member of the team is best suited for this assignment.

5. The other team members should be interviewing the witness, or witnesses, about the events in the case. The questions should be asked by one interviewer at a time and all of the interview should be recorded on tape and if possible, video. One team member should also be taking notes of everything that is said. It is essential to get all of the details of the case in this first interview.

6. An investigation report should be written from all notes and findings in the case, even if it turns out to have a natural explanation. If you plan to publish any of the results, make sure that you get permission from the witness.

7. After the interview, an additional team member should begin another scan of the house with detection equipment, also noting any strange locations that may come up using the equipment. Particular attention should be paid to those areas where the witness recalled an experience or sighting.
At this point, it is also a good idea to compare notes with the first investigator who walked through the house. Try and determine if any of the locations where this person noted something unusual match anything from the witness testimony or from the use of the detection equipment.

8. Another team member should make a photographic record of the location with his camera, documenting each of the locations, particularly the area where the witness reports seem to gravitate. Using a video camera, a team member should also document the location in this manner also.

9. If the phenomena occurs on a regular basis, or has a set pattern, you should obtain permission from the witness to do a surveillance of the area for an extended period.
I like to refer to this as a "ghost watch", because it gets away from actual ghost hunting and becomes more of a "wait and see what happens" experience. In these situations,

it benefits the researchers to come to the location, set up their monitoring equipment and then wait to see what they can record. This type of investigation should be done once you are relatively sure that you cannot explain away the reports of the witnesses, or after your own investigations have turned up something beyond the ordinary. (see later in the chapter for more on this)

10. Remember that after the investigation is over, you may not have turned up anything on that occasion. It does not mean the location is not haunted. If you have tracked down all possible natural sources for the phenomena and have ruled them out, it could mean that the ghost was simply not active while you were there. This is the reason that follow-up calls and repeat visits are important.

If you have established a good relationship with the witness, they will not mind hearing from you again. Be sure to ask and make sure they are willing to call you if anything else happens and make sure that they keep a record of it. If anything occurs, go back and conduct another investigation. Who knows what might happen?

THE GHOST WATCH

Earlier in this chapter, I referred to a certain type of experimental investigation as a "ghost watch". In short, it actually means just sitting around and waiting for something to happen. It is not your proactive type of ghost hunting and for this reason, it is often overlooked by researchers. In all honesty, I feel that sidestepping this part of the investigation (mostly because it is mind-numbingly boring at times) can be a huge mistake. And it's also imperative when dealing with what you believe is a human agent poltergeist case.

The idea of the "ghost watch" comes into play when the ghost research team has become relatively sure that they cannot explain away the reports of the witnesses at the location. It can also be planned when the ghost hunter's investigations have turned up something beyond the ordinary. In these situations, the investigation veers away from interviewing witnesses and scanning with equipment and becomes a game of "wait and see what happens". In this type of experiment, the ghost hunters come to the location, set up monitoring equipment and then wait to see what they record. As mentioned, it can be time-consuming, and more than a bit boring, but the researcher might be surprised at how well it pays off.

Before getting involved in this sort of research, it helps to be able to establish a set pattern for the reported activity. In other words, the witnesses might tell you that certain incidents occur around the same time of the evening. It is also useful research in a fairly active location where phenomena has been widely reported. Every ghost hunter wants to be present when something that cannot be explained actually occurs. Believe it or not, a "ghost watch" offers your best chance of that.

There are a couple of different ways to conduct this type of experiment. The first method is the use of monitoring equipment. While I feel that both methods require equipment, the first method that I want to discuss requires more equipment than the other. Using this method, the ghost researcher can literally place himself outside of the area of the investigation and monitor it with cameras that will record any activity.

This can be useful for several reasons and there is a system involved for setting things up. Let me give you some ideas to work with:

1. Find a location in the house that is best suited for monitoring. It may be an area where the witnesses report the most activity, or perhaps an area where an earlier sweep of the house picked up some anomalous readings that you could not rule out as artificial disruptions or interference.

2. Using your video camera (or in this case, more than one), you will need to be able to run video cables to a monitoring system outside of the room or area. You can pick up any of the equipment that you need for this at a local electronics store and you may want to consider hooking up a recorder that can also record any activity that occurs. Usually, I recommend using more than one monitor for this experiment, perhaps one for each camera.

3. As an alternative, there are a number of companies that offer security and monitoring systems, most of which were designed for retail stores and companies. Some of them even offer night-vision capabilities and infrared filming in total darkness. The systems often come with several cameras and professional monitors that offer multi-screen viewing on one unit. You can also hook up a recorder to these units as well so that you can go back and watch the tape later.

4. Recording the "ghost watch" is essential. As mentioned, you will need to go back and watch the tape later (perhaps even frame by frame) to see what may have occurred that didn't immediately register with the watchers. This is the same as with any investigation that you do, when watching hours of tape may be imperative to your investigation results.

5. After getting your cameras placed, you will need to set up the rest of the equipment. I recommend using Tri-Field Natural EM Meters, which can be used as stationary monitors of energy disruptions in a room. By pointing one of your cameras (and/or sound recording equipment) in the direction of the meters, you can see any changes that might occur in the location.

You should also consider using a temperature and humidity gauge that can be monitored on camera too. During any investigation, the ghost hunter needs to make note of the temperature of the location and if possible, the humidity levels. Both readings may have an effect on the outcome of photos, video and monitoring. As any sudden drops in temperature may signal the presence of something anomalous, this might be vital to the experiment's result.

I also recommend the use of infrared motion detectors as well. These units have more than one benefit. By monitoring the infrared spectrum of the location, it's possible that the units might pick up something that is unseen by the human eye. On more than one occasion in the past, ghost hunters have reported inexplicable alarms from these units, even when there was nothing to see. Later, they were surprised to find strange images had appeared in their photos or on video. They also sometimes noted corresponding readings with their detection equipment. In addition, the units can be used to monitor the area for living persons, effectively sealing the area from entry. This is very important when fraud is suspected or when conducting a "ghost watch" experiment where none of the investigators are in the immediate area.

This brings us to the main benefit of this type of experiment. By sealing off the area to everyone and monitoring it from a remote location, the investigator has effectively ruled out a source of activity that could be mistaken for paranormal. As most of us know, the human body does emit its share of electromagnetic energy and this could have an effect on the more sensitive meters, including motion detectors and the Natural EM Meter. Also, since no one will be moving through the area, we have a perfect opportunity to monitor an area without human movement. We have then eliminated not only small temperature changes caused by the human body, but we have also eliminated the chance for minute dust particles to be blown into the air. That means that any anomalies that appear on the film from that location have a much better chance of being paranormal.

In many cases though, this type of "ghost watch" may not be practical. Not all ghost hunters are as fully equipped as this method requires and not all home owners are as agreeable as this process would need them to be. Some witnesses are happy to have you at the location, but not in such an invasive manner. As we are always required to honor the wishes of the location owner, we have to adapt our investigations to suit their mood and desires.

For this reason, another method of the "ghost watch" is most often used and I always recommend it to researchers with a more limited budget. In my experience, a "ghost watch" is an essential part of every investigation, or at least those investigations where natural and artificial explanations have been ruled out. If you have managed to get that far with your research, then being present and "waiting for something to happen" should always be the next step. And even if you don't have the funds and equipment for the first type of "ghost watch", you can easily handle the second.

This method can be just as important to the overall investigation and while you will still want to record as much of the event as possible, usually one video camera (or at the most, two) will do the trick. This method depends more on the alertness and common sense of the ghost hunter than on high-tech equipment. Since it does not involve completely sealing off portions of the house, it is usually more palatable to the home owner too. Here are some details on how best to handle this:

1. As with the previous system, seek out an area of the house / location that you want to monitor. The good news is that this does not have to be a single room, hallway or staircase. Because the monitoring here is done more by man than machine, the investigation team can actually be scattered throughout the location. In this way, you can observe almost the entire house and perhaps even everyone who is in it. By stationing the group in different rooms, the team is in perhaps a better position than any other to decide if the case is genuine or not.

By doing this, you may actually be able to authenticate much more. In the case that I was involved in with a human agent poltergeist (detailed in Chapter 3), the family was experiencing what appeared to be a poltergeist outbreak that was centered around a young woman in the family. During the evening investigations, the team was stationed downstairs, interviewing the family, and we heard movement coming from the second floor. No one was on that floor at the time. Also, at one point, we heard the rapid slamming of cabinet doors in the kitchen, which was the room adjacent to where we were conducting the interviews. I immediately checked the room and while I found that it was empty (and was able to determine the doors had moved without physical assistance), imagine what we would have discovered if one of the other team members had been stationed in the room during a "ghost watch"?

2. If possible, it can't hurt for each of the team members to have their own video camera to record anything (supernatural or otherwise) that might occur in their designated area. If this is not possible though, it is imperative that the team member keep track of everything that occurs, and everyone who enters, their portion of the house. If it cannot be video taped, then they must make a written or tape-recorded note of what happens. In this way, you will know the exact whereabouts of everyone should anything occur during the experiment.

3. In spite of the fact that sitting around and waiting for something to happen can be excruciatingly boring over a long period of time, the researcher must stay alert and be prepared for anything. For this reason (if no other), I suggest that team leaders carefully choose group members for investigations. If you know a member is prone to falling asleep, or becomes easily bored, they may not be your best choice to take part in this kind of experiment. For those team members who are videotaping their area, they should keep the camera running at all times. If using night vision technology, I suggest monitoring the camera screen for anything not visible to the human eye. (Because this will more rapidly drain the camera battery, consider plugging in to a nearby power source, if possible). Those members who are monitoring their areas visually should also remain on high alert and should keep their still camera available at all times. They should also keep a notebook and pen, a tape recorder, and any other ghost hunting equipment close at hand. As I have learned the hard way in the past, you never know when something remarkable might happen.

This type of experiment might last for hours, or it might last all night. Obviously, there is a very good chance that nothing out of the ordinary will happen but you have to be prepared for it if it does. Team members should be sure to have a good supply of "energy drink" along with them, be it coffee or their favorite soda. It is bound to be a long night and a largely uneventful one.

It is also recommend that one of the team members (a designated leader) check in with the other investigators on a regular basis. This person can provide not only assistance, but perhaps extra film, batteries, refreshments or even encouragement when needed. This can keep the investigators on their toes and wide awake during a lengthy investigation.

I always feel that a designated leader is important to any investigation, and not just so that everyone stays awake. This person can coordinate the investigation, dealing with the owners and planning when everyone should arrive and who should be in charge of what task. This person becomes doubly important during a "ghost watch" because the team has to be properly organized for the experiment to have the most benefit.

There are some other things worth thinking about too, no matter what type of "ghost watch" that you decide to experiment with. These are simply some odds and ends and items that are worth keeping in mind:

1. If a "ghost watch" is worth doing once, then it is worth repeating. To get the point where one of these methods becomes worthwhile, you should be reasonably sure that something is taking place at the location that you cannot explain away as ordinary. Just remember that you should not be disappointed if nothing happens on the first investigation. This is why I always insist on follow-up research at presumably haunted spots. It's likely that your vigilance and persistence will pay off with something in the end. Even if it doesn't though, you will have managed to establish a good pattern for future experiments. Or at the very least, you have done as I have often done --- you have established what not to do the next time.

2. As part of the standard investigation, I always recommend that the team members prepare a diagram of the location on which they can mark questionable areas and spots where they may have picked up anomalies of any sort. These diagrams are especially important during a "ghost watch" and a map of this type can be used to mark designated areas for team members as well as any odd happenings.

3. You will need to decide what the investigators should be doing in their designated areas. For the method one "ghost watch", the area is sealed off and there are no investigators present in the monitored location. However, in the second method, the researchers are literally interacting with the location. There has been much debate as to what works better --- silence or normal behavior. Opinions vary on this and I feel that it really depends on the location itself. In a place where sounds carry in unusual ways (like an old theater), it is probably best that the investigators remain completely silent, or as much so as possible. On other occasions, they might be able to behave normally and quietly in whatever area has been designated to them.

Keep in mind though (especially if you are a leader of an investigation team), your group members will remain much more alert and ready if they are allowed to move about to some extent and behave normally. Working under conditions of silence, and sitting still for hours at a time, can be exhausting. This can lead to errors in observation and leave the investigators stressed out and irritable, which are not the best conditions for a well carried out investigation. A compromise that I might suggest would be to alternate the periods of silence and restricted movement with periods of more normal behavior. You will find that your "ghost watch" can continue much longer this way.

4. Another element to keep in mind during your "ghost watch" is the lighting of the location. While working with the first type of experiment, which depends mainly on the use of cameras and equipment, you may consider working in near or total darkness. This may increase the activity and also increase your chances of recording it. Many ghost

hunters prefer to work this way and it can be useful in situations where no one will be walking or moving around in the monitored areas. There are no concerns of anyone being injured in the dark and your infrared cameras should be able to pick up any anomalous activity, as well as being able to still check the read outs on the equipment that is also under observation.

Obviously, in the other type of "ghost watch", total darkness is not always practical. In the past, I have experimented in both darkness and in low light. While conducting investigations inside of private homes, I have found low lighting to be the preferred method. By keeping the lights low, the investigators will be able to see but their vision (and any photographs that are taken) will not be affected by glare from harsh or too much lighting.

Low lighting is also of assistance in avoiding unwanted attention to your investigation. By having all of the lights turned off and on at a location and having flashlights bouncing around and moving past the windows, the investigation could attract the attention of the neighbors or in the worst case, the police. You can understand how this might look suspicious to someone passing by and this is yet another reason to suggest that the lights remain on but at a discreet level.

Finally, let me make one last mention of a type of "ghost watch" that has not been talked about here so far. This type of "ghost watch" differs from the others because it is designed to be used during a reported poltergeist outbreak. In a situation like this, the investigator has to quickly decide if the reported events are connected to actual ghosts or to one of the people residing in the house. To reach this point, a lot of interviewing and investigation has to be done. If the case is an active one, it is very possible that sounds might occur or physical items might be moved while the investigators are present.

In a situation like this, your "ghost watch" skills become very important. It is essential that team members are stationed throughout the house and that cameras and recording devices are running constantly. In this way, you have the best chance of actually documenting the activity. The most important thing to remember (whether you suspect the case is genuine or a hoax) is to keep the family members under constant observation. Remember the incident with the cabinet doors that I referred to in that earlier chapter? In that case, it was a partial failure because I had not stationed a team member in the kitchen where the event occurred. On the other hand, since everyone in the house was in the living room with me, I was convinced that no living hands had moved those doors. By keeping track of the movements of everyone present, you can actually authenticate the events that occur.

However, keeping the family under constant watch does present some problems. Since you do not want to seem like a kidnapper who is holding a group of hostages, you have to be subtle about how you do this. If the homeowners feel that you don't trust them or that you think they are faking the whole thing, then they are likely to become offended and ask you to leave. This is where your repartee with the witnesses comes into play and why every ghost hunter has to have some amount of "people skills", or they should not be dealing with the witnesses.

Rather than herd them into a group and stand over them, you should try and engage the family in conversation or explain to them that they should not move around too much with the idea that it might interfere with your testing equipment. Since people don't move around as much when you are talking or interacting with them, I suggest getting them to talk about their interests, school, their jobs, whatever it takes. You might also consider allowing them to "help" with the investigation, keeping notes or making diagrams --- anything that will keep them busy.

If for some reason the "haunting" turns about to be a hoax, this is your best chance of finding that out. There have been many cases that start out with great promise and eventually are revealed to be the antics of an adolescent in the house whose playful pranks went just a bit too far. Although it may be the hardest thing that you have to do, revealing to the parents that you have a video clip of the prankster at work will certainly cure all of the fears that they had of their house being haunted. And if the phenomenon does turn out to be real, then your hours of "ghost watching" have certainly paid off!

With all of that in mind, I hope that you can take at least a portion of this section and put it to use. I have long been of the belief that the "ghost watch" is one of the most important parts to any investigation and one of the methods of research that both amateurs and experienced veterans can most easily put to use.

EXAMINING THE HOUSE

As has been often stated, it is best to approach each investigation with the idea that the reported phenomenon has a natural cause, rather than a supernatural one. Such care will provide you with the best results because "true" haunted houses are rare and elusive creatures. Most ghost hunters learn this by trial and error, discovering that many people who feel their houses are haunted are merely misinterpreting normal sounds for unnatural phenomena.

One of your main jobs is to check out the allegedly haunted house to see whether there are leaky or rattling pipes that could be causing strange noises. Electrical problems, plumbing, weather conditions outside and a variety of other natural occurrences can sometimes convince a property owner that they are being haunted. The investigator however, can often quickly learn the truth.

For instance, if the "ghostly noises" in the house seem to always occur at the same time each night, this usually means they have a natural cause. A few years ago, I investigated a house where the owners reported the sounds of "phantom footsteps" in the house every night around 9:30 pm. After listening to the family's spine-chilling accounts of the ghost, I actually heard the footsteps myself. It wasn't until the next night when we realized that the footsteps corresponded to the same time when the youngest daughter in the family went to bed.

Each night, around 9:30, she flushed a toilet in the downstairs bathroom and this caused the pipes beneath the floor in the "haunted" hallway to rattle, just as though an unseen figure was walking down the corridor. Water pipes can play other tricks as well. In fact, even water pressure in a kitchen faucet can seem like a ghost. The water pressure can build up to the point that the faucet begins to seep water, as though it was turned on by itself.

Faulty electrical work can also cause all sorts of seemingly bizarre manifestations, from tapping inside of the walls to light switches that turn on and off. I once investigated a house where electrical outlets, lights and appliances turned on and off and behaved erratically. A quick check of the electrical box in the basement revealed (even to a non-professional like myself) that the fuse box had been installed in the house in 1926 and had not been updated. Besides being a fire hazard, it was also determined to be the cause of the supernatural events.

As in this case, most houses where only electrical disturbances are reported will usually have a normal explanation for the odd happenings. You may want to recommend that the family call in a good electrician rather than a ghost hunter. Be careful though. Sometimes electrical and otherwise normal disturbances can actually be the first sign that poltergeist-like phenomena is about to begin. There could be more here than meets the eye, so remain open-minded about the location.

Checking into the house should not stop there either. Other questions should be addressed. What kind of soil was the house built on? Are there any underground rivers or water sources nearby? Could there be caves, tunnels or even mine shafts beneath the house? All of these answers make up the geological aspects of the property. They can show if the house might shift on its foundation, making noises occur or making objects move about. Imagine that the homeowners tell you that the phenomenon normally occurs after a rainstorm. If so, you might check to see how much clay or chalk is present in the soil. As this kind of soil settles after a storm, it can put stress on the house, causing it to creak and shift. Needless to say, these sounds and happenings could certainly make even a reasonable person believe the house was haunted.

EQUIPMENT FAILURES

The annals of paranormal research are filled with accounts and incidents of equipment failing at crucial times during the investigation. Many readers may have had this happen to them and I can certainly tell you that it has occurred during my own research on several occasions. The stories usually recount flashlights mysteriously turning off, cameras failing and most especially, batteries being mysteriously drained without explanation. In many cases, the failures seemed to be strangely "cured" several hours (or even minutes) later or when the equipment is tested again away from the location.

During one investigation that I conducted at an old jail, former employees took me down to the basement. Each of them had experienced strange and ghostly happenings in an area referred to as the "hole". This narrow punishment cell was reserved for prisoners who had broken the rules of the jail and many of the men were caged here, in total darkness, for sometimes days at a time. Since the jail had closed, there had been a number of accounts of screams, crying and moaning coming from inside the cell. With a flashlight in one hand and a video camera in the other, I climbed down several stone steps and entered the dark cell. Moments later, the flashlight blinked out and the video camera inexplicably shut down. Startled and plunged into complete darkness, I fumbled for the door and back up the stairs I had just descended. Almost as soon as I left the staircase, the flashlight came back to life. When I tried the video camera, I found that it too was functioning again. How or why this had happened I didn't know, but theory suggests that the energy enclosed in the cell had somehow affected the equipment that I was carrying.

In this same way, many feel that ghosts (or at least paranormal energy) can have an effect on the equipment that we use in our investigations. There have also been reported cases when batteries have drained completely and no longer function at all. For this reason, I always recommend that investigators carry extra batteries for all of their equipment in their "ghost hunter's kit".

Of course, not all of the failures of equipment are due to paranormal energy. I always suggest that investigators check all of the equipment before arriving at the investigation site. You may even want to leave the equipment running one evening as a trial, just to see how long the batteries last. That way, there are no surprises later on.

AFRAID OF GHOSTS?

As mentioned already, paranormal events can range from slightly spooky phenomena, such as knocks and footsteps, all the way up to furniture being moved about and full-blown ghost appearances. Any of these things can happen during an investigation and under these circumstances, all that the ghost hunter can do is react as professionally as possible.

When things do happen during an investigation, it is essential that the researchers remain calm and try to be as objective as possible. Obviously, this isn't easy but the ghost hunter should try to verify just what it is he is hearing or seeing and, when possible, take notes. Even though a video camera or tape machine will hopefully be operating, it is important that the researcher be sure that his own thoughts and feelings are recorded. However, it's not a good idea to simply shout "what the hell is that?". In order to avoid some hint of group hallucination, it is important not to lead the other witnesses who are present with even a small description of the phenomena that is being encountered. One technique that has been suggested during an outbreak of activity is to simply state that you are "experiencing something". If anyone else is also experiencing anything, they are to write it down. Afterwards, the written statements can be collected and compared with one another.

Of course, this is the ideal way of operating but rarely does anyone know just how they might react in the heat of an active investigation. This is where we begin to talk about what might happen when the witness (or the investigators) becomes frightened during the course of the investigation.

In many cases, the witnesses at the location do become frightened about the activity that might be occurring and have been known to occasionally call a halt to the proceedings. They may have called in ghost hunters to help decide whether the phenomena taking place at the location is genuine or not. As soon as they see that something strange is happening, and that others are seeing it too, they may want to end the investigation. This often happens because the location owner is afraid that by prolonging the investigation, they might make the ghosts "angry" or "upset". It is quite common for them to change their view and decide that they want to leave it alone or that they want to get rid of the phenomena and refrain from making things worse. When this happens, the ghost hunter must go along with the owner's wishes.

In some cases, the researcher might be able to reach a compromise with the owner. He might consider asking to continue his research on the condition that he helps to find someone who might be able to get rid of the ghost. This is usually an ideal compromise, but it might not always be possible. No matter what you decide to do, the wishes of the location owner or witness must be of the utmost importance.

A researcher will also find that the fear threshold for members of his team is bound to vary. Thanks to the fact that a team member is drawn to investigate this sort of thing in the first place, he is likely to not be afraid at the first sign of anything unusual. However, intense activity can have a remarkable effect on a person that you might have once thought was a solid and fearless investigator. In my own experience, I have had fellow researchers who have actually dropped out of the team and stopped ghost hunting altogether after being involved with a case they found especially frightening. Different people will respond to things in different ways.

There have been many cases where ghost hunters have screamed, wept or have run in fear from a location because they are afraid. There is no way to know how a person might react in a specific situation. You might even find yourself the member of the team who becomes inexplicably unnerved by an experience that you thought would never bother you. Personally, I can't count the number of times when I have had the hair raise on the back of my neck or when I have shuddered because of some weird encounter. A time or two, I have stopped investigations short because of some element of fear that I could not easily explain. It's easy for us to rationalize everything and say that "ghosts can't hurt us" or that "there's nothing to be afraid of" but sometimes the energy of the location may affect us in a way that we could not have imagined.

If this does happen to you, try to remain calm. Your fear will quickly spread to other members of the team and will possibly ruin the investigation. It is best to segregate yourself from the group (and especially from the location owner) until the feeling passes. If it does not pass, you may want to consider sitting this one out. If another member of the team becomes frightened, take this person aside and get them away from the others present. As stated, fear is contagious and anyone who asks to be removed from an investigation should step out immediately.

INTERVIEWING THE WITNESS

Interviewing a witness may be the hardest thing that you have to do during an investigation. As any law enforcement officer will tell you, two witnesses rarely see the same incident in the exact same way. Paranormal investigators run into the same situation but in a different manner. In paranormal cases, a witness will see and hear something totally alien to them, something frightening and something they don't understand. This makes our job even tougher. A witness should be handled in a careful and deliberate manner. They have to be made to feel comfortable with the investigation and the entire situation. The paranormal may seem like "old hat" to us, but it is something completely bizarre to the ordinary person.

The following are some hints and tips that will help you through a proper interview with a witness. These are some things to watch out for:

1. Check all of the details of the account with the witness and make sure that all of the outside facts are in order and not just their immediate encounter. If they recall that

it was snowing that night, check the weather conditions and see, because if it wasn't, that might not be the only problem with their memory.

2. Attempt to recreate the events if possible. Place each witness in the same position they were in when the encounter occurred. If they reported a strange noise, try to recreate that noise by natural means and make sure the normal possibilities are ruled out.

3. Try to get a full and complete report of everything that happened. This might be important later as the mind tends to forget slight details as time goes by.

At this point, let's suppose that you have followed all of the rules of investigation and the case seems genuine. It appears that the witness statement holds up to scrutiny, but does it really?

I can't stress how important it is to be careful when assessing this testimony. Being careful is the best way to discover what really happened. You have to make sure that you are objective when writing up your report. Don't let yourself be influenced by information that you may have run across in other cases, or while reading.

Your assessment of the witness testimony may be imperative to the case. Is the witness believable? If you have any doubts about what may have happened, you need to rule those out while you are at the location.

The following is a list of testimonial problems that can occur with the witness and again, some other things that you need to watch out for when conducting an interview:

1. A witness may be totally unaware of how some phenomena may occur. Check into the details! There may be something natural about the house that is causing the lights to go on and off or something like nearby train tracks that could be causing things to move about.

2. Eyewitness testimony is not always what actually happened --- but what the witness believes to have happened. It is good to find out ahead of time if the witness is already "sure" the house is "haunted" or not. This kind of thinking can easily color their testimony.

3. A witness can be influenced by information you give them. Be careful about what you say before the interview. Even joking about paranormal events can be bad. You could laugh and say "that sounds like the Amityville Horror" and the next thing you know, the witness is reporting blood coming from the walls! Don't laugh about this one, it happens.

4. The witness may be mentally unstable. This also happens, and more frequently than we would care to admit. I have been called to houses where the residents are just plain "nuts". Obviously, we are not health care workers, so there is little we can do in this situation but try to extricate ourselves from the predicament as politely as possible.

5. The witness may deliberately fabricate events. This is a two-fold problem. On one

hand you have a person who has made the whole thing up and on the other, a person who actually had a real experience, but can't recall all of the details, so they have "filled in the blanks" with less honest information. Don't let yourself get pulled in by this. It is easy to allow this to occur and it happens to the best investigators sometimes. Following through on a case like this could be disastrous for your reputation. You have to learn when to tell if someone is lying. It will become identifiable by asking pointed and direct questions about the events.

QUESTIONS TO ASK THE WITNESS

The following list will certainly not contain every question that you should ask a witness, but I think it will give you a good starting spot to add your own and to subtract those that may not really fit the particular investigation you are conducting. You will want to add any questions that are pertinent to your case and then you can customize your own questionnaire.

Before getting started with the list of questions, let the witness tell the entire story as they remember it. Then, start asking your questions and you will notice that more details will start to emerge from the story. After that, try recreating the events in the locations where they occurred.

Also, before working your way through your list of questions, I would advise apologizing in advance for the intrusive (and sometimes even offensive) nature of the questions that you will be asking. Explain that while many of them may not seem relevant, they have to be asked. By having a complete picture of the person's experiences and beliefs, you will be able to have a complete documentation of the case. Remember to stress that the answers they give you are completely confidential. This may help them to be more forthcoming with their information.

1. How was the phenomenon experienced? Were you alone at the time? Were others present? How many people saw the event?

2. If the phenomenon was visual -- did it move or was it stationary?

3. How would you describe the visual phenomena? Was it a shadow? Was it light? Was it a recognizable form? Did it seem to have any form at all?

4. If it was sound phenomena --- how would you describe it? Was it quiet or loud? Was it a sound that you recognized?

5. How would you describe the phenomena in general? Did you feel frightened by it? Disturbed? At ease?

6. Was there a smell involved with the phenomena? If so, how would you describe it? Strong or faint? Did you recognize the smell?

7. If there was a sensation of touch, how would you describe it? Was it slight or strong? Was it violent? What sort of feeling did it give you?

8. How would you describe the encounter as an experience? Did you sense that you were being watched? Did you sense a presence close by?

9. If any physical objects were moved --- did you see it happen directly? Did you see movements of objects, or anything else, out of the corner of your eye?

10. Have you had any problems with electrical items? If so, describe them and where

are they located? How are they located in conjunction with your encounter? Was there any disturbance of electrical items during your encounter?

11. What was your mood prior to the encounter? What was your state of mind? How were you feeling physically?

12. What activity were you involved in at the time of the encounter?

These questions are used to determine the background and the belief systems of the witness. They may be telling if there comes up a question about any of the information gathered from the witness.

1. Do you believe that ghosts and other paranormal entities exist?
2. Did you believe in them before your encounter?
3. Do you ever visit allegedly haunted location in groups or alone?
4. Are you actively involved in a church or a religion?
5. Do you agree with most of the teachings of your religion?
6. How does your church feel about ghosts and the paranormal?
7. Do you believe that angels have contact with people on earth?
8. Does your family believe in the existence of ghosts?
9. Do you have any knowledge about ghosts and the paranormal?
10. Where does that knowledge come from? (books, TV...etc?)
11. Did you believe this location was haunted before your experience?
12. Has a member of your family recently died?
13. Are you currently taking any medication?
14. Have you been treated recently for any serious illnesses?
15. Were you drinking any alcohol near the time of your experience?
16. Have you been treated for any mental illness?
17. Do you believe that ghosts are real?
18. Do you believe that people can influence mind over matter?
19. Do you believe that people can effect their health through positive thought?
20. Have you ever experienced "deja vu"?
21. Have you ever dreamed of events before they happened?
22. Have you ever had a "near death experience"?
23. Do you believe that other people's paranormal experiences are real?
24. Have you ever been involved in a religion that "speaks in tongues"?
25. Do you believe in reincarnation?
26. Have you ever used a Ouija Board?
27. If so, have you ever used the board in this location?
28. Have you ever experimented with witchcraft or black magic?
29. Do you believe that UFO's are a possibility?
30. What was the time and exact location of your encounter?
31. What were the weather conditions at the time of the event?
32. Overall, how has this experience left you feeling? Scared? Confused? Interested in learning more?

After asking these questions, the investigator should make any related notes about the answers the witness gave and ask them if they can recall any other details about the experience. They probably would have given you those details while you were asking the questions, but it never hurts to inquire.

I also should mention again that it is imperative to record this entire interview and to have one of the other investigators, not the main interviewer, marking replies to the questions in a separate notebook. This gives you several accounts that can be corroborated.

AFTER THE INVESTIGATION: RESEARCHING THE LOCATION

The purpose of this section of the book is not to explain how you can tell if the house is haunted but to assist you in one of the most important parts of the investigation -- finding out why the house is haunted and who might be haunting it. At this point, you will have already determined that what you have is a genuine case and not a residual haunting or even a case of jangled nerves or an overactive imagination. You will have taken all of the precautions to insure that the phenomena is authentic. You may have found that your photographs have come back with strange images on them or your EMF and temperature scans may have picked up strange anomalies. You have done everything that you can to prove the house is NOT haunted -- and yet it seems to be. Your next step is to find out why.

Unfortunately, this is something that all of the technology and gadgets in the world cannot accomplish. I have often been asked whether or not I believe that modern technology has influenced the belief systems of the non-believer or not. Do the gadgets, cameras and sensitive meters actually convince skeptics that ghosts really exist? Honestly, I don't think that technology has done all that much for the non-believers, other than to convince them that a lot of people don't know how to use cameras correctly. Technology has really done more for those who already believe than for anyone else. Unfortunately, so many things can go wrong with these meters and cameras that many mistake their readings and their mysterious "orbs" for ghosts -- when they are actually not. Don't get me wrong, I think technology certainly has its uses but I think that many ghost hunters are ignoring the skills that they really need in favor of "gee whiz" gadgets.

Technology is unlikely to ever "prove" that ghosts exist. The only way that we can do that is through history. In other words, find a house that the current occupants allege to be haunted. Then contact past owners of the house and in a perfect situation, they can tell you the exact same things were happening in the house that the current owners claim -- even though these people have never met, do not know one another and have not compared stories. How can we dismiss such claims?

But to make and research these claims, this is where ghost hunting becomes even more like detective work. You have eliminated the impossible and it seems the house you are investigating is truly haunted. This is where historical research comes into play. The following is a how-to list or guide for finding out the history of a house or building. If you are researching a public building, your job just got easier. Many public buildings, including famous homes in your region, will often be mentioned in local history books.

Even some of the strange events of the past (including ghostly ones) might be mentioned.

Sometimes however, the owners or the curators of the place will give you some resistance about ghosts unless they called you in to investigate in the first place. This is to be expected, but don't let it deter you in your research. As long as the material has been presented as public record (newspaper articles, magazines... etc.) you are welcome to read and write about it if you like.

But let's get back to the history of the haunted house we are investigating.

All houses, just like people, have a past. You may find clues to what you are looking for right under your nose -- like a child's growth chart that is hidden under layers of paint or wallpaper or even initials that are carved into a tree in the front yard. And you don't even need an old house to make fascinating discoveries. Even new housing developments have a past. Think of the horror movies that we have all seen about houses that have been built on old cemeteries and then remember that stories like these are not just for the movies. As mentioned, local legends, as well as land records, will often help to uncover a compelling story.

All you need to get started is a little direction and a few tools -- sturdy notebook, a sharpened pencil, a magnifying glass for examining documents, a lot of curiosity and plenty of energy. Searching through the past can be a tiring job but well worth the time and effort.

Start off easy and check out what the current occupants know about the house's history. Be prepared for some inaccurate information though. There is a chance that the occupants, unnerved by the strange activity that is taking place, could shadow their information in a suggestive way. You should also find out if there are any neighbors who may have been in the area for a long time. This is often a great source. The little old lady who has lived down the street for fifty years will remember many of the former occupants of the property. These local residents may also know if there is any local folklore about the place. This type of information is rarely scientific and usually only partially accurate, but don't discount it totally. Folklore can often point the researcher in the right direction, although sometimes by a meandering path.

The next step should be checking to see if anyone else has ever traced the history of the house in question. Each state has a State Historic Preservation Officer who nominates structures that are "significant in American history, architecture, archaeology, engineering and culture" and then gets them listed on the National Register of Historic Places. You can get a list of historic buildings in your state by visiting the State Historic Preservation Office.

There are other places to look too. The Historic American Buildings Survey and the Historic American Engineering Record have documented more than 37,000 historic structures and sites since 1993. Their reports contain measured drawings, photographs and historical information, which is a wealth of knowledge for any ghost researcher who is lucky enough to find the house he is checking out included in the survey. The data is available on microfilm and at the Library of Congress.

You also might find a history of the house at the local library or at the local newspaper. Many newspapers have a research division, but they will also charge exorbitant prices for assisting you.

LAND DEEDS & DIRECTORIES: In most cases though, especially with "ordinary" homes that are not historic locations, you will likely need to start your research from scratch. You should begin by locating the land records in your area and dig in. If you have ever done any genealogical research, you will find that researching a house is much the same process -- starting with the present and then working backward. The best place to find the house's history is through the land deed, which can be traced from the current owner to the first owner of the site. Deeds record the transfer of ownership from a grantor (seller) to the grantee (buyer) and will give you the grantor's name, marital status and address (usually only the town and state); the grantee's name and address; price of the property; and a property description. Sometimes the deed will also list restrictions for the property, such as a ban on chicken or pig farms, sale of alcohol on the premises and in older records, even a ban against property buyers of a certain race or religion.

Deeds can make for both invaluable resources and even fascinating reading. Keep in mind though that deeds record ownership of the land, not of the houses. Most deeds don't even mention the buildings on the property and you will have to use the price of the property to guess whether or not it was vacant at the time of the sale. Also remember that just because someone's name does not appear on the deed does not mean that he did not live there. The house might have been rented out and only by tracking down other listings will you be able to see who actually lived in the house.

In order to do this, try checking through what most towns call city directories. They are books that collect the names, addresses and occupations of the people who lived in a city during a certain year. They usually also offer a "reverse" directory , which will allow you to look up the address of the house and then find out the owner of the property, instead of the other way around. This is an excellent way to find out the owner / occupant of the house for each successive year to the time that it was built. City directories are a great reference for ghost hunters and genealogists alike. You can find out from the directory who the former occupants of the house were. What were their names? How long did they live there? Be sure to make copies of whatever documents you discover, so that you can refer back to them later. If you can't make photocopies, take the time to write everything down. Place each new piece of information on a timeline so that you will have an outline of whatever you find.

One research complication that you might encounter is a change in a street name or the house's street number. Don't worry though -- when these changes were made, maps and directories usually included the old and new numbers for the next year or two. Just be sure to write down all of the street names and numbers for future reference.

Once you have a detailed timeline from the city directory, you'll have a listing of those who lived in the house and an idea of how long they resided there. Using this list, you will have an idea of who the most recent occupants of the house were and whether or not they are still living. If possible, consider sending a letter that requests information about any strange events that occurred in the house. It is not a good idea to call them but you should be sure that your letter (which should be as professional-sounding as possible) contains your telephone number. In most cases, the former residents are going to be uncooperative and it is rare to get a letter or call in reply. If they did not experience anything out of the ordinary, they are probably not going to feel the need to tell you that. However, if they also experienced the haunting that is reported by the current occupants, you may hear from them. If they can verify the strange happenings and will state that they also occurred during their occupancy, then you have an excellent record of a genuine haunted house -- and what constitutes historical "proof" of the ghosts. Unfortunately though, the previous family may have actually moved out of the house because of the strange things that were going on and may not want to talk to you about them.

Even if you are unable to speak with the former residents, your timeline and list of occupants will continue to serve you well. Start by checking the local obituaries for the people who once lived in the place. Libraries will often have a directory for obituaries and what date they appeared in the newspaper. Often, Genealogical and Historical societies will also keep copies of obituaries or at least may have a record of when they appeared in a newspaper. Once you find the obituary, try to find out how the person connected to it died. If the death was eventful in any way, there will also likely be a story in the general section of the newspaper for that day as well. As ghost hunters are aware, murders, suicides and traumatic deaths can certainly lead to a house becoming haunted.

Also, if the death involved a murder, suicide, or was under other questionable circumstances, then there was undoubtedly a police report filed about it. In this case, you are also in luck as police and coroner's reports are public record and can be obtained by anyone. In most cases, there may be a small fee involved and likely you will have to wait for a short period of time to get a copy of the reports but you can get them.

CLUES & DOCUMENTS: In addition to city directories and telephone books, there are other records that can provide interesting details about the house and can assist you in developing a complete portrait.

Architectural drawings: A great source of information about the history of the house can be the builder's plans, although they can often be hard to come by. Some builders (especially with older homes) may have just kept the plans in their heads and modified them when needed. The best place to find them though is in the house itself. Homeowners often kept the plans in the attic, basement of tucked away in a closet somewhere. If your research leads you to past occupants of the house, they might have accidentally taken the plans with them. Sometimes tracking down the heirs or descendants of the former occupants will help to find the drawings. You can also check with the state historical society and see if they have a drawing of the house or would know who to contact to get one. Many archives collect plans of architecturally significant buildings or those drawn by noteworthy architects. You might also consider looking in a book of house plans if all else fails. Many older homes were modeled from basic plans.

Maps: No house history research is complete without checking out the maps of the neighborhood. As you move backward through records and property changes, a map of the area will help to keep you oriented. Ask the Register of Deeds (or a related office) for maps that cover the neighborhood, such as surveys that were conducted when roads were widened or moved. In any older town, the roads were changed (especially in residential neighborhoods) at least once to accommodate the coming of automobiles, as opposed to the horse and buggy. The house you are researching may appear as a small dot on the map or may be complete with details on a fire insurance map. It simply depends on what type of map you find.

A great resource is a plat map. When a piece of land is subdivided into streets, blocks or lots, this information gets recorded on a plat map. Originally, these maps were hand-drawn and contained only a few details. Printed maps usually show streets, significant buildings and houses and rural maps will show who owned what plots of land, cemeteries and much more. Plat maps can be found at the office where deeds are filed or usually at the local library.

Many researchers also turn to birds-eye view maps, which are panoramic scenes of cities and towns that show buildings, trees and homes from an overhead vantage point. Thousands of them were created for cities all over America between 1850 and 1900 but they show few details and while striking and beautiful, are only of assistance when dealing with well-known or highly visible locations.

Another type of map, which is quiet useful but only if you location happens to be listed on one, is a Sanborn Map. Beginning in the 1860's, the Sanborn Fire Insurance Co. created maps to assess the fire hazard of buildings. The maps list construction details, such as windows and doors, and depict the size and shape of the insured structures. They also detail property boundaries and usage for about 12,000 cities and towns in the United States. Check with your local library to see if these types of maps are available in your area.

Biographical Encyclopedias: If the people who lived in the house you are researching were notable in the community, then they may be listed in the county or city biographical encyclopedia. These books were created for communities around 1870 to 1905 and list the accomplishments of local businessmen, bankers and pioneers. Many of them will also contain a portrait of the individual. Again, they are a great resource if you are lucky enough for the occupants of the house you are researching to be listed.

Building Permits: Generally, before owners can make any major changes to their home, they need to obtain a permit from the town's building department, which may also be called the planning department or code enforcement. These permits record the vital statistics of the home from number of bathrooms to bedrooms, porches, window locations and more. Permits also include the names of the homeowners, when the work was done and the contractors for the job. The information contained in a permit could play an important role in your research and provide clues to hidden aspects of the house, such as the location of former doors or windows -- prime suspects when occupants report unexplained chills and drafts.

Photographs: A wonderful addition to your research would be a vintage photo of the house. You can often find photo files at local historical societies, libraries and newspapers. Search under the name of a previous owner or the street address. You might also contact local real estate agencies to see if they have any photos of the house on file. When you visit a library or historical society, it's always a good idea to bring a current photo of the house with you. It might jog someone's memory and you can also use the photo for reference when looking through books of house styles.

THE STYLE OF THE HOUSE: Another element of the house's history is the style -- from Tudor, to Cape Cod, Victorian or even a combination of several. Like clothing styles, architectural styles in America are often changing and reflect both ethnic and immigrant influences. Many early New Englanders built two-story dwellings with over-hanging upper floors because that was the style in England of the day. In an entirely different part of the country, the American Southwest, you'll find many homes that reflect the Spanish influences on traditional Native American adobe dwellings. In the Midwest, you'll find scores of ranch-style homes that were modeled after the Prairie style homes of the early 1900's.

To discover the style of your house, you'll need to make note of both the exterior and the interior details and then consult a guide like *A Field Guide to American Houses*. Check out the details like molding, window framing and interior trim. Colonial homes, for instance, have wide floorboards and were put together with hand-forged, square nails, which makes these homes quite easily identified.

But don't be surprised if you think you have nailed down the style of the house you are investigating and then find some inconsistencies. The style of a home can change as owners update and add on and finding old photos of the place can help you trace the progression of the house's style.

Here are some basic types of American homes:

Cape Cod: This is a style of Colonial Revival architecture, which expressed a renewed interest in America's colonial past in the 1800's and early to middle 1900's. The Cape Cod's style history goes back to the British colonists who arrived in America in the late 17th century. They used half-timbered English houses with a hall and parlor as a model, and adapted it to New England's stormy weather and natural resources. Over the course of a few generations, a modest, one- to one-and-a-half-story house with wooden shut-ters emerged. In the 1930s, when the trend was for small, economical, and mass-pro-duced houses, Cape Cod style homes became popular throughout the United States. In the twentieth century version of the style, the chimneys were often placed at the side rather than the center and the shutters were strictly decorative.

Federal Style: Federal (or Georgian) style became popular in New England and in the southern states as early as the 1700's. Stately and symmetrical, these homes imitated the larger, more elaborate Georgian homes, which were being built in England. Both Georgian and Federal styles have square, symmetrical shapes and centered doorways that often have decorative crowns. The houses also usually have paired chimneys and medium-pitched roofs. Most homes of this type are made from brick. The only main dif-ference between the two is that Georgian style homes are always square and straight, while Federal homes will often have curves and decorative flourishes.

Greek Revival Style (Antebellum Period): Antebellum isn't so much an individual house style as an architectural time and place. Antebellum, Latin for "before war," refers to elegant plantation homes built in the American South in the 30 years or so preceding the Civil War. Antebellum homes are essentially in the Greek Revival style, which is grand, symmetrical, and boxy, with center entrances in the front and rear, balconies, and columns or pillars. In the mid-19th century, many prosperous Americans believed that ancient Greece represented the spirit of democracy. Interest in British styles had waned during the bitter War of 1812. Greek Revival architecture began with public buildings in Philadelphia. Many European-trained architects designed in the popular Grecian style, and the fashion spread via carpenter's guides and pattern books. Colonnaded Greek Revival mansions sprang up throughout the American south. With its classic clapboard exterior and bold, simple lines, Greek Revival architecture became the most predominant housing style in the United States. During the second half of the 19th century, Gothic Revival and Italianate styles captured the American imagination. Grecian ideas faded from popularity. However, front-gable design -- a trademark of the Greek Revival style -- continued to influence the shape of American houses well into the 20th century.

Queen Anne Style Victorian: Of all the Victorian house styles, the Queen Anne is the most elaborate and the most eccentric. The style is often called romantic and became an architectural fashion in the 1880s and 1890s, when the industrial revolution was building up steam. North America was caught up in the excitement of new technologies. Factory-made, precut architectural parts were shuttled across the country on a rapidly expanding train network. Exuberant builders combined these pieces to create innovative, and sometimes excessive, homes. Also, widely-published pattern books touted spindles and towers and other flourishes we associate with Queen Anne architecture. Country folk yearned for fancy city trappings. Wealthy industrialists pulled out all stops as they built lavish "castles" in the Queen Anne Style. Popular during the time of Britain's Queen Victoria, Queen Anne architecture has little to do with the 18th century Queen Anne. Moreover, the exuberant style bears little resemblance to the formal architecture which was popular during her time. Rather, British architects borrowed ideas from the earlier Medieval era and were first adopted by wealthy Americans. However, Queen Anne flourishes may also be found on less pretentious houses. In American cities, smaller working-class homes were given patterned shingles, spindlework, extensive porches and bay windows. Many turn-of-the-century houses are in fact hybrids, combining Queen Anne motifs with features from earlier and later fashions. The expansive and expressive buildings proved expensive and difficult to maintain. By the turn of the century, Queen Anne's had fallen out of favor. In San Francisco and other cities, flamboyant homeowners have painted their Queen Anne's a rainbow of bright colors. Purists protest that the colors are not historically authentic but the owners of these "Painted Ladies" claim that Victorian architects would be pleased.

Second Empire Victorian: The Second Empire Victorian, or Mansard style, house is the perfect setting for a horror film and has become the Hollywood standard of the "haunted house". It's the haunting hilltop architecture seen in spooky movies such as Alfred Hitchcock's Psycho, and indeed, with its tall mansard roof and wrought iron cresting, a Second Empire home may create a sense of looming height. But, in the nineteenth century, the style was not viewed as foreboding. This was a majestic fashion, inspired by Napoleon III. These homes were especially suitable for urban settings and remain a highly ornamental style. In describing these buildings, French architects used the term "horror vacui" -- the fear of unadorned surfaces. In the United States, private homes in this style often have an Italianate flavor. A Second Empire house may have U-shaped window crowns, decorative brackets, single story porches and an overall square shape. Most notable though is the distinctive mansard roof. In the middle 1800s, when Louis Napoleon (Napoleon III) established the Second Empire in France, Paris was transformed into a city of grand boulevards and monumental buildings and interest in the tall, majestic mansard roof was revived. Second Empire architecture spread to England during the Paris Exhibitions of 1852 and 1867. Before long, French fever spread to America. When the Second Empire style was applied to residential architecture, builders created interesting innovations. High mansard roofs were placed atop houses in a variety of contemporary styles. Also, older buildings were often renovated to include trendy and practical mansard roofs. For this reason, Second Empire homes in the United States are often composites of Italianate, Carpenter Gothic and other styles. During the presidency of Ulysses Grant, Second Empire was a preferred style for public buildings in the United States. In fact, the style became so closely associated with the prosperous Grant administration that it is sometimes called the General Grant Style. When the age of prosperity turned into the economic depression of the 1870s, flamboyant Second Empire architecture fell out of fashion.

Bungalow Style: The Craftsman Bungalow (aside from being my personal favorite style of home) is an all American housing style. Strangely though, it has its roots in colonial India, when British colonists adopted the style of native thatched huts to use for their summer homes. For their comfortable "bangla", the British arranged dining rooms, bedrooms, kitchens, and bathrooms around central living rooms. This efficient floor plan became the prototype for America's Craftsman Bungalows. The first American house to be called a bungalow was designed in 1879 by William Gibbons Preston. Built at Monument Beach on Cape Cod, Massachusetts, the two-story house had the informal air of resort architecture but was not what we consider today to be the true Bungalow style. Two California architects, Charles Sumner Greene and Henry Mather Greene, are often credited with inspiring America to build simple one-and-a-half story bungalows. Homes designed by the Greenes were publicized in magazines, and a flood of pattern books followed. True Bungalows represent structural simplicity, efficient use of space, and understated style. Most of the living area is placed on the ground floor. Seventy-five years after Bungalows took America by storm, the style remains a popular favorite and you'll find these comfortable and elegant little houses in towns and cities all over America.

Ranch Style Homes: These homes (perhaps the most common type of home imaginable for suburban America) were inspired by the rambling, single level designs of Frank Lloyd Wright's Prairie School of architecture, but the modern Ranch is a far cry from Wright's designs. Traditional Ranch homes reflect a hard-working, simple life and are often considered an expression of the informality of Western culture. Because these homes are uncomplicated, critics often say the Ranch style has no style. The style is also dismissed because it has become so common. "Ranches" are found in the suburbs throughout North America, making the style synonymous with the concept of tract housing: fast-built, cookie-cutter homes. The first Ranch home, designed by Cliff May, was built in San Diego, California in 1932. Over the next 20 years, thanks in part to the popularization of the automobile, Ranch-style houses spread to other states and were the dominant home style of the 1950's and 60's. Today, many new homes have characteristics of the relaxed, informal Ranch style.

Split Level Ranch: This type of house, perhaps even more than the traditional Ranch Style House, has become more equated with the suburban housing development than any other. Even the more luxurious and expensive homes that can be found in developments across America are little more than variations on this theme. A traditional Ranch Style house is only one story, but a split level, "Raised Ranch" house places the living space on two floors. A finished basement with large windows creates extra living space below, while a raised roof leaves room for bedrooms above. Critics may say that a Raised Ranch house lacks personality, but there's no question that this style fills a need for space and flexibility in these moderns times (the Spilt Level has been around since about 1932). The main living areas and bedrooms tend to be located on the main floor, while the garage and a large room are in the basement. Thanks to the placement of large windows in the lower level, the basement can be a pleasant living space.

Neoeclectic/ Modern Style: If your home was built in the past decade, chances are it incorporates many different historic styles. Decorative details borrowed from the past and selected from a construction catalog create a mixture that can be difficult to define. For lack of a name, critics call this the modern Neoeclectic style. During the late 1960s, a rebellion against modernism and a longing for more traditional styles influenced the design of modest tract housing in North America. Builders began to borrow freely from a variety of historic traditions, offering neoeclectic houses that were "customized" using a mixture of features selected from construction catalogs. These homes are sometimes called postmodern because they borrow from a variety of styles without consideration for continuity or context. Critics use the term "McMansion" to describe a neoeclectic home that is oversized and pretentious. Coined from the McDonald's fast food restaurant, the name "McMansion" implies that these homes are hastily assembled using cheaply-made materials and a menu of mix-and-match decorative details.

Hopefully, all of this information will be of use to you and even if only a small part of it assists you in your hunt for the history of the house, then it has served some purpose. Even if you follow it closely though, there is no guarantee that you will not run into a dead end, even using the material, but I have had good luck with it and hope that you will also. If the ghost in the house can be connected to a person who once lived there, especially by details that were not known before researching the location, then you have a pretty powerful case and excellent evidence of life after death.

AFTER THE INVESTIGATION: GETTING RID OF A GHOST

Unless you happen to be a psychic, you are probably a ghost hunter just like I am. I don't see ghosts or hear voices from the astral plane. I have experienced a number of ghosts, but I don't carry on conversations with them.

So, what do you do in a situation where the family in a haunted house wants to get rid of the ghost? This can be a touchy thing. First of all, you have hopefully reassured the family that there is nothing here that can hurt them and that they can live peacefully with the spirit (at least in most cases). On the other hand, what about the ghost itself? Wouldn't it be better off passing over to the other side, or "going to the light" as some mediums say?

As a ghost hunter, you are going to run into some people who want the ghosts to be gone from their house, for whatever reason. Therefore, we have to be pro-active in trying to find these people some relief from their problem. This is what we signed on to do, so to speak, when we took the case in the first place.

Start off by just continuing your own work, which does have some positive benefits. You can help these people, through their own belief systems, to realize that they have nothing to fear. This will help to reduce their stress about the paranormal because they now understand it better.

If this doesn't work to their satisfaction, then it is time to take the next step. In this situation, I attempt to turn to a member of the clergy or someone who may be experienced in this sort of thing. There are advantages to both types of people.

If there is a minister that you know personally, so much the better. Ask this person to come into the house and pray for the soul of the deceased person. Never have them try and tell the ghost to leave and never refer to this as an "exorcism", because it is not. This is simply a psychological banishment that often works in convincing the spirit to leave. If you don't know a minister, you can ask the family if they have a clergy member who might be comfortable in this situation. This person can also come into the house and bless it and pray for the soul of the deceased. This will often have great benefit.

It is also a great psychological relief for the residents because they have much more control over the spirit leaving then they first thought they did. In some cases, just the owners of the house asking the spirits to leave will do the trick. If the occupants are comfortable with this, and can be convinced that it will work, have them give it a try.

If there is no minister available, or the family is not willing to try that approach, then your next step is to find someone who is an expert in getting rid of ghosts. They don't have to be a professional medium, as there are many fellow ghost hunters out there who are sensitive to spirits and do this on a regular basis. If you do contact someone, make sure that it is someone you are comfortable with or someone you have worked with before. If you have never done this before, ask for a referral from another ghost hunter. There are too many "quacks" out there with whom you do not want to get mixed up.

The difference between someone who is a ghost hunter and a person who gets rid of ghosts is that this person uses no equipment in what they do. They operate only with their senses and their minds. Remember though, these persons cannot get rid of residual hauntings. The only way this can happen is for the haunting to just wear itself out, or you could completely dismantle the house, which is something that most home owners would not be entirely in agreement with.

As discussed earlier, intelligent hauntings are made up of the soul, or the personality, of a person who was once alive. For some reason, this spirit did not move on to its proper place after death. The sensitive who comes into this situation must convince the spirit to move on through communication. They will talk to the spirits and help them to realize they are causing a problem by remaining behind. In most cases, the spirits do not even realize that they are dead and by developing a rapport with them, they can be convinced of this fact and assured that something better awaits them on the other side.

A medium, or person who can communicate with the spirits, may come from any walk of life and they believe they have a gift. There is usually a complete lack of ceremony when a sensitive of this nature comes to call. They are not "exorcists", merely ordinary people with an extraordinary gift. They may want to sit down and talk to the witnesses first, or they may want to walk around the location and get a feel for the place.

Beware of any medium that tries to pump you or the witnesses for too much information up front. It is much more convincing, and legitimate, if the medium gathers impressions that match the information you already have. Also, beware of psychics who talk of "possession" and "evil spirits" --- they are going into an area that will probably have no basis in anything that you have already discovered.

The sensitives that you can count on will behave in the same manner that you have, suggesting natural explanations for the phenomena if they receive no impressions. If they do detect that a spirit is present, they will try and convince it to move on.

How effective is this? It's hard to say. It has been my experience that sometimes it works and sometimes it doesn't. It almost always has a positive effect on the residents of the house, so that does give it merit in my opinion. I think that it all depends on the person you use and the job that you do as the mediator between the residents and the medium. It is up to you to make sure that the residents understand what is going on, just as it was during the investigation.

I often get calls from people, and talk with people after investigations, in which they ask for the name of someone to come in to their home and get rid of the ghosts who are present there. In the years that I have been involved with the paranormal, I have found very few people whom I would recommend as someone trustworthy enough to be given this task. Before I can recommend anyone, I have to get to know him or her first and know they are someone who can be trusted. I recommend this same approach for you as well.

9. THE GHOST VIGIL

CONDUCTING INVESTIGATIONS IN CEMETERIES & OTHER OUTDOOR LOCATIONS

A few years back, in an earlier edition of the *Ghost Hunter's Guidebook*, I wrote some rather scathing comments about the so-called "ghost hunters" who spent their time running about in cemeteries, snapping photographs and calling what they were doing investigations. I received a number of responses to my comments and while some were harsh, many of them were simply looking for more information. If this was not the best way to conduct ghost research in cemeteries, then what was?

When this book was revised in 2001, I added an entirely new section on conducting investigations in cemeteries and other outdoor locations. For the most part, the response for this was positive but many well-established researchers began to criticize me for encouraging people to carry out what they called "useless research". They believe that no legitimate investigations can be carried out in cemeteries but this is mostly because of the way that such investigations were handled in the past.

However, I believe that conducting paranormal research in cemeteries really shouldn't be that much different than conducting an investigation in someone's home or in a building. Every investigation has to be organized and there has to be a point to it, otherwise we can't legitimately call it "research" or even an "investigation". To be able to conduct an actual investigation, we have to have rules and criteria to go by. The ghost hunter should have his own checklist of items to be studied at the site because while wandering around in a cemetery taking pictures is fun, it does not constitute an actual investigation.

The first thing to do when preparing for a cemetery vigil is to choose the site. This should not be done by simply picking a cemetery at random. Despite what some people apparently believe, not every cemetery is haunted. However, there are hundreds of sites where strange stories have been told, dark history has taken place and where people have encountered things that cannot be explained.

Once you do find a place that seems promising, start looking into the history of it so that you can decide if it is a location for legitimate research. You can make your decision based on the information learned by answering the following questions:

1. What is the history of this location?
2. What events have taken place here to lead you to believe that it might be haunted?
3. What paranormal events have been reported in the past?

If the answers to these questions lead you to suspect that something ghostly may be taking place at the location, then you should consider organizing an investigation. Hopefully, the following chapter will assist you in carrying out that investigation and obtaining some authentic evidence of the paranormal.

But the question remains as to how we can do this?

As discussed in an earlier section of the book, ghost researchers can provide historical evidence of hauntings by gathering witness testimony and details about a ghost that may be present in a location. We can then research that gathered information and match it to the alleged ghost when it was still a living person. Better yet, we can collect previous resident's testimony of events that occurred in the house and then match that evidence to current events that are now taking place. Having independent witnesses, of different time periods, with matching experiences makes for some very convincing evidence. Technically, we have "historically proven" that the house is haunted and that ghosts exist.

Many researchers have come to accept this way of thinking and have adopted it for their own investigations. The problems with graveyard ghosts arise though when we try and provide historical proof of the ghosts in cemeteries. Few researchers have been able to gather the data needed to explain why a cemetery might be haunted, which is why many established researchers think so poorly of this type of investigation.

Hopefully, this chapter will provide you with some of the tools needed to do this and soon, the graveyards that you research and investigate will no longer be enigmas where strange phenomena occurs but no one seems to know why.

As mentioned already, conducting paranormal research in cemeteries really shouldn't be that much different than conducting an investigation anywhere else. Choosing cemetery sites to investigate is much like choosing other types of sites, although in this case, you will not have the home owners around to help you out with their experiences. Your best bet is to keep your ears and your options open. You may be surprised at how many people have ghost stories to tell about local cemeteries, what might be around in the old folklore or what might be heard by everyday people who have encountered the unusual.

In the past, the one thing that has set the investigation of cemeteries apart from investigations of homes and buildings is that researchers have had such a hard time tracking down the history of the sites. This has been one of the reasons why this type of research has never really been considered "legitimate". Hopefully though, the information in this chapter will help to change that.

The section ahead has been designed to help ghost researchers compile as complete and as accurate a picture of the haunted graveyards they are investigating as possible.

After the researcher has learned of the possibility of the haunting, it is now up to him or her to try and discover why the place might be haunted. In many cases, as has been pointed out already, no real reasons may exist but the historical background of any location is essential to the investigation. Obviously, we cannot jump to the conclusion that the cemetery is haunted because it is a "portal" spot or crossover location without examining all of the facts at our disposal. It's possible that the haunting activity might have a cause behind it after all. Perhaps the ghost that has been seen stalking the grounds is not a nameless spirit from another dimension at all but rather a convicted murderer who was buried there in an unmarked grave after his execution? In this case, as with haunted houses, the history of the site may be the key.

TRACKING DOWN GRAVEYARD HISTORY

If you have heard about a cemetery that may be haunted, you are going to want to do two things: first, visit the cemetery for yourself and second, research the history of the place so you can get a better feel for its background.

Once you have decided on your possibly haunted cemetery, and believe that it seems worthwhile to organize an investigation, you should start the investigation by visiting the location in advance during the daylight hours. There are many things that need to be studied in detail and since most investigations take place at night, the option of studying the place will not be available to you then.

If there is a caretaker's office at the cemetery, be sure to stop in and ask for maps and any available literature about the cemetery. We'll discuss permissions for your investigations later on in the chapter. If you plan to do any headstone rubbings, ask the caretaker's permission for that as well. Technically, the stones belong to the family members of the person buried beneath them, but it never hurts to establish a good rapport.

Later on, we'll discuss more in detail about what you should do during the daytime to prepare for the investigation but in your first scouting expedition, you'll want to get an overall feel for the place. Be sure to take plenty of photographs, stroll through the graves and try and search out the older sections. Take your time in doing this and get a feel for the different kinds of markers that are on the grounds, the landscape and anything else that might play a role in the history of the place.

As a method of determining a complete history of the graveyard, you will want to discover what type of cemetery it is. The following is a breakdown of various types of burial grounds:

1. Church Cemetery
America's first cemeteries were the churchyards of New England and the East Coast and it's here that you will find the oldest burials. The tradition of church burials was started in Europe and carried on in America. When the churchyards became too crowded and the conditions unsanitary, town cemeteries were started. After that, land was usually set aside on the borders of towns where the cemeteries would be located. The early churchyards will not usually be laid out in neat rows like later cemeteries. The alignment of the graves tended to be haphazard and close. In many cities, and often in

rural settings, churchyards are still in use today but those located away from the East Coast tend to be more organized and less crowded than the original sites.

2. Family Plots

Family plots, or private burial grounds, would often hold the remains of not only the immediate family who owned the land, but also friends, neighbors and extended relatives as well. Family burial grounds were most common in the old South, where plantation living made it impractical to take a body for miles to churchyard or town cemetery, but they can be found in other locations as well. The burial plots were normally located on a person's property, usually in a garden or an orchard, and often on high ground. In towns and cities, many private burial grounds were absorbed by larger ones or bodies were moved to new locations as the town grew around them. Many others were lost altogether and were built over, often leading to gruesome finds in later years. In some states, it is still legal to bury the bodies of loved ones on private property (especially in the South) and so it's not uncommon to find homes with small fenced-in graveyards in front.

3. Garden Cemetery

The Garden Cemetery movement began in Paris and later extended to America. The popularity of the movement came at a time when American attitudes toward death were changing from the grim reality of it, as typified by the skulls, wings and dark characters of early tombstones, to finding beauty in death. This beauty was portrayed in the statuary and monuments and soon in the landscape architecture of the cemetery itself. Garden Cemeteries are easily identified by the park-like setting of them, with pathways, ponds, trees, foliage and benches for visitors. Before public parks were common, people came to the cemeteries on weekend afternoons to relax, walk, have picnic lunches and even make love under the shade trees. Even the names of the cemeteries began to emphasize the beauty and back-to-nature settings with names like Greenwood, Laurel Hill, Spring Grove, Forest Lawn, Oak Ridge and others. Garden Cemeteries tend to be huge, sprawling places and maps are always suggested if one is available.

4. Rural Cemetery

Growing up in the country in Illinois, rural cemeteries were the first types of graveyards that I was exposed to. These types of cemeteries are a true piece of Americana and are easily found on the highways and back roads of the country. On many occasions, you'll find them well hidden along gravel roads and at the end of dirt tracks, abandoned and forgotten by the local populace. Other times, they will be on the edge of a small town, or a mile or two from town, and often on small hills to protect them from spring floods. It is rare to find large monuments or mausoleums in them because most of these cemeteries are small, which makes them simple to investigate but difficult to research the history for. In these cases, it's best to check with the local genealogical society for information or to talk with some of the old-timers in the area.

5. Urban Cemetery

Most modern urban cemeteries are "public" cemeteries that are operated by the cities in which they can be found. Because most of them are not very historic or pictur-esque, they have largely been ignored over the years by researchers. The rows and rows of mostly ordinary markers tend not to get too much attention and for this reason, lit-tle documentation is available about them, even at the cemetery office itself.

6. Memorial Parks

The first Memorial Park was established in Southern California in 1917 (Forest Lawn) and the movement has since spread all over the country. There is nothing inspir-ing about this type of cemetery -- which is really the point. The flat, grassy lawns with their flush, stone tablets were designed to eliminate all suggestions of death. There are no monuments and no grave mounds and the markers are all situated against the ground so that lawn mowers will pass right over them. The goal was to give the ceme-tery a more park-like landscape but what it succeeded in doing was erasing all of the personality from the graveyard.

7. Military Cemetery

The first large military cemetery in the country was established in Pennsylvania in 1863, shortly after the Battle of Gettysburg doomed the fate of the Confederacy. It was here that President Abraham Lincoln gave his famous "Gettysburg Address" and conse-crated the place as hallowed ground. There are currently 119 National Cemeteries in the United States, including Arlington Cemetery, and all of them are filled with rows and rows of identical stone markers, indicating the graves of men killed in battle and who were discharged from military service. The history of these cemeteries, especially those associated with the battlefields, can easily be obtained and offer a rich tale for the researcher. Many of them are as haunted as the battlefields that are located nearby.

8. Potter's Fields

Potter's Fields are graveyards where the country or the city buries the poor, the unknown, the unclaimed, criminals, suicides and illegitimate babies. Most often they are buried in mass graves or in individual graves with no marker. A potter's field is the greatest example of anonymity, a place where the names of the dead, if known, are usu-ally placed only on the coffin itself. A pit is loaded with caskets until it is full and then the entire mass grave is given a single, numbered marker. No mourners are present when the earth is smoothed over this grave and no clergyman is there to offer a prayer for the dead. They can be stark, forbidding places.

As you are exploring the cemetery, you will want to try and get oriented with the gen-eral design of the site. One of the most common customs regarding cemetery layout is that most are on an east-west axis. The inscription on the monument might face east or west though. Many times, they face west so that visitors are not standing on the grave to read the inscription but they can be anywhere, so check the back and all of the sides too. Many ornate monuments, or those with lengthy stories to tell about the people buried beneath them, may have inscriptions on practically every surface. Some graves also have footstones, which makes it obvious which direction the body was placed, but most are laid with the head to the east and the feet to the west. This tradition follows the idea that the eastern sky will open on the Day of Judgment and the dead will rise from their graves to face the east.

GRAVE STONES & MARKERS

Grave stones and cemetery markers provide us with the greatest amount of information that we will be able to find about the history of the graveyard, while we are actually at the site. For this reason, it's best that we understand as much as we possibly can about them. Listed below are the items that you are most likely going to find on cemetery stones:

- The name of the deceased
- birth date and date of death
- birth place and place of death
- relationships / marriage information
- artwork and / or epitaph

Other information may appear as well, including service in the military, fraternal or service orders, life accomplishments and perhaps even a short biography of the deceased but the items above are the most common. Many graves will have footstones as well, which may have no engravings or perhaps only the initials of the deceased.

It should also be noted that just because there is a stone in the cemetery, it does not mean that the person is actually buried there. The marker could be simply a memorial that was placed there by loved ones. The body could have been lost in an accident or disaster and never recovered. Cemetery records, if they exist, should reveal that information. You can watch for clues on the tombstones that say something like "Sacred to the Memory of.." and while this is not a sure indicator, stones are usually inscribed with certain words and phrases for a reason.

Cemetery gravestones act as a road map to the past but unfortunately, vandals, pollution and the weather can destroy these vital links. Weathering is a natural decaying process that affects porous objects that are left outside. When water gets into the cracks of a tombstone and freezes, it tends to expand, causing stress on the marker, especially older and more fragile ones. This makes the stone much more susceptible to accidents and damage from lawn mowers and rakes that are wielded by cemetery caretakers. Wind, rain and sun can do damage also and since the force of our weather patterns seem to move from west to east, many markers, especially marble ones, become eroded and are no longer legible. Be sure to note whatever information you can find on the markers in the section of the cemetery that you plan to investigate. There is no way to say just how long the stone might actually have been there.

SURVERYING THE CEMETERY

One of the best ways of finding out about the cemetery is through records, newspapers, local census records and county histories but you can also get an equally good sense of time and place by surveying the cemetery itself. When you do this in conjunction with your research on paper, the cemetery will literally come alive for you. By surveying the site and reading though the tombstones (especially in smaller cemeteries) you should be able to determine many details about much of the following:

1. On some headstones, you will find information on where people buried in the cemetery migrated from, such as places of birth or inscriptions that tell of moving from one place to another. You can also use such information, including family names, to determine where their country of origin may have been.

2. In many cemeteries, you will find family plots conveniently marked by fences or stones that separate them from other parts of the cemetery. You may also want to note the names of those buried within the plots whose names do not match. Later research will likely reveal they are part of the family by marriage. I once discovered some interesting facts when I found a large family plot on the edge of a cemetery. Research revealed that it actually pre-dated the rest of the graveyard and had been a private burial site that was eventually absorbed by the larger cemetery. As it turned out, the family's mansion was actually right behind the private plot through a patch of woods and a path had once led to it from the house. I was glad that I checked into it too --- because family lore had it that the place was haunted!

3. A survey of gravesites can also give you an idea of how the people buried in the cemetery were affected by epidemics that swept through the region. If you find a number of graves that are dated 1918, it's possible that many of the deceased died during the Spanish Influenza epidemic of that year. A number of graves that share the same date means that a check of the records could reveal a cholera, smallpox or any other common frontier epidemic could also have occurred.

Floods, hurricanes, tornadoes, fires, mine accidents and other tragedies often claim the lives of a large number of people. On many occasions, the victim's tombstones will tell the story of the disaster, or at least that it occurred. If not, another check of records from a date that appears on many stones will likely provide the information that you need.

4. While you are in the cemetery, use your notebook to take a random sampling of about 40 gravestones that belong to adults that were at least 21 years of age when they died. Write down just the birth and death years and then sort them out by sex. Total the ages of the men and women and then divide that number by the number of individuals of each sex. This number that you come up with will give you an average age at death for men and women of the community. To be totally accurate, you would have to go through the entire cemetery and do this but this random sampling will at least give you an average for the community.

HISTORY OF THE CEMETERY
& ITS OCCUPANTS

Surveying and exploring the cemetery grounds is likely to give you pages and pages of information and believe it or not, most of it will be worthwhile, no matter how confusing it might seem at first. A few years back, I spent nearly a week in a large cemetery, going over every section of it, a grave at a time. I photographed everything of interest and used a large notebook to write down the names and inscriptions of those I believed would be of interest to the history of the town and cemetery. Keep in mind, that I did this with a fairly practiced eye -- meaning that I knew what kinds of monuments and burial plots to look for. However, most of the names that I jotted down meant nothing to me at the time.

After I finished exploring the graveyard, and had completed my survey, I began to research the names that I had compiled. Even though very few of them meant anything to me when I was trudging through the cemetery, the names on the list ended up belonging to politicians, city founders, early pioneers, generals, Civil War heroes, a famous Methodist circuit rider and even an ambassador to a South American country! I learned more about the history of the area from my trip to the cemetery than I had previously learned from books and documents about the town.

More importantly (at least for our purposes here), I was also able to track down some authentic history behind some of the ghost stories that I had heard about various parts of the cemetery. I was then able to actually link the tales to some real people who were buried there. For this reason, I continue to believe that, even with cemeteries, the history is the key to determining the ghostly activity at a place.

As with a haunted house, city directories can also provide information about the graveyard with not only listing those in charge of the cemetery in the past but also the local funeral homes, undertakers and monument companies. All of these companies have the potential to have records for the cemetery. If they are no longer in business, the local historical society may have access to their past records.

County, Local and Family histories may also provide information and as mentioned before, the local genealogical society can provide a wealth of information about the cemetery, from burial lists to epitaphs and even maps.

Here are some other areas worth checking to glean some additional information about the graveyard and about the people buried there:

1. Cemetery Plat Maps: While it may be hard to find plat maps (check the genealogical society) for old and defunct cemeteries, those graveyards still open for interments should have a map or register so that grave diggers don't accidentally dig a grave where another is still in use. You can check for copies of such maps at the cemetery office or at a town or county office. Cemetery maps normally give the names of the person or persons occupying the graves and other details, such as the date of burial. This may be important if your survey of the cemetery pointed toward evidence of some unmarked graves in some areas.

In other cases, and with most maps that I have run across, the plots on the map are numbered and to find out who is buried where, you have to compare the map to the cemetery deeds.

This type of information is vital when visitors and workers at the cemetery are experiencing phenomenon in one particular area and are unable to link it to any one person or event in particular. By tracking down the owners of the surrounding plots, this is the first link in the chain to establishing who might be haunting the spot. From there, more detailed information will be needed about the owners, which is more research in itself, but this will at least get you started in the right direction.

2. Cemetery Deeds: In the same way that purchasers receive a deed showing the ownership of a piece of property they have bought, those who purchase a cemetery plot also received a deed. A copy of it is usually recorded with the town or county where the cemetery is located and the other copy is stored with the cemetery sexton. In the record, you will find the names of the buyer and seller, the amount paid for the plot, the lot number and where it is located in the cemetery. This is the next likely step in research following the obtaining of a cemetery plat map.

3. Cemetery Transcriptions: As I have mentioned already, one of the best places to find more information about the cemetery is at the local genealogical society. Genealogists love cemeteries and graveyards are, in addition to records rooms and in front of their computers, the place where they spend the bulk of their time tracking down family histories. Over the years, many genealogists have taken the time to copy down cemetery inscriptions -- and I mean from entire cemeteries -- and have often had them privately printed into books that are stored in the local library or genealogical society so that others will have access to them. However, since this has been done on a hit and miss basis, not all transcriptions are the same, as some may be in manuscript form while others may be only index cards.

4. Cemetery Records: The superintendent's records typically give the name of the deceased, the date of the burial and often, the exact location of the grave in the cemetery. In addition, the records sometime list the original purchaser of the burial plot and who is responsible for the upkeep of it, such as a relative living in the area. When researching stories from a ghostly viewpoint, this just may be vital information if that person's relative is suspected of being the resident haunt. You can often find these records in the cemetery office itself or filed at the town or city hall.

I should add though that cemetery records, deeds and transcriptions may not always have all of the information that you need. As I mentioned at the start of this chapter, the information here will not provide all of the answers and over time, I have found that no matter how hard you search -- sometimes the answers are just not there. In one case, I was looking for information about an entire cemetery that had been closed down and moved. The company that constructed on the original site of the cemetery had not only found human remains while they were building, but the structure that was completed on the site was known for being haunted.

The only records that I could find stated that the cemetery, which had been a potter's field for the local poor house, had been closed down in 1913 and moved to a larger cemetery. The remains from the old site had been buried in a common grave on the grounds. Strangely, I was completely unable to find any records of the relocation (only that it had been done) and despite an extensive check of the cemetery records and plat maps, I was unable to discover where the mass grave was located on the grounds. The cemetery superintendent, who had been at his position since the early 1970's, was just as stumped as I was and even took it upon himself to continue the research and see if the remains were actually sent to another cemetery in the area. To this day, they continue to be "missing"!

BRINGING THE DEAD TO LIFE

After you have been to the cemetery and have pored through the records trying to link the burial plots or sections to those buried there, you now have to try and find out more about the people whose identities you have discovered. There are many ways to find out more about their lives, including at the library, through city directories and of course, at the local genealogical society but our focus here will be on their deaths. As most readers are undoubtedly aware, the majority of those who return to haunt the earth do so because of their death and usually when and how it occurred. I have pointed out several times already that most cemetery ghosts are linked to events that happened after death, rather than before, but our research should be complete enough to delve into the final days of those buried within the cemetery ,or section of the graveyard, in question.

For the purposes of our example here, we will assume that you are trying to track down more information about a single person that is buried in a section of the graveyard. As part of the example, let's assume that there is a private burial plot where visitors to the cemetery and cemetery workers have reported seeing a ghostly figure. After tracking down as much information as you can about the cemetery, and prior to conducting an on-site paranormal investigation of the spot, you will want to learn all that you can about the life and death of the individual who is interred in the plot.

If the subject died since the early years of the Twentieth Century, when statewide vital registration became common, you will probably find a death certificate on file for them in a local office. If the person died before that though, there are still other records that you can find to establish dates and information about his death. Following are different types of sources for death-related information that may assist you. Not all of them will be relevant to your individual search but each will help you to get a little closer to what you are looking for. Here are some excellent places to start the search:

1. City Directories: As the reader may have noticed already in this book, city directories are an excellent place to begin an investigation into the history of a person or a site. Information will vary in the books from city to city but you may find the person's death listed or, as in some cases, a list of all the deaths that occurred in the city over a given year. A clue to watch for is a man's name being listed and then disappearing from the following year's directory with his wife listed as "widow" or "widow of..." Remember though, just because a name is removed does not mean the person died. He could have simply moved or was missed for that year, so be sure to check the next several years as well.

2. Obituaries: Your next likely step, after determining a death date and a place or residence for the subject, is to check for information listed in the newspaper obituary. Obituaries are like small biographies and are often written for the newspaper by funeral homes or by the relatives of the deceased. They will often tell something about the deceased and his remaining family, as well as details about funeral services and where he was buried. The cause of death may or may not be listed in the obituary but you can watch for clues within the notice as to what may have happened. Words like "died suddenly" might indicate an accidental death, a murder or suicide or possibly just a heart attack or a stroke. The words "lingering" or "long illness" could suggest cancer, heart disease or tuberculosis.

The best news might be when someone who ordinarily would not end up on the front page of the newspaper ends up there because they died in an unusual way. If your subject did die in a strange way, be sure to look for an article to go along with the obituary.

3. Death Certificates: Death certificates are the official documents that record people's deaths and were first created to determine the frequency and distribution of fatal diseases. Many states did not have such a plan in place until the early part of the last century but modern death certificates are completed by several people. If a person dies in a hospital or other institution, then a nurse or staff member fills in the time and date of death. The doctor fills in the cause and then the funeral director, or one of their staff members, fills in the rest. The information then is retyped onto a new, blank form and then is returned to the doctor for their signature. After that, the funeral home then goes to the registrar for a burial permit. Usually, the funeral home will keep a copy of the certificate on file.

Death certificates, which are filled with vital information, can be confusing and hard to decipher but the more modern they are, the more they are likely to contain. Sometimes, information can be in error and often the cause of death can be obscured or covered up to protect a person's reputation or privacy. This is especially common with older certificates. For example, instead of "suicide", you might find the cause of death was listed as "accidental" or instead of "abortion", you might find "uterine bleeding". On older certificates, causes of death will often use archaic words for diseases so be sure to have some sort of glossary on hand while attempting to decipher them.

4. Funeral Home Records: While this is a possible source for research, it's not a likely one. While many funeral homes will not have a problem accommodating you for research on people who have been dead for many decades, they are unlikely to grant you access to anything recent. Funeral home records are private and so they are within their rights to restrict or deny access to records. And because they are private, the content in the records will vary from one location to another and from one time period to another as well.

5. Institutional Records: If your subject died in a hospital, asylum, tuberculosis sanatorium, poor house or prison, then his death would have been noted in that institution's records. These registers, which usually predate state ward registrations, may be kept in a separate death book or among the other entries in the main register book. Information is going to vary in them from one place to the next and certainly from one time period to another. In many cases, the institution (especially with asylums and tuberculosis hospitals) will have closed down years ago and so finding the records may be tricky. To find out if the records still exist, contact the town, city or county, or even the state historical society. They may have some idea to help you find them.

6. Autopsy Records: Many death certificates can tell you if an autopsy was performed on your subject and if that record was then filed with the hospital or with the coroner's reports (see next section). Hospital records are considered private and you can usually only get access to them if you are related to the deceased. Each hospital has its own policy as to how long it keeps records. An autopsy is performed when a cause of death is uncertain, questionable or suspicious. If the medical examiner suspects something unusual, then no consent is needed from the family for an autopsy. The details of these records are fascinating and just may provide many clues to the researcher in search of the strange.

7. Coroner's Records: If you should learn from your research that your subject died in an unusual way or under strange circumstances, you will want to check and see if a coroner looked into the case. Both medical examiners and coroners investigate suspicious deaths and the position of coroner predates that of medical examiners. The coroner, an elected position, was responsible for examining dead bodies for any sign of foul play. No special education was required and it was not necessary to be a doctor. By the late 1800's, many states and cities began replacing the position of coroner with that of medical examiner, who is required to be a physician. Some locations still use the elected coroner position or a combination of both.

If the coroner decided that the death appeared to be from criminal negligence or murder, then he held what was called an inquest and the records of these affairs hold huge amounts of information for both crime buffs and ghost researchers. Juries were appointed and witnesses were called to testify. The postmortem findings (autopsy records) were included as well. Most coroners' reports are open to the public and should be followed up with newspaper research. There might be an obituary that was written or if the death was unusual, an entire report. If the death turned out to be murder or linked to a crime, there would also be subsequent articles and possibly even court records if the case went to trial.

As you can see from the preceding pages, research and investigation into possibly haunted cemeteries can be just as "legitimate" as the research that is being done in other haunted sites -- as long as it is done the right way. As mentioned, wandering aimlessly through a graveyard at night, just snapping photographs, is not the way to do worthwhile research. However, we have been able to show that by using even a fraction of the information that we have listed here, your cemetery research can go in all sorts of new and fascinating directions.

PREPARING FOR THE INVESTIGATION

Once all of your preliminary research has been finished, there is still much to be done before the actual investigation takes place. Some of that will mean returning to the cemetery for some additional surveying and exploration, although this time it will be specifically in regards to the vigil that your investigation team will be carrying out on the grounds.

You will need to return to the cemetery again and, once more, bring your notebook and pen with you. There are a number of things that have to be noted about the grave-yard and the surrounding area before you can return at night. Make sure that this step is carried out during the daylight hours so that everything can be seen in detail. You will be coming back after dark for the investigation, so all of this data will need to be compiled now. Here are some steps for you to follow:

1. Draw a map of the location, as close to scale as possible. Be sure to mark any land-marks or noticeable spots on the map so that other team members will be able to easi-ly locate them. This may mean trees, mausoleums, easily identifiable grave markers and monuments and anything else that the team can use to orient themselves between the cemetery and your map.

2. Take note of the location's surroundings. Be sure to notice what might be seen from the location during the investigation. If woods surround the cemetery, check and see if there are houses on the other side of the trees. Even a small amount of light (or sound) from a home or farm could appear to be anomalous in any photos that might be taken or on any recordings that your group might make.

3. Take many photographs of the site in the daytime. That way, any night time pho-tos can be checked for location and compared to areas that might be active.

After leaving the site, there is more preparation work that needs to be done. One of the most important things can be accomplished by speaking with local authorities. It is imperative that if you are planning to conduct an investigation in a public location, that you find out what the state and local laws say about trespassing in a cemetery after dark. In most cases, unless the site is otherwise posted, you will be asked to leave the ceme-tery by law enforcement officials. If the cemetery is posted, then you could be arrested or fined. Never go into a cemetery that is posted against night time trespassing unless you have permission to be there.

4. Try to get permission in writing from the owners of the location to conduct inves-tigations at the site. Few cemeteries are privately owned and most belong to the local community (or the township in rural areas). You can speak to the on-site superintendent about this. You might also contact the local police department and let them know that you will be at the site as a courtesy. This may be very important if you are unable to get written permission. If you can get permission, take the letter with you to the site.

5. After selecting the site and getting your clearances (if applicable), carefully put together a team of people to accompany you to the location. As with any other investigation, you will want to put together people who can take photographs, run the equipment, use the video camera, etc. Be sure not to tell them what to expect before the vigil. If they witness anything at the site that matches previous reports, this will strengthen your suspicions about the place being haunted.

6. Once your team has been put together, I recommend preparing a variety of equipment that you want to take with you. Your team should be no larger than 7-9 people and no less than 5. Here is a list of some equipment that I believe is worth taking along (in addition to extra batteries and essential items from your "ghost hunter's kit"):

- Flashlights (one for every team member)
- clipboard, paper, pencil & copies of the location maps
- EMF detectors and IR temperature probes
- Cameras (one for every team member)
- At least one video camera, capable of IR filming in total darkness
- PIR (Passive Infrared) motion detectors
- hygrometer (measure humidity in the area)
- Thermometer (check weather conditions for the vigil)

Beyond this basic list, you should add whatever pieces of equipment that you feel would be useful in your particular location or investigation. Just be sure that you have a practice run with any new or unfamiliar equipment prior to the investigation. This is also suggested with new cameras and probes as well. Most likely, you will be working in uncomfortable and dark conditions and it is important that the investigators be familiar with the equipment before arriving at the location.

7. Before you leave for the investigation, consider using the map that you have already made to decide where you would like to first set up the equipment. This might be based on previous reports from the location or insights by the team member who previously visited the site. No matter what, it will give you a place to start from and a "game plan" for the investigation.

THE CEMETERY INVESTIGATION

Before the investigation actually begins, you may want to go over some ground rules with your team. Here are some suggestions for things to keep in mind while getting the investigation organized:

1. Never take on an investigation like this alone. A good team is required for legitimate research. Not only is safety important in an outdoor or an isolated location, but it is essential to have more than one person to authenticate evidence and incidents that might occur.

2. Never trespass in a location without permission. As mentioned earlier, you should try and get permission from the caretaker of the cemetery, or county officials, before the investigation. If this cannot be done, get in touch with the local police department or sheriff's department about the investigation. This is a good idea to do no matter what, even if for nothing other than courtesy and professionalism.

3. Do not drink or smoke prior to or (especially) during the investigation. The majority of evidence from the night comes in the form of photographs that have been obtained with corresponding evidence. If a team member is smoking, even if the smoke does not appear in any photos, it can destroy the credibility of any evidence that might be obtained.

4. As with any other investigation, arrive at the scene with skepticism and make an effort to find a natural explanation for any phenomena that occurs.

5. During the investigation, be sure to write down and make a note of anything that occurs, no matter how small it seems. I suggest creating a logbook for the investigation. A logbook can be prepared in advance and should contain the following information:

- Date and Time of the Investigation
- Name and location of the site
- Investigators / team members present
- weather conditions (temperature / humidity / barometer readings and even the wind speed... check the local weather service before leaving home)
- Detailed list of the equipment being used

Each of the team members should receive a copy of the log sheet, along with the map of the location. An additional sheet should also be added with times listed along the left side. On the right, blank spaces should be inserted so that any phenomena that occurs can be noted next to the corresponding time. You need to consider a photographic log as well (especially when working with infrared film) so that you can keep track of when and where your photographs were taken.

6. Finally, leave the location exactly as it was when you found it. Be sure that you do not leave any trash behind and also be sure that nothing is done to physically disturb the site, such as knocking over a tombstone. Even accidents can have a grave effect on the opportunity that you might have for future investigations at this site and others.

Once you arrive back at the cemetery that night, you are going to want to get a "feel" for the place and to set up a base of operations. I suggest finding a central location that is easily recognized by all of the team members. Here, you can leave your equipment cases and any non-essential items that do not need to be carried about the cemetery or location. If possible, try to arrive at the site before dark so that all of the team members can get a look at the place. Hopefully, the map that you made will have noted any hazards that might be encountered (like an open grave) but if not, this will give everyone a chance to see things for themselves.

Once this is done, you should start setting up any stationary equipment that you plan to use, like Tri-Field meters and motion detectors. Position the instruments in locations where they will not be moved and have each team member make note of where everything is so that they will not stumble over it later. Make sure the equipment is in a place where it is most likely to encounter phenomena. If nothing occurs after a set period of time (say, one hour), then try moving it to another spot. If hand-held equipment encounters something in a different place, try moving the stationary equipment to that area as well.

Once the equipment is in place, it is time to get started.

1. It is best to try and split the investigators into separate teams. You may have noticed that when I noted the ideal number of investigators that I suggested an odd number of people. I feel that one person should always be in charge of monitoring the stationary equipment. It does not have to be the same person for the entire investigation, but this should always be someone's job. He or she should take notes of anything that occurs and if more than one camera is available, keep a video camera monitoring this equipment.

2. The rest of the researchers should be split up into teams of two and should begin checking out the rest of the location with various other types of equipment. Remember that you are not here to randomly snap photographs! You should be searching for all manner of activity and photographing any anomalies that may occur in order to provide corresponding evidence. It might be best that one member of the team handles the equipment and the other team member holds the flashlight and the investigation log. This person can keep track of anything unusual that occurs and mark the location of the occurrence on the map.

3. Ideally, the vigil will last from 2-4 hours (depending on the amount of activity recorded) and this means that the location will have to be covered almost continuously during this time. Try to refrain from too many breaks and from leaving the equipment unwatched. There is no pattern as to when something paranormal might occur and the investigator has to be constantly aware.

4. If strange activity is found during the course of the night, the investigators should compare notes and try to pinpoint the most active areas of the location. Using the map that you have drawn, it becomes possible to see what areas of the location boast the most anomalies. For the last hour of so of the vigil, it is suggested that all of the equipment and the cameras be focused on this area.

It has been my experience with cemeteries in the past, that much of the activity seems to center around a particular area. There may be no reason for this, unless we consider the theories of "portals" or "doorways", as we discussed in an earlier chapter. It is possible that you might discover a lot of strange phenomena is taking place in a localized section of the graveyard.

Even though the investigation ends for the night, it is far from over. All of the data that you collected has to be gone over, the tapes watched and the photos developed. In an investigation such as this, you have a unique situation in that you rarely have any eyewitness testimony to collect. For this reason, the material that you have collected becomes even more important and essential to any theories that you might develop about the haunting.

If something paranormal does occur in the cemetery you are researching, definitely plan to do follow-up investigations. And when you do, you might consider working with different investigators (as well as the same team members) and try to focus your investigations on the areas of the location that were the most active. You might see an increase in activity, or possibly even a decline. If this occurs, continue the same methods that you used in your initial vigil and see if the phenomena has moved to a different area.

Just remember that an investigation of this sort can quickly deteriorate into a circus if it is not handled properly. It is extremely important that the goals of the group remain focused and that the vigil is organized and well thought out. This is the only way that an outdoor, or cemetery, investigation can be considered successful and the only way that it can be considered to be legitimate ghost research.

10. BEYOND GHOST RESEARCH

WORKING WITH OTHER GHOST HUNTERS, THE MEDIA & THE GENERAL PUBLIC

Over the past several years, I have often gotten questions from people about how to get started on their first case. How do you find out where to go? How do people get in touch with you?

The first thing that you want to do is to make contact with other ghost hunters and possibly get involved with a research group. As I have mentioned many times, it is not a good idea to try and research cases by yourself, so you might consider putting together a small local group of like-minded friends and individuals to hunt down cases.

You can start by going to the library or local newspaper and trying to find out about any ghost stories, legends or alleged haunted spots in your area. If they are public locations, then you are ready to begin experimenting with your newfound ghost hunting knowledge. Try taking some readings and photographs and then you will have some idea what you are doing when you make contact with other groups.

The best way to do this is through the Internet. You can meet and talk with ghost hunters from all over the country who are often interested in sharing news and ideas about ghost hunting and investigations. Once you start to know your way around, you may also consider setting up a web site, either big or small. There are several companies on the Internet who host free web pages and this might be the perfect place to start. This way, you have a "base of operations" where people can get in touch with you.

Remember though, web surfers are not going to come knocking down your door the moment you launch your web page. It takes quite awhile to establish a presence on the Internet. You can get your name out by going to other ghost-related sites and asking them to include your web site in their section of linked pages. As long as you have a credible site, with decent information, most of them will be glad to.

Another thing to think about though is to not get caught up in the idea of trying to post nothing but "ghost photographs" on your page. People are looking for information! The problem with the photos is that so many web designers are interested in sheer numbers and will post anything to compete with people like you. Remember that quantity does not mean quality and if you look at some of these pages you will find ludicrous examples of what are purported to be ghost photos and yet are clearly not. Go for the quality web page, with lots of information about ghost hunting, haunted places and a nice collection of carefully picked photos, and if you stick around long enough, you will begin to attract the visitors.

Now, you have established a ghost research group and have a base of operations in cyberspace. The next thing to do is to get yourself established in your local area. You have knowledge about several haunted places in your area and you should put together a small packet with this information. Include photos and any stories that you might have and collect it into something that looks as professional as you can manage. You don't have to be able to write to do this, just recount a few of the stories and your basic interest in the locations.

Then, put together another packet of information about yourself and your new group. It doesn't have to be a complete biography, just some items of interest about you and about your goals with the group. Again, go down to your local copy shop if necessary and make sure that the entire package is very presentable.

Next, go to your local newspaper and present the entire packet to a reporter who is assigned to the local area. If possible, you might even want to talk to the highest-ranking editor who is available (call first for an appointment if necessary) because this will be the person who ultimately will decide how much, if any, coverage that you will get.

Be sure to dress conservatively and make the best impression that you can. You do not want to come across as a "nut" with your packet and your presentation. As long as they know you are serious about the subject matter, you have a much better chance of success with them.

Obviously, the best time to do this is in late September or early October, and I don't think that I have to tell you why. As far as the media is concerned, Halloween is the only time of year the general public is interested in ghosts. Now, we all know this is not the case, but for some reason, the media is a little narrow in their focus sometimes (to say the least). Believe me when I tell you there is nothing you can do about it though and that you are just better off going along with their reasoning. To many of us, the Halloween season with the media has become the "necessary evil" to cope with so that we can continue to do ghost research the rest of the year.

Now, once you have accomplished this, next comes the interview. Hopefully, you will get the chance to present your thoughts and investigations in a positive light. When you are just starting out, you often have to take whatever publicity that you can get, but my advice is to be cautious about what you say and how you word things when talking with any reporter. I have found that your quotes in the article often turn out to be the off-handed remarks that you didn't think were being recorded. Learn from my past mistakes and try not to say anything that you don't want to see in print. This isn't easy and chances are, you will still be a little disappointed in what is written about you. I will also wager that the article will mention the word "ghostbuster" at least once and will either begin or end with the phrase, "Who ya gonna call?" or "He ain't afraid of no ghosts!"

As anyone who has dealt with the media can tell you, your initial attempts at publicity are bound to be disconcerting. Let's face it --- to most newspapers, the coverage of "ghost hunters" is not taken too seriously. Most likely you will be stuck with either a new reporter, someone very low on staff roster or a free-lancer. No matter what, most of these people seem to have a few things in common:

1. They are writing for the newspaper, or articles in a weekly feature paper, but what they really want to do is write novels and stories and / or screenplays.

2. They usually are not very good writers and no matter what they write, it will always appear to be in newspaper style and format.

3. They have no control over what the finished piece will look like when it goes to print.

4. They will make no attempts to "fact check" with you or to get you proofs of what the article may look like.

5. They all share an uncanny ability to get things wrong.

This is not the case with all reporters but if there are any of you who are reading this that have been interviewed by the press at some point in the past, you are likely nodding your head and smiling right now. In all fairness though, I have worked with many good reporters over the years and as you become better known in your area, you will start to see them take you a little more seriously. Here are some suggestions that might help:

1. Always ask if it might be possible to see the article before it goes to print. It's unlikely that they will let you do this unless you make a lot of noise about it. Here, you have to decide what is more important -- the article running as is, or the chance of alienating the newspaper reporter and features editor. If there are concerns though, it might be worth it to ask rather than have something really atrocious written about you.

2. When you sit down to the interview, consider taping it yourself. That way, nothing bizarre can be attributed to you and if it is, you have proof that what was written was not what you said. Since many reporters only rely on their notes (which they never hesitate to quote you from), offer them a copy of the tape when you are finished since they obviously "forgot" to bring their own recorder.

3. Unless you are given some input about any photos that are going to be taken for the article, suggest that you provide the reporter with one of your own. You might consider having some decent publicity photos taken (which do not have to be fancy, just a good photo of you) and you can let the editor know that you'll provide the reporter with something appropriate - in other words, something that does not make you look like a mass murderer!

When it's all said and done, we usually just have to be happy with what we get and we can only hope for the best. I suggest just trying to keep a sense of humor and remembering that (almost) any publicity is good publicity.

Once the article makes the paper and the paper hits the newsstands, you will hopefully begin to see some attention and results from it. It will be from this article (and any that follow) that people will learn about you and your research. After that, the calls are going to start coming in. Finally, you will have the chance to put your investigative skills into action. From this point on, it will be much easier to attract new members to your group and to get information about haunted places.

Good luck with your research and happy hunting!

HOW TO DO A GHOST TOUR

One of the great ways to meet the public and to generate publicity for your research is to offer a ghost tour of your local area. As Harry Price knew, the only way to get the general public involved in paranormal research is to make it entertaining. Ghost tours provide great entertainment and also serve to introduce the public to not only local hauntings but in many cases, to ghost research in general.

Over the last several years, while traveling around the country, I have noticed that ghost tours of various communities have become more and more prevalent. It seems that almost every town, large and small, that has ghost stories and haunted places to offer now has a tour that takes visitors to these spooky spots. Many of the tours that I have had an opportunity to take have been great, others not so great, and some, downright terrible. Every guide has his own style of hosting tours, just like every writer has his own way of telling a story. Like a ghost book, a ghost tour can run the gamut between entertaining and uneven, with just about every level in between.

I have had many requests from people that ask for assistance in starting their own ghost tours in their various parts of the country. This is not because I am an expert at it, for like ghost hunting itself, there really aren't any experts when it comes to offering a ghost tour. However, I have been doing tours for quite awhile and have been lucky enough to start and host two very successful (and award winning) tours in two different cities in Illinois, Decatur and Alton. I also put together the very first ghost tour of St. Charles, Missouri, which I have unfortunately not had much of a chance to continue, and have offered tours to other locations, including St. Louis, and a number of trips and excursions as well.

I love doing ghost tours and I think that this is the main reason why I have been successful at it. What I may not possess in skill and expertise, I think that I make up for in enthusiasm and a love of the subject matter. I have been fascinated with ghosts and hauntings for as long as I can remember. In addition, I am also fascinated with history and it's this ingredient that I believe is vital to any successful ghost tour. Just as no haunting can exist without a history behind it, so should no ghost tour. The only locations that I have ever had trouble with during a tour have been locations for which no interesting history exists. No matter how active the haunting may be, the story behind the location cannot be of interest to the casual tour attendee if there is no history involved.

And make no mistake about it --- the average attendee of a ghost tour is not a ghost hunter or researcher, but rather a person with a casual interest in ghosts. Most tour attendees are looking for "thrills and chills". They are not interested (for the most part) in the science of the investigation. They are interested in what happened at the location the past, who it happened to, what is happening now, who that is currently happening to and most importantly -- will they have the chance for that to happen to them?

A successful ghost tour is all about interaction. It's about how the guest can interact with the location (or rather the ghosts!) and even more important, how you (as the host) interact with them. You have to be a "people person" to be able to host a tour. If you are shy, backwards and don't like public speaking, take my advice now and don't consider trying to start a tour. The worst tours that I have ever experienced have been hosted by people who have been awkward with their presentations and have been unable to answer questions and to have a good time. Trust me, if you are not having a good time as the host, neither are the attendees. Hosting a tour is just like performing on stage for the audience is only going to get out of it what you decide to put into it.

The other problem that I have encountered is with hosts who don't know the material. If you are planning on hiring people to help you with your tours, be sure that they know every location on the tour backwards and forwards. Scripts are a bad idea, especially if your host sounds as though he is reading from it. I understand that in very busy, tourist-centered areas, one person can rarely handle all of the tours that are needed to meet the demand but no one wants to see a badly prepared college student fumbling with his lines. Make sure that if you do hire someone to help that they know their material or the tour is bound to suffer.

Of course, I can't say that everyone is that discriminating. In fact, many people aren't. A lot of people will take any kind of tour, they don't care, but for the most part, if someone takes one lousy tour, they certainly aren't going to take it again. I have always been able to be happy about the fact that I often get repeat customers on the tours that I have done over the years. I believe this is because I try to offer an entertaining and authentic tour and one that is more believable because it's hosted by the person who started the tour and wrote the book that it's based on. In their eyes (and in mine), I have much more to lose than just some guy off the street offering a tour. It's my credibility that suffers if the tour is bad but on the other hand, my credibility improves if the tour is done well. Keep that in mind if you are planning on starting a tour, especially if you are considering hiring someone to help you with it.

What follows is a number of hints and tips to help you start and put together a successful ghost tour. Remember, I do not claim to be some sort of expert on tours, any more than I claim to be an expert on ghosts. I am basing this information on my own past experience with doing tours. As of this year, I will have been hosting tours for 12 years and believe me when I say that I have learned a number of lessons the hard way during that time. If you are planning on starting a tour in your area, I hope that the information contained in this article will help you, at least a little bit. Please feel free to take this information, change it, cut it up and make it work for you. If there is anything that you get out of it that helps, I will feel that it has served a purpose. Good luck!

WALKING TOUR OR BUS TOUR?

This may be one of the greatest dilemmas that you will face when starting a tour. For a number of years, I always offered bus and / or trolley tours because the haunted locations that I visited in various towns were very spread out. No matter how much I liked the method of transportation, I would much rather offer a walking tour than a driving one. A couple of years back, I switched to strictly walking tours and have never regretted it.

There are a variety of reasons to not use a bus or vehicle, not the least of which is the overhead for the tour. As soon as you book a vehicle of any sort for a tour, you have automatically created an expense. Once you sell a ticket for the tour, you have committed to that expense and no matter how many people now attend the tour, you still have to pay the vehicle costs, no matter how many attendees actually show up. This can be very disconcerting for someone just starting out.

In addition, I also feel that you create a distance between yourself and the attendees when on board the vehicle, especially if it is a large vehicle and some of the passengers are unable to see you. Everyone wants something to look at, they don't want to just hear your voice. If you do have to use a vehicle though, there are ways to combat this. First, be sure to stand and speak where you can be seen by everyone aboard. Be sure that the passengers feel that they are a part of the tour by making sure that you speak "to" them, not just "at" them. This is very important!

I would also try to combine my driving tour with as much off the vehicle walking as possible. This allows the passengers to feel as though they are visiting more of the locations first hand and not just driving by and looking at them. They will also feel that they are more connected to the host as well. I would much rather have everyone gathered around me, involved in the story, than just sitting in their seats starting at me. This helped me to enjoy the tour more and in return, the attendees enjoyed it more as well.

So, my advice would be that if you have a chance to offer a walking tour instead of a driving one, do so. It's possible though that the haunted locations in your area may be widespread and if this is the case, make the best of it by referring to the information that I just mentioned. No matter what sort of tour that you offer, you have the chance to make it a great one but it all depends on what you do with what you have to work with.

DO I HAVE TO WRITE A BOOK?

That's another big question that I am often asked --- do all ghost tours have to be based on a book? The answer to that is "no", although there are big advantages to doing so. I realize that this is a tough question for me to address because I am a writer, it's what I do for a living, and because of this, the tours that I have hosted have been based on books. I have always felt that, in a large part, the tours have enjoyed the success that they have because I have based them on my books. Having a book that the tour is built upon gives a tour credibility and substance. In addition, it makes the tour more financially successful because people have something to purchase with which they can "re-live" the tour if they enjoyed it. By reading the book afterwards, they feel that they have gotten more out of the experience and also that they have a souvenir of their experience that they can take home with them.

However, not everyone has the ability to write a book, or the chance to publish one if they do write it. Just because your tour may not have a book that it is based on, does not mean that you can't offer a great tour. I have hosted tours in a few locations that have not had books written about them. However, I will admit that I have included both locations in other books that I have done, usually about broader subjects. All that I did was to take the research that I did for the tour and put it into written form.

You might consider doing this if you do not have the time or the finances to publish an actual book. You might consider a small booklet instead. This can be done by putting all of your stories into written form and having a small quantity put together for you at a local printer. They do not have to be fancy or expensive, just something nice that the attendee can take home with them afterwards. By charging a few dollars for them, you will have recouped your expenses for the printing and may have even made a buck or two. You have also given your tour even more credibility and made it all the more desirable for a newspaper reporter or local television station looking for a good "Halloween" story. You have just become a published author and that is infinitely more desirable to the media than just "a person who does a tour".

HOW DO I GET STARTED?

Let me answer that question by first stating the obvious --- you need to find the haunted places in your town or area. Honestly, it's almost that simple but after that, you still have plenty of work to do. It's very important that after finding the locations that you do your own research into the history of the site and the history of the ghost activity as well. Earlier, I attempted to stress how important it is that your tour includes as much history as possible about each of the locations that you plan to visit. This not only gives your tour more credibility but it also opens it up to people who might not necessarily be just "ghost buffs". Over the years, I have been lucky enough to host tours for many people who were not really interested in the ghosts but in the history that was included in the tour. I feel that the history is so important that we even listed that aspect of the tour first when we put together our tour company as the "History & Hauntings Tours".

In addition to researching the history, it's also imperative that you research the ghostlore of the location as well. Talk to the people at the location and find out as much as you can about the stories yourself. Never, never base your tour on the stories that you have heard around town unless there is absolutely no other source. When I first moved to the town where I currently live, I heard a number of ghost stories about haunted locations around the city but when I began researching the stories myself, I found that the information I had been given was highly inaccurate and in fact, have spent the last several years trying to correct the stories for people who had heard the earlier, misleading versions.

After talking to the people and researching the locations, you will need to start compiling a list of places that you plan to visit on the tour and should begin working on your tour route. This will need to be as smooth a process for the attendees as possible. You need to have a starting location for the tour and then work the tour around so that you end up at the same location again. This will be important to your attendees, who will obviously need to return to where their cars are parked. You should then try and guess how long you will be visiting each location and then add up the times to determine the length of the tour. Remember to overestimate, especially with a walking tour, because the speed of the tour attendees will either make or break your schedule.

Once you have the locations that you want to visit, you should determine how many of these are public spots and how many are privately owned homes and businesses. With public places, you can always visit the spots, even during the evening hours, and should run into no problems as long as you have the proper clearances. You may need to get permission from someone in authority for historic sites, parks and especially cemeteries. With private spots, you have an entirely different set of issues.

First, let's start with homes. I usually try to discourage tour operators from including private residences on their tours. There are a lot of reasons for this but the most important is that most home owners do not want to deal with what comes AFTER the tour --- namely having people knocking on their door asking to see the ghosts! You may laugh about this, but it is sadly the case. Most of my dealings with home owners, even those who granted permission for me to include them on the tour, eventually came to an end because they usually did not realize what they were in for when they granted permission. Even those who are excited about the tour and even welcome the attendees into their homes, will eventually tire of the attention. Trust me on this!

Of course, if the residence has advertised the fact that they are haunted and the place has perhaps appeared in books or articles, then they have become a matter of public record and are fair game for any tour that wants to feature them. If this home owner does not grant permission to have you on their property though, be sure to feature the spot from no closer than the sidewalk.

Private businesses are bound to offer a greater potential for the tour operator. In many cases, as long as you do not wear out your welcome, you can often coax business owners into opening their shop, hotel or restaurant exclusively for the tour. Not only is this great for the tour, but it's great for the business owner as well. Here are potential sales, especially for coffee shops and restaurants, that they would not have had otherwise. By bringing a group into their business, you have added something extra for the tour attendees and have also earned the goodwill of the business owner. Be sure to make time for this in your schedule but if possible, include a locations (or several locations) like this on your tour. Everyone involved will thank you!

GETTING THE WORD OUT

Once you have the tour established the way that you want it, have the route planned out and have confirmed the locations with the owners or anyone who needs to grant permission, you need to attract the attendees. There are many ways to do this but start out by trying to work with your local tourism or visitor's bureau. For the most part, I have found just about every one of these types of organizations to be fairly ineffectual but it's a place to start. And occasionally, you will even find the stray employee (who must have been hired by accident) or a worthwhile volunteer who will get behind what you are trying to do. More and more, cities are starting to realize the potential traffic from ghost tours and haunted places, so hopefully, you will get lucky in your area. Talk over your plans with someone there who will listen and perhaps you can get them to help you spread the word. Don't be disappointed if they talk a good game but then never come through for you but if nothing else, make sure that they have flyers and posters for the tour to hand out or to put on display in the visitor's center.

Next, make sure that the same posters and flyers are distributed to the shops and businesses in town who have expressed a willingness to work with you. If there are other shops in town that would be willing to hang up the flyers, make sure they have them too. By bringing more people to town, it's good for everyone, even if it's tough sometimes to get people to realize this.

If you have a popular website on the Internet, this is also a good place to advertise. I will caution you against this being your only form of advertising when you are just starting out though, especially if your website does not receive many visitors. Even so, it makes an excellent way to get the word out about the tours to people outside of your immediate area, especially those who are traveling and might be passing through.

Unless you are in a heavy tourist area, I would also discourage you from starting the tours at any time outside of the October / Halloween season. In some areas, tours can be held every weekend and even sometimes on a nightly basis, but this depends completely on the number of tourists and visitors to the area. If you are a new tour and a ghost tour is a new thing for your city or town, consider starting it for the Halloween season (on a limited basis) and see how it goes. If it is successful, there is always next year and perhaps even a limited number of tours that you can do during warmer weather.

Once the tour is ready to go and you are ready to announce the dates when tours will be held, you will also need to figure out how admissions will be handled. If possible, consider selling the tickets through a local shop or business (especially your own), a cooperative visitor's bureau or even over the telephone. Established walking tours can often simply announce that a tour will leave at a certain time and place each night and just take along everyone who shows up. This is a dangerous way of doing things for a tour just starting out though and I advise against it. Your best bet, especially with a tour using a vehicle, is to sell tickets in advance.

At this point, your advertising must go beyond posters and flyers and it's time to turn to the local newspaper and television stations. However, I again discourage you from paying for advertising, especially when starting out. This is far too expensive! Besides that, if you plan the timing of the tour correctly, you will never need to pay for advertising at all!

By taking the idea to the newspaper in advance of Halloween, you have pretty much guaranteed yourself publicity for the tour. All papers are looking for local Halloween stories in October and a new ghost tour in town in just the thing. Once the story appears in the newspaper, you are sure to hear from the television stations as well. Just be sure to put together a professional presentation when approaching the newspaper (try not to sounds like a nut!) and your plan for free publicity is almost guaranteed to work.

Now, you are on your way to ghost tour success! Good luck with it and happy hauntings!

- AFTERWORD -

I hope that this new edition of the GHOST HUNTER'S GUIDEBOOK will prove to be of merit to you as an investigator of the paranormal and the unknown. As I stated in the introduction, I did not intend this book to be the final word on the subject of ghost hunting. This volume was meant to be a map and a guide to hopefully point you in the right direction or to give you some ideas that you may not have considered before. Take as much, or as little, of the book and put it to use --- change it, adapt it, mark out sections, tear out pages, or do anything else that you like to help you to be comfortable with the information, methods and suggestions presented within.

Obviously, this will not be my final word on the subject as there is much still to discover about ghosts and spirits and I truly believe it is up to all of us as researchers to discover it.

Thanks for reading this GUIDEBOOK and I hope that you will let me know what you thought of it and whether or not it had any practical use for you. Also, let me know if you have anything that you would like to see added to possible future editions! Send your comments and feedback to the address below:

Troy Taylor
c/o Whitechapel Productions Press
515 East Third St. - Alton, Illinois - 62002

Or email me from our website at: **http://www.prairieghosts.com**

ADDITIONS TO THE GHOST HUNTER'S GUIDEBOOK

The following sections are intended to provide further useful information to readers of the **GHOST HUNTER'S GUIDEBOOK**. Our bibliography and our books for recommended reading will follow these sections.

APPENDIX 1

WHAT TO DO IF YOUR HOUSE IS HAUNTED -- A guide for home owners that can be given out to those seeking information about whether or not their house is haunted, how to handle the haunting and the paranormal investigation that follows. This is essentially a how-to guide for those who live in a haunted house. Feel free to make copies of the article and give them to those who make inquiries about investigations.

APPENDIX 2

Investigation forms and releases for paranormal investigations. The reader is invited to use these forms as a basis for creating forms for your own research local group. You are more than welcome to copy the forms and substitute the of your own local group in place of the American Ghost Society. Please do not use the forms as they are unless you are a member of the American Ghost Society. Thanks!

APPENDIX 3

A dictionary and glossary of ghost-related terms and information. For a complete encyclopedia of ghostly material, see the book THE ENCYCLOPEDIA OF GHOSTS & SPIRITS by Rosemary Ellen Guiley.

APPENDIX 1:
WHAT TO DO IF YOUR HOUSE IS HAUNTED
A Guide for Home Owners who Believe
They Are Experiencing Paranormal Activity

Thanks to the type of work that I do, I meet people on what seems an almost weekly basis who have, or believe they have, a ghost in their house. These otherworldly encounters may not be occurring at the present time, or may have happened in a house where they used to live, but they assure me that strange things did, or do, occur at the place they inhabit.

Perhaps even more frequent than these chance, fact-to-face encounters are the phone calls and email messages that I receive from people who also claim to be going through the same predicament. All manner of strangeness may be reported and on many occasions, the callers and correspondents will ask what they should do about their uninvited and often spooky guests. Should they move out? Should they stay? Should they talk to the specters or ignore them? What is the best thing to do in this situation? And most of all, should they contact a ghost hunter to come in and investigate?

First of all, let me say that over the years that I have been involved in ghosts and ghost research, the vast majority of the cases that I have been involved in have perfectly natural explanations. These explanations may not be immediately realized, but they can be discovered. Of course, that is not to say that I have not been involved in some cases that did puzzle me and which did leave me feeling that (based on the witness accounts and my own research) the location really was haunted.

As the witness to a series of what could be ghostly events, you (the reader this article is aimed at) have to first determine whether or not you think the odd happenings in your house (or business, theater, etc.) are natural or supernatural. In order to do this, you should try and relax and be a good observer. Even if you are scared by what you have seen or heard (or what someone else has seen) you have to give the occurrences some rational thought. Could those "phantom footsteps" have been simply the house settling or the floorboards creaking? Could that "cold chill" have been merely a draft? Could the "ghost" that you saw out of the corner of the eye have been nothing more than a trick of the light?

Maybe the events have explanations, or maybe they don't. Believe me, I know that it's easy to let your imagination get away from you. All it might take are a few harmless comments to someone else in the house and before long, you have a "haunted house" made to order. Here's how that works:

Let's say that you and your family just moved into an old house in a neighborhood in your town. You don't know anything about the history of the house but unknown to you, a family of mice lives quite comfortably in the cellar. One night, you wake up and hear strange noises coming from under the floor. Since you don't know that the sounds are caused by the mice, you jump to the conclusion that the house is haunted. Of course, it's not haunted --- but that's not the point. What is important is that you think the house is haunted! In fact, you get quite caught up in the idea and begin to think that every bump and creak that you hear is something ghostly. An odd reflection or a curtain moving in the wind might even look like a ghost. Combine all of these things together and you have a haunted house on your hands.

At this point, you have come to believe that you have a haunted house with bumps, rappings, ghostly footsteps and even apparitions that roam the hallways. It's not long before your family begins to pick up on your fears, either consciously or unconsciously, and they also begin hearing the "unexplainable" sounds and seeing the resident "ghost".

You can see why it might be easy to feed off one another's fears and literally "invent" a haunted house. That's why I try to ask the people who contact me to step back for a moment and try to look at the events they describe to me as a skeptic. I ask them to try and consider some other possibilities for the events besides supernatural ones. Sometimes this can be done and sometimes it can't. I never tell the witness that their house cannot be haunted! Obviously, there is no way that I can know that and for several reasons:

1. I was not present at the time the reported events occurred.
2. At this point, I have never visited the location.
3. I cannot claim to be an "expert" on all things paranormal because no such thing exists.

What I am trying to do at this point is to simply assist the witness in looking at what they feel is a supernatural event in another manner. As a witness, you should not take offense at this. In fact, you should welcome the skepticism of the investigator. A legitimate investigator will not accuse you of lying but he will also not immediately accept your story as fact, based on the idea that he really has very little evidence to work from at this time. It is not that he doesn't believe you, but only that he is keeping an open mind to everything, including the idea that the house may not be haunted. This is the sort of investigator that you should be looking for --- not the one who immediately accepts your story at face value. This is a sure sign of inexperience with real cases and one best to be avoided.

However, at this point, I may have gotten ahead of myself a little bit. As mentioned already, it is best for the homeowner to try and determine for themselves if the possible ghostly activity has some natural cause. In many cases, if they do contact an investigator, that investigator may try and suggest some natural causes for the activity and it would be best to try and rule that out ahead of time. You might save yourself some embarrassment down the line, although a good investigator would never try to make you feel silly for some misidentified happenings.

Another thing that I recommend doing is to try and keep a log or a journal of any activity that occurs in the house. This will be extremely helpful and as a rule, I always suggest it to people who contact me about their possible haunting. It's a great way to not only recall the events while they are fresh in your mind (so you don't have to try and remember them for the first time in a later interview) but also to see if a pattern of activity exists. The determination of such a pattern would be extremely helpful to an investigator. It could show a natural cause for the activity (such as a furnace kicking on or a nearby freight train passing by) or might make it possible (if the activity turns out to be real) to decide when might be the best time for a paranormal investigation to take place. Obviously, if it looks like the ghostly events are occurring at a certain time (or day), then this would be the time the ghost hunter and his team would want to be present.

When you are compiling your journal or logbook, here are a few things that you want to be sure to include:

1. Note the exact time and date when the activity occurred.
2. Make a note of everyone who was present and what they saw. If possible have each witness record their thoughts in their own words.
3. Try and note the weather conditions at the time.

The journal will be an invaluable piece of research if an investigator comes to call and it will go a long way in establishing evidence about the haunting in your home.

Now that you have been able to try and rule out natural explanations for the events in your house and perhaps have even kept a log of the weird things that occurred, you have to decide what you want to do next. Admittedly, many witnesses will not have gotten this far with their own research. Many people are frightened by what is going on and very few of them understand it. The fact that (if you think your house is haunted) you have gone as far as to read this article is something you should be commended for. People are frightened by the unknown and by things that they don't understand. I should tell you though, that in all of the years that I have been involved in ghost research, I have never run across anything that I would consider to be "evil" or "demonic". Yes, I have run across some cases that are outside of the norm, and were certainly strange, but they were not "demons" disguised as ghosts! Despite what some people would have you believe, the cases of people actually being hurt by ghosts are very, very rare. There is an extremely remote chance that you have anything at all to be afraid of, so try and relax and keep your eyes and ears open to any other developments.

At this point, you have a choice of what to do next. You can either learn to live with the novelty of a ghost in your house, or you can get in touch with a legitimate ghost researcher to help you understand it better. You may also decide that you can't abide the idea of sharing your house with a ghost and we'll talk about what you can do about that later. Even if you decide that you want to "get rid of" the ghost, it's likely that an investigation team would need to determine the veracity and extent of the haunting first.

This leads up to you getting in touch with a qualified ghost hunter, who can come into your home and determine what sort of activity is taking place. This is not as easy as it sounds. There are literally hundreds of websites on the Internet that claim to be affiliated with paranormal research and it would seem that you have scores of ghost hunters to choose from. Unfortunately, this is not the case. Once you discard the inactive groups who still have websites, the "wanna-be" ghost hunters who offer all sorts of services and yet have never actually done a real investigation and the ones who think that wandering around in cemeteries with cameras makes them "researchers" --- you don't have near as many to choose from as it first appeared.

But here's some information that may help when it comes to actually choosing a ghost hunter to do an investigation at your location:

1. Make sure they offer a phone number. While there is nothing wrong with making contact through email, make sure that the group or ghost hunter you are contacting offers a phone number where they can be reached. This does not insure credibility but it does at least rule out the wishful ghost hunters who are living in their parent's basement. In many cases (as with the American Ghost Society), larger organizations may not offer the phone numbers of their area investigators but they should offer a main number where information can be given out.

2. Make sure that the contact information on the ghost hunter's website lists a first and last name of the persons who are actually doing the investigations. If they are listed by their first names only, then it's likely that they are not serious investigators but rather more wishful ghost hunters looking for thrills.

3. Try and determine from the website if the investigators are people that you would like to have in your home. Remember, the website is the method of advertising that they chose to offer their services through and if the site is questionable, the ghost hunters are likely to be as well. Anyone can put up a website but the quality of the material on it will speak volumes about who is behind it.

4. Avoid ghost hunters who dabble in magic, the occult or offer "magical cleansings" of homes. All of these things are the ghost hunter's own business but should not in any way be a part of a legitimate investigation. If anything like this appears on the website, move on. And be sure to ask about this when you speak to the person on the phone because solid researchers will not employ these methods.

5. Legitimate ghost hunters will not charge for their services. If you are asked to pay for an investigation, then you should look for something else. Only services that produce concrete and tangible results are worthy of payment and paranormal research is too unpredictable for that. In most cases, very little may occur in an investigation and no one should be expected to pay for that. It should be noted however that if the ghost researcher is expected to travel (especially overnight) to reach your location, it should be expected for you to offer that person reimbursement for their expenses.

6. Remember that legitimate ghost hunters will come to your home by invitation. If you are contacted and are asked if an investigation can be conducted in your home, quickly decline. Trustworthy ghost hunters don't go where they are not wanted! This may not be the case in public locations though, so if you are involved with a location that has a reputation for being haunted, you may be contacted by someone. At that point, you should simply judge the researcher on his merits.

7. Once you believe you have found an investigator that you are comfortable with, you need to check his qualifications for an investigation. Ask how long he has been involved in paranormal research and about investigations in the past, especially those involving private residences. If he claims to be some sort of "doctor", ask where this certification may have come from. Just because he chooses to pay for a questionable "doctorate" from

an Internet university, does not make him qualified to interact with people. Believe it or not, many ghost hunters have never conducted an investigation in a home (no matter how experienced they seem) and you have to decide if you are comfortable with this person starting out in your house. They may turn out to be great investigators, but you have to decide if you want to be their first one.

8. Also ask the researcher if they are affiliated with a research group or a national organization. Just because they are not does not make them less legitimate, however being affiliated with a group that has a good reputation can help you make a decision about allowing the researcher into your home. You can also get in touch with the main number for the group and check this person out before working with him.

Just remember though, once you have decided on the person that you want to contact, you have to be patient when requesting help. Although there are people out there claiming to be legitimate and charging large sums of money to "bust your ghost", genuine researchers do not charge for investigations, being more interested in collecting evidence. Because of this, there can be a shortage of funding for most people involved and witnesses are often asked to wait until the investigator can be freed from his "real job".

Once you have a ghost hunter to work with, they will need to determine if an on-site investigation of your home is needed. They will do this by asking a lot of questions and by referring to information that I mentioned you should gather. They will need to know that you have already tried to rule out natural explanations for the phenomena and perhaps even that you have compiled dates and times for the reported events.

Should the researcher then decide that an investigation of the house is warranted, then prepare to be invaded! Even though legitimate research groups will consist of no more than 5-6 individuals, a good team can seem like many more. An investigation can be very invasive and there will be photographs taken of the house and hundreds of feet of video shot. The investigators will ask you to describe the events that occurred (perhaps several times) and your statement will be recorded. They will ask you dozens of questions and many of them will seem unconnected and perhaps even embarrassing. Bear with them however, because the questions do have a purpose and the investigators will be working to try and not only legitimize your story but also to try and determine if the reported activity is real.

Here are some things that you should be aware of when it comes to legitimate paranormal investigations:

1. The investigating team should be no more than 5-6 people in your home. If the group is larger than this, then they have no idea what they are doing and should be questioned by you.

2. The investigators should not be drinking or smoking at any time.

3. Remember that they should arrive at your home with healthy skepticism. No one is trying to debunk your reports but they have to keep an open mind to all possibilities.

Good investigators must remain non-committal until they have had a chance to gather their evidence.

4. Make sure that the investigators seem to know how to use all of their equipment. If there is anything that you don't understand, be sure to ask them to explain what it is used for. If they cannot, you may have a problem.

5. Unless the investigation was set up through you with a local television station or newspaper, the investigators should not be accompanied to your home with a reporter or media person. This should never occur without your permission! The investigators are duty-bound to keep all aspects of your case confidential unless they have your permission to disclose anything.

6. As mentioned already, the investigators should be able to explain to you what they are doing and don't be afraid to ask. If there is anything that you want to know or need information about to feel comfortable, a legitimate researcher will give it to you. Just remember that any natural explanations that are discovered that might show the "haunting" has nothing to do with ghosts should be properly explained. This is not an indictment against your honesty, so don't be offended. You asked this person in to give you an honest opinion and you have to be prepared to accept it.

7. You can also help by making sure that everyone who experienced anything unusual is present on the night of the investigation and that you keep out friends and relatives who want to come over to watch the proceedings. This can be very distracting to you and to the investigators and can interfere with an accurate investigation.

8. Also remember that if you become uncomfortable with what is going on at any point in the investigation, you have the absolute right to call a halt to everything. The investigators are present at your request and are "guests" in your home. They should be given the respect that such a title signifies, but they also have to respect your feelings and fears as well.

As the investigation continues in your home, the team members will divide up their duties and while you are being thoroughly interviewed, other investigators will be filming and mapping the house, taking photos and looking for any anomalies with their equipment. They will likely ask you to show them where any odd happenings took place and may ask you to recreate what you were doing when they occurred.

If the phenomena that you have reported occurs on a regular basis, or has a set pattern, the investigators may want to conduct a vigil or "ghost watch". This means that they will set up themselves and their gear in hopes that the activity might occur again. This can be a long process and can be very boring for you and the investigators. At this point, you may want to consider quietly going about your activities and to let them work.

You may have noticed in this article that I mentioned several times that activity rarely occurs during the investigation. In some cases it does though, and this can be exciting for everyone involved. However, in most cases (if the investigator has determined that there seems to be a strong possibility that the reported phenomena is genuine) a follow-up investigation will be required. This usually means a return visit that will be much less "painless" than the first, as the initial groundwork has already been laid.

It should be stressed that a legitimate researcher will always follow up on a case. If you do not hear from him, and the phenomenon persists, then call him yourself. Don't be afraid to get in touch with him and ask him to come back.

The information that has come before has been mostly geared to the witness who has experienced something out of the ordinary and while not completely frightened by it, is curious enough to contact someone who can tell them more. Truthfully, I have worked more often with this type of person than any other. They aren't necessarily afraid of the activity they have reported, but are bothered by it to the point that they decided to seek some help.

This is not always the case though. As a witness, you may call in a researcher to decide whether or not your house is truly haunted and once you realize that something is actually happening (and that others are seeing it too!), you may want to call the proceedings to a halt. This can happen when the witness is afraid of making the ghost "angry" and you may decide that you want to just leave well enough alone, who knows? Some witnesses also may decide that they want to get rid of the ghost and if this happens to you, the investigators that you have contacted have no choice but to go along with your wishes.

But unless the investigator is a psychic (and I don't recommend contacting a psychic for your investigation unless they are accompanied by a legitimate team to back up their findings), they will not be equipped to get rid of the ghosts that may be haunting your house. Most ghost hunters are merely investigators. We do not talk to ghosts and we don't see them around every corner. If we are going to be able to help you, we are going to have to contact an outside source.

Let me reassure you again though that ghosts are not present to hurt anyone and in almost every case, a family can peacefully coincide with a spirit. Obviously though, not everyone wants that and some even insist that the ghost itself would be better off passing on to wherever we go at the time of death. In this case, the ghost hunter should be proactive in helping you with your wishes.

If you have a family minister, the ghost hunter will likely suggest that you get in touch with this person and ask them to come to the house and to pray for the soul of the spirit that is present. This is not an "exorcism" but simply an attempt to get the ghost to leave in peace. It can be of great benefit to you and your family as well.

If a willing minister is not available, then the ghost hunter should be able to suggest or find an expert in getting rid of ghosts. They may not be a professional medium or psychic but someone who is sensitive to spirits and who has a good reputation. It should be someone the ghost hunter has either worked with before or someone who was referred through a legitimate source. There is usually a complete lack of ceremony with this type of person as they are not a phony psychic or exorcist. They are likely going to want to look over the location and sit down and talk with you before proceeding.

Remember though to beware of any medium that tries to pump you for too much information up front! It is obviously more legitimate if this person can gather impressions that match the information you already have. If they come up with weird things that you have not experienced and seem to be making things up out of thin air, they most likely are.

If an authentic medium detects a spirit that is present, they will try and convince it to move on. How effective is this? It's hard to say. It has been my experience that sometimes it works and sometimes it doesn't. It usually has a positive effect on the house though, no matter what else it manages to accomplish. I often get calls from people who ask for this service but in my years in the paranormal field, I have found very few people that I can recommend as someone trustworthy enough to be given this assignment. They are out there though and if you request it, the ghost hunter you work with should do all they can to get you in touch with them.

In closing, I hope that this article has been worthwhile for you and has provided you with some of the essential information that you need in order to find a legitimate ghost hunter. I always say that ghost hunting has several goals. Not only is the ghost hunter seeking evidence of ghosts, but he is also there to help the person who called him in to investigate the case. It is the ghost hunter's main responsibility to alleviate the fears of the witness and to help them deal with the activity they are experiencing. The home owner should never be shut out of the investigation but should be treated with the utmost respect --- for man always fears what he does not understand.

If you are experiencing a haunting and have been thinking of contacting a ghost hunter, then I hope that you now know what to expect from this experience. In some small way, I hope that this knowledge can contribute to the end of people being taken advantage of by the questionable and inexperienced ghost hunters who are out there. A little knowledge can go a long way and now that you know what to look for, you can avoid the problems that so many have encountered in the past. Good luck!

AMERICAN GHOST SOCIETY

Headquarters
515 East Third Street
Alton, Illinois 62002
(618) 465-1086 / www.prairieghosts.com

INVESTIGATION PERMISSION FORM

I, _____ have the authority to allow access to investigators from the American Ghost Society to conduct research at _____ located in _____ in the state of _____. Permission is being granted to the American Ghost Society to conduct research into the history of the location and into possible occurrences and sightings related to ghosts and the paranormal. All parts of the investigation have been explained to the owners / trustees of the location and we have given permission for research to be conducted.

The American Ghost Society investigation team releases the owner of the location from any liability for injuries that occur during the investigation. In addition, the investigators present assume responsibility for any damages to property that take place during the investigation.

The investigating team also assumes responsibility for proper releases of information from the property owners. No information about the investigation will be released without signed copies of the current release forms.

Signed _____ Date _____
(Property owner / trustee)

Signed _____ Date _____
(Investigation Team Leader / Organizer)

Please Contact the American Ghost Society Office at the number above for Information on Investigators and Representatives.

AMERICAN GHOST SOCIETY

Headquarters
515 East Third Street
Alton, Illinois 62002
(618) 465-1086 / www.prairieghosts.com

INFORMATION RELEASE FORM

This form is intended to insure the privacy of all individuals associated with the investigation conducted on _____ at the location owned by _____. All personal information connected to this investigation will be kept confidential by researchers from the American Ghost Society. Use of this form is to allow permission from those involved with the investigation to grant the use of the location on our website, in books or in future media venues.

All information that is released will only be used on the condition that the identity of witnesses and clients are protected and the exact location of the site is not used.

Other comments and requests:

_____
_____
_____
_____
_____
_____

Signed _____
(property owner and / or witness)

Date _____

AMERICAN GHOST SOCIETY
Paranormal Vigil Log

Date of the Investigation _____ Time Started _____
Name and Location of Site _____
_____

Investigators & Team Members Present:

_____   _____
_____   _____
_____   _____
_____   _____
_____

Weather Conditions:
Temperature _____
Relative Humidity _____
Barometer Readings _____
High Pressure _____ Low Pressure _____
Wind Speed _____ mph

Investigator's Log Sheet _____

Equipment Being Used by Investigator:

_____
_____
_____
_____

Film Speed Loaded in Camera: _____ ASA
Number of Exposures: _____

Phenomena Personally witnessed by Investigator:

_____
_____
_____
_____

LOGBOOK TIME & INFORMATION SHEET

Time of Event	Phenomena Witnessed	Photo Taken:
_____	_____	_____
_____	_____	_____
_____	_____	_____
_____	_____	_____
_____	_____	_____
_____	_____	_____
_____	_____	_____
_____	_____	_____
_____	_____	_____
_____	_____	_____
_____	_____	_____
_____	_____	_____
_____	_____	_____
_____	_____	_____
_____	_____	_____
_____	_____	_____
_____	_____	_____
_____	_____	_____
_____	_____	_____
_____	_____	_____
_____	_____	_____
_____	_____	_____
_____	_____	_____
_____	_____	_____
_____	_____	_____
_____	_____	_____
_____	_____	_____
_____	_____	_____
_____	_____	_____

APPENDIX 3:
DICTIONARY OF GHOSTLY TERMS

AGENT: A living person at the site of a haunting. Some human agents act only as witnesses to paranormal events while others are believed to be the method by which the hauntings occur. Some agents may cause phenomena to increase, while others may be the entire source of the activity. How this works is as yet unexplained.

APPARITION: A spectral image that is sometimes referred to as a ghost, but is more like an imprint with distinct features that enables the witness to recognize it as a person or specific shape. They are usually connected to residual hauntings rather than spirit-related ones.

APPORT: A physical object that can materialize and appear at will and can include coins, watches, jewelry and even food. They are often connected to spirits who interact with the living as the spirits cause items to appear and disappear in an effort to make themselves known.

AUTOMATIC WRITING: A method used by spirit mediums to obtain information from the next world. It is believed that spirits take control of the medium and cause them to write unconscious information on paper.

BANSHEE: A death omen or spirit that attaches itself to certain families.

COLLECTIVE APPARITION: A type of ghost sighting that occurs when one or more people see the same apparition.

CONTROL: A spirit who acts as a medium's connection with the next world. Also referred to as a "spirit guide".

DEMATERIALIZATION: The sudden disappearance of a person or spirit in full view of witnesses.

DOPPELGANGER: Meaning "double image", it is thought to be an exact spirit double of a living person. They are considered to be very negative in nature.

EARTHBOUND: Refers to a ghost or spirit that is unable to cross over at the time of death. Many spirits make the decision to remain behind by choice while others are too confused or frightened because of a sudden death or suicide to make the crossing.

ECTOPLASM: An organic material that was supposedly exuded by physical mediums during seances as a way of proving contact with the spirit world. It would often take certain shapes. The substance was supposed to appear from just about any orifice of the medium's body. In more recent times, many researchers believe the substance had a natural form, created by fraudulent mediums during the Spiritualist era.

ELECTRONIC VOICE PHENOMENA: Voices and sounds that are alleged to be from the dead and that are captured by electronic mediums on tape.

ELEMENTALS: A term used by Spiritualists to describe angry or malicious spirits. Others refer to them as "earth spirits".

EXORCISM: A ritual used primarily by the Catholic Church as a way of driving out demons or evil spirits from a living person. Some fundamentalists also use this term to describe the expelling of spirits from a home or location.

EXTRA: A shape or a face that is said to have supernaturally appeared on film and cannot be explained away as fraud, faulty film or developing flaws.

GHOST: Generic term used for a number of different supernatural entities.

GHOST HUNTING: Various methods of investigating reports of ghosts and hauntings and determining their authenticity.

GHOST LIGHTS: Strange balls of light that appear in specific locations, often for an extended period of time but which have no explanation. They are thought to be of natural origin, possibly pertaining to earthquakes, fault lines, railroad tracks or water sources, but remain a mystery.

HAUNTING: A repeated manifestation of supernatural phenomena in a specific location. The activity may appear as physical apparitions, sights, sounds, smells or cold areas. Hauntings may continue for years or may only last for a brief period of time.

INTELLIGENT HAUNTING: Activity that takes place around people or locations that is caused by an intelligent or conscious spirit. Best defined as the personality of someone who has died and whose spirit has not crossed over to the other side. This spirit will interact with witnesses at a location and attempt to make its presence known through repeated phenomena of sights, sounds, feelings and the movement of physical objects.

LEVITATION: The raising of physical objects without assistance. Thought to be caused by ghosts, levitations were always popular during Spiritualist seances, when tables, chairs and many other items were said to have moved and lifted from the floor.

MATERIALIZATION: The sudden appearance of a person or object in front of witnesses.

ORBS: Round, opaque lights that are captured on film and believed to be spirits, or some sort of paranormal activity. Although a number of legitimate orbs have been witnessed and photographed, the majority of the ones shown in photographs are nothing more than faulty photography and light refractions imprinted on film.

PARANORMAL: A word meaning "unknown" or "beyond the normal" that has come to refer to events that are unexplainable.

PHANTOM: Another name for "ghost" or "spirit", although interestingly, many use the word "phantom" to refer to ghosts that have been seen wearing cloaks or robes.

PHENOMENON (PHENOMENA): An event that is an outward sign of the working of the laws of nature or an extraordinary happening.

POLTERGEIST: Literally means "noisy ghost" in German. Although it actually refers to Traditional ghosts and hauntings and in other cases, it can be used to describe the work of a human agent. In this situation, the knockings and the movement of objects is caused by an outward explosion of kinetic energy from the human mind. Most poltergeist outbreaks are short-lived.

PSYCHIC: An all-encompassing word that is used to describe a person who is allegedly sensitive beyond the normal means. Such a person may be able to see and hear things that are not available to most people.

PSYCHOKINESIS (PK): The ability to move physical objects using only the power of the mind. In many poltergeist-like cases, human agents affect objects in an unconscious manner.

RECIPROCAL APPARITION: A rare type of ghost sighting when both the spirit and the human witness see and respond to one another.

SEANCE: A sitting that is held for the purpose of communication with the dead. At least on person in the circle is preferred to be a medium (or psychic), with the power of contacting the spirits.

SIMULACRA: A word used to describe the faces and shapes that are often reported in photographs and in almost every kind of inanimate object including doors, buildings, clouds, trees and bushes. Usually, it is nothing more than the imagination of the witness making the texture of the object into a face or a figure.

SPECTER: (OR SPECTRE) Another term for a ghost.

SPIRIT: A discarnate being, or ghost, that exists in an invisible realm.

SPIRIT PHOTOGRAPHY: A term used for both legitimate attempts to capture ghosts and paranormal energy on film and also for the work of fraudulent photographers during the Spiritualist era.

SPIRITUALISM: A faith based on the idea that life continues after death and that communication between the living and the dead can, and does, take place.

SUPERNATURAL: Events or happenings that take place in violation of the laws of nature, usually associated with ghosts and hauntings.

TALKING BOARDS: A piece of wood bearing the letters of the alphabet that is used as a tool to make contact with the spirit world. Sitters place their fingers lightly on the planchette (or pointer) by which the spirits can spell out messages on the board.

TELEPORTATION: The appearance, disappearance or movement of human bodies and physical objects through closed doors or over some amount of distance using paranormal means. Such events often are reported to take place during hauntings.

WRAITH: An apparition that is generally supposed to be an omen of death.

BIBLIOGRAPHY & RECOMMENDED READING

Auerbach, Loyd - ESP, Hauntings and Poltergeists (1986)
Auebach, Loyd - Ghost Hunting (2004)
Baker, Alan - Ghosts and Spirits (1999)
Baker, Robert A. And Joe Nickell - Missing Pieces (1992)
Banks, Ivan - The Enigma of Borley Rectory (1996)
Bardens, Dennis - Ghosts and Hauntings (1965)
Brandon, Ruth - Life and Many Deaths of Harry Houdini (1993)
Brandon, Ruth - The Spiritualists (1983)
Brown, Slater - The Heyday of Spiritualism (1970)
Brugioni, Dino - Photo Fakery (1999)
Buckley, Doris Heather - Spirit Communication for the Millions (1967)
Cannell, J.C. - Secrets of Houdini (1932)
Chambers, Paul - Paranormal People (1998)
Clark, Jerome - Unexplained! (1998)
Coates, James - Photographing the Invisible (1921)
Cohen, Daniel - Encyclopedia of Ghosts (1984)
Cornell, Tony - Investigating the Paranormal (2002)
Crowe, Catherine - The Night Side of Nature (1854)
Doyle, Sir Arthur Conan - History of Spiritualism (1926)
Doyle, Sir Arthur Conan - Memories and Adventures (1924)
Doyle, Sir Arthur Conan - The Coming of the Fairies (1922)
Doyle, Sir Arthur Conan - The Edge of the Unknown (1930)
Evans, Henry Ridgely - Hours with the Ghosts (1897)
Evans, Henry Ridgely - The Spirit World Unmasked (1902)
Evans, Hilary & Patrick Huyghe - Field Guide to Ghosts and Other Apparitions (2000)

Fiore, Dr. Edith - The Unquiet Dead (1987)
Fisher, Joe - Hungry Ghosts (1990)
Fuller, John G. - Ghost of the 29 Megacycles (1981)
Gaddis, Vincent - Mysterious Fires and Lights (1967)
Gettings, Fred - Ghosts in Photographs (1978)
Guiley, Rosemary Ellen - Encyclopedia of Ghosts and Spirits (1992 / 2000)
Haining, Peter - Ghosts: The Illustrated History (1987)
Hall, Trevor - The Medium and the Scientist (1984)
Hall, Trevor - The Spiritualists (1962)
Hauck, Dennis William - Haunted Places: A National Directory (1996 / 2002)
Hope, Valerie & Maurice Townsend - Paranormal Investigator's Handbook (1999)
Houdini, Harry - A Magician Among the Spirits (1924)
Huyser, Barb - Small Town Ghosts (2003)
Jackson, Jr., Herbert G. - The Spirit Rappers (1972)
Kaczmarek, Dale - Field Guide to Spirit Photography (2002)
Lodge, Sir Oliver - Raymond, or Life after Death (1916)
McHargue, Georgess - Facts, Frauds and Phantasms (1972)
Melton, J. Gordon - Ency. of Occultism and Parapsychology (1996)
Michaels, Susan - Sightings (1996)
Moore, L. - In Search of White Crows (1977)
Mulholland, John - Beware Familiar Spirits (1938)
Nickell, Joe - Camera Clues
Nickell, Joe - Entities (1995)
Northrop, Suzane - The Seance (1994)
O'Donnell, Elliot - The Great Ghost Hunter (1956)
O'Donnell, Elliot - The Menace of Spiritualism (1920)
Ogden, Tom - Complete Idiot's Guide to Ghosts & Hauntings (2000)
Owen, George and Victor Sims - Science and the Spook (1971)
Peach, Emily - Things that go Bump in the Night (1991)
Pearsall, Ronald - The Table Rappers (1972)
Permutt, Cyril - Photographing the Spirit World (1983)
Picknett, Lynn - Flights of Fancy (1987)
Price, Harry - Confessions of a Ghost Hunter (1936)
Price, Harry - End of Borley Rectory (1946)
Price, Harry - Haunting at Cashen's Gap (1936)
Price, Harry - Poltergeist over England (1945)
Price, Harry - Search for Truth (1942)
Price, Harry - The Most Haunted House in England (1940)
Rawcliffe, D.H. - The Psychology of the Occult (1952)
Reader's Digest Books - Into the Unknown (1981)
Rogo, D. Scott - An Experience of Phantoms (1974)
Rogo, D. Scott - The Haunted House Handbook (1978)
Rogo, D. Scott - The Haunted Universe (1977)
Roll, Michael - Scientific Proof of Survival of Death (1995)
Roll, William Ph.D. & Valerie Story - Unleashed (2004)
Saltzman, Pauline - Strange Spirits (1967)
Somerlott, Robert - Here, Mr. Splitfoot (1971)
Spencer, John and Anne - Encyclopedia of Ghosts and Spirits (1992)
Spencer, John and Anne - Poltergeist Phenomenon (1997)
Spencer, John and Tony Wells - Ghost Watching (1994)

Spraggett, Allen - Arthur Ford: Man who Talked with the Dead (1973)
Stashower, Daniel - Teller of Tales: Life of Sir Arthur Conan Doyle (1999)
Stead, W.T. - Real Ghost Stories
Stein, Gordon - The Sorcerer of Kings (1993)
Steinour, Harold - Exploring the Unseen World (1959)
Stirling, AMW - Ghosts Vivisected (1958)
Tabori, Paul - Harry Price: Biography of a Ghost Hunter (1950)
Taff, Barry E. - Aliens Above, Ghosts Below (1996)
Taylor, Troy - Confessions of a Ghost Hunter (2002)
Taylor, Troy - Field Guide to Haunted Graveyards (2003)
Taylor, Troy - The Ghost Hunter's Handbook (1998)
Taylor, Troy - The Ghost Hunter's Guidebook (1999 / 2001)
Thurston, Herbert - Ghosts and Poltergeists (1953)
Underwood, Peter - Borley Postscript (2001)
Underwood, Peter - Ghosts and How to See Them (1993)
Underwood, Peter - Nights in Haunted Houses (1994)
Underwood, Peter - The Ghost Hunter's Guide (1986)
Weisberg, Barbara - Talking to the Dead (2004)
White, Laurie - Infrared Photography Handbook (1995)
Wilson, Colin - Poltergeist: Study in Destructive Haunting (1993)
Wilson, Ian - In Search of Ghosts (1995)

Personal Interviews & Correspondence

Special Thanks to:

Kim Young - Proofreading & Editing Services
David Betz
Vince Wilson
Orlando Pla
Chris Moseley
Scott Denning
Dan Quaroni
Jim Carter

ABOUT THE AUTHOR

Troy Taylor is the author of 33 books about ghosts and hauntings in America, including HAUNTED ILLINOIS, THE GHOST HUNTER'S GUIDEBOOK and many others. He is also the editor of GHOSTS OF THE PRAIRIE Magazine, about the history, hauntings & unsolved mysteries of America. A number of his articles have been published here and in other ghost-related publications.

Taylor is the president of the "American Ghost Society", a network of ghost hunters, which boasts more than 600 active members in the United States and Canada. The group collects stories of ghost sightings and haunted houses and uses investigative techniques to track down evidence of the supernatural. In addition, he also hosts a National Conference each year in conjunction with the group which usually attracts several hundred ghost enthusiasts from around the country.

Along with writing about ghosts, Taylor is also a public speaker on the subject and has spoken to well over 600 private and public groups on a variety of paranormal subjects. He has appeared in literally dozens of newspaper and magazine articles about ghosts and hauntings. He has also been fortunate enough to be interviewed hundreds of times for radio and television broadcasts about the supernatural. He has also appeared in a number of documentary films like AMERICA'S MOST HAUNTED, BEYOND HUMAN SENSES, GHOST WATERS, NIGHT VISITORS, GHOSTS OF MIDDLE AMERICA, the television series MYSTERIOUS WORLDS and in one feature film, THE ST. FRANCISVILLE EXPERIMENT.

Born and raised in Illinois, Taylor has long had an affinity for "things that go bump in the night" and published his first book HAUNTED DECATUR in 1995. For seven years, he was also the host of the popular, and award-winning, "Haunted Decatur" ghost tours of the city for which he sometimes still appears as a guest host. He also hosted tours in St. Louis, St. Charles, Missouri and currently hosts the "History & Hauntings Tours" of Alton, Illinois.

In 1996, Taylor married Amy Van Lear, the Managing Director of Whitechapel Press, and they currently reside in a restored 1850's bakery in Alton. Their first child together, Margaret Opal, was born in June 2002. She joined her half siblings, Orrin and Anastasia.

ABOUT WHITECHAPEL PRODUCTIONS PRESS

Whitechapel Productions Press is a small press publisher, specializing in books about ghosts and hauntings. Since 1993, the company has been one of America's leading publishers of supernatural books. Located in Alton, Illinois, they also produce the "Ghosts of the Prairie" Internet web page and "Ghosts of the Prairie", a print magazine that is dedicated to American hauntings and unsolved mysteries. The magazine began its original run from 1997 to 2000 but was revived as a full-cover, bi-monthly magazine in 2003. Issues are available through the website or at the Alton bookstore.

In addition to publishing books and the periodical on history and hauntings, Whitechapel Press also owns and distributes the Haunted America Catalog, which features over 500 different books about ghosts and hauntings from authors all over the United States. A complete selection of these books can be browsed in person at the "History & Hauntings Book Co." Store in Alton and on our Internet website.

Visit Whitechapel Productions Press online and browse through our selection of ghostly titles, plus get information on ghosts and hauntings, haunted history, spirit photographs, information on ghost hunting and much more.
Visit the Internet web page at:

www.historyandhauntings.com

Or visit the Haunted Book Co. in Person at:

515 East Third Street
Alton, Illinois 62002
(618)-456-1086

The Alton Bookstore is home to not only Whitechapel Press and the Haunted America Catalog but is also the home base for the acclaimed History & Hauntings Ghost Tours of the city, which are hosted by Troy Taylor. The bookstore features hundreds and hundreds of titles on ghosts, hauntings and the unexplained, as well as books on American, regional and local history, the Old West, the Civil War and much more.

Printed in the United States
64515LVS00001B/49-87